Navies in the Mountains

J. R. HARLE

Navies in the Mountains

The Battles on the Waters
of Lake Champlain and Lake George

1609 - 1814

HARRISON BIRD

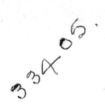

New York OXFORD UNIVERSITY PRESS 1962

To the memory
of
Stephen H. P. Pell

Acknowledgments

The vast number of interested and interesting people encountered in the research and organization of material for this book may be placed, roughly, in three categories.

First, there are the people, long dead, who during all the years of wars and troubles found their way, for one reason or another, up and down Lake George and Lake Champlain. In their journals and letters, and in the mute objects related to their trades and crafts and artistry, they left the mark of their ambitions, their motives, anxieties and hopes, their comforts and discomforts.

In the second group are those persons of long memory and patient research, who, to preserve the tales of old men, wrote them down to constitute what, today, are called "secondary sources." Their work forms the links of the chain joining the present to the past.

In the last category are those whom I have met face to face as I sought out the acquaintance of the others. To them I offer my appreciation and my thanks. They are many.

At Fort Ticonderoga there is John H. G. Pell, its President, who wholeheartedly made available to me all the resources of that remarkable storehouse of history. Eleanor Murray, of Fort Ticonderoga, not only made the original suggestion that I write a history of naval action in the Lake Champlain Pass, but turned over for my use all her intimate knowledge of the Fort and its library, as well as the results of her own profound research.

In technical naval matters, I have been fortunate in being able to discuss tactics and strategy with Admiral H. Kent Hewitt and with Captain P. P. Bassett, both USN.

The Mystic Museum, and the Marine Historical Society, at Mystic, Connecticut, the Peabody Museum of Salem, Massachusetts, The Company of Military Collectors & Historians, the New York Public Library, the Mariners' Museum of Newport News, Virginia, all contributed generous help.

Some few of the people who have helped in divers ways, and to whom I am grateful, are: Robert Adamson, Glens Falls, New York; John Bakeless, Seymour, Connecticut; Mrs. P. P. Bassett, Huletts Landing, New York; John R. Cuneo, Westport, Connecticut; John Jay Cunningham, New York City; Col. Donald L. Dickson, USMC; Robert Flack, Lake George, New York; Elbert L. Huber, Navy Branch, The National Archives, Washington, D.C.; the late Lawrence W. Jenkins, Salem, Massachusetts; Arthur S. Knight, Lake George, New York; the late Col. Harry C. Larter, USA, Retired; Professor Marine Leland, Northampton, Massachusetts; Captain F. Kent Loomis, USN, Retired; Colonel John H. Magruder, III, USMC; Edward Mann, Huletts Landing, New York; Miss Joan Maxwell, Fort Ticonderoga, New York; Mrs. Walter J. Newell, Whitehall, New York; Daniel G. Olney, Vera Cruz, Mexico; Godfrey J. Olsen, Staatsburg, New York; Julius Rauzin, New York City; Kenneth Robbins, Whitehall, New York; Harold L. Peterson, Washington, D.C.; Mr. and Mrs. Nils G. Sahlin, Jr., Rowayton, Connecticut; Henry I. Shaw, Historical Section, USMC; Captain LeRoy Taylor, USN; Lawrence Phelps Tower, New York, H. O. Werner, U.S. Navy Institute, and R. F. White, The Mystic Museum.

Contents

Illustrations

Maps

France in the Ascendancy

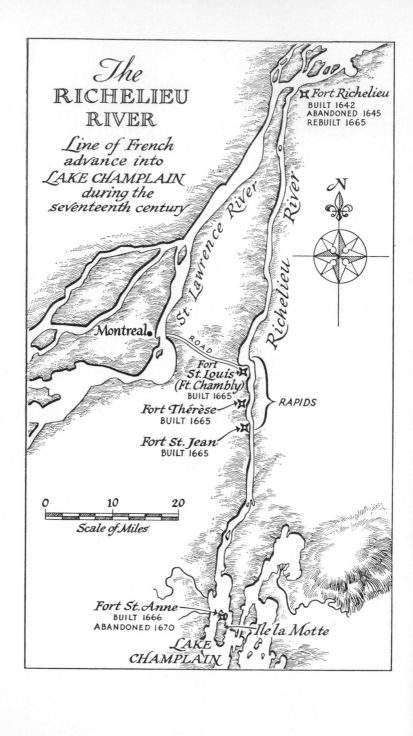

The
RICHELIEU
RIVER

*Line of French
advance into
LAKE CHAMPLAIN
during the
seventeenth century*

Fort Richelieu
BUILT 1642
ABANDONED 1645
REBUILT 1665

St. Lawrence River

Richelieu River

N

Montreal.

ROAD

Fort
St. Louis
(Ft. Chambly)
BUILT 1665

Fort Thérèse
BUILT 1665

RAPIDS

Fort St. Jean
BUILT 1665

0   10   20
Scale of Miles

Fort St. Anne
BUILT 1666
ABANDONED 1670

Ile la Motte

LAKE
CHAMPLAIN

Men of Iron

Fifteen miles up the River of the Iroquois, the shallop rode at taut anchor. The blunt-bowed craft could go no further, so strong was the spring freshet carrying an immensity of water from the mountain-fed lakes and emptying it many miles below, into the St. Lawrence River and the Atlantic Ocean. François de Pontgravé, diplomat, trader, and leader of the French expedition to Canada in 1603, awaited only the return of his lieutenant, Samuel de Champlain, to hoist anchor and be off for France and home. Pontgravé had acquiesced somewhat reluctantly to Champlain's wish, in bringing the shallop even this far up the unfamiliar river, and it was with even greater reluctance that he had agreed to wait while the younger man ventured further up the river in a skiff.

Now, while Pontgravé impatiently awaited his return to the shallop, Champlain, already five miles ahead, was eager to press on still further. The force of the river held him back, as though resentful of intrusion by these alien men in their strange craft. The skirted French sailors strained at their oars, while at the stern tiller, Champlain attempted to gain an advantage, however small, over the strength of the current. If only he could see around the next bend of the river, where lay another vista into the unknown, another reach into the unexplored—the revelation, perhaps, of truths hinted at but as yet undiscovered.

A bold thrust of the rudder drove the skiff close inshore, where the rush of the spring water veered out around a point of land. A tree in full foliage leaned out over the river, its leafy branches brushing over the backs of the sailors as they hauled at the oars. The cool leaves touched Champlain's eager face, blinding him for a moment. Then the next reach of the river came into view: it was like the last, a long stretch of smooth, dark-flowing water, coming from somewhere unknown to any European, and leading on to yet undiscovered places.

But on that June day of 1603, there was no hope of going on. Time turned Champlain back to the waiting Pontgravé, and six long years of time would pass before Samuel de Champlain again traveled up the River of the Iroquois — to its beginning.

The French expedition of 1603 was for the purpose of allying the Algonquin Indians to France and to select a site for a permanent trading post and a base for exploration and the commercial exploitation of the Algonquin lands. Two vessels set out in April to cross the North Atlantic. Of these, one had turned south after reaching Newfoundland, to scout the Atlantic coast line. The flagship, commanded by the expedition's leader, François de Pontgravé, continued westward and inland, bound for Tadoussac. This was the principal village of the Montagnai Algonquins, at the confluence of the Saguenay and St. Lawrence rivers. The bluff old Mâlouin sailor had traded at Tadoussac before.

Samuel de Champlain had come with Pontgravé as second-in-command, charged with the specific duty of making "a true report of what should befall."

Born in 1567, at Brouage, on the Bay of Biscay, Champlain had grown up in the last years of the decrepit Valois dynasty. As a young man he had followed Henry of Navarre through the bitter campaigns of the civil and religious wars that ended in time to begin a new and splendid century for France, under the four great Bourbon kings, of whom Henry IV was the gallant first.

With peace in his country, and an established regime, Champlain, like many another veteran seemingly past his prime, was confronted with the bleak necessity of putting his heart into a new career. He turned to the sea on which he had fought, and on the shores of which he had spent his boyhood. Brouage was then a great salt port where fishing boats, bound for the Grand Banks off Nova Scotia, loaded for the westward passage, and all eyes looked toward the New World of the Americas. In these questing years, Champlain voyaged to the Spanish Main and saw the empire building there, but he found in it no place for his talents, his energies, or his loyalties.

The wars had trained Samuel de Champlain in only one marketable quality, and for that there was a limited demand: he was a servant of Henry IV, who was France. In 1603, Champlain re-engaged himself to his adored king, as an inspired explorer and a tenacious colonizer in the New World of North America. It was in his capacity as Geographer Royal and Captain-in-Ordinary to the King in the Marine that Champlain came with Pontgravé to the Algonquin lands of Canada.

Pontgravé's ship, the *Bonne Renommée*, seventy-three days out of Honfleur in the Kingdom of France, had made the last landfall of her outward voyage on May 27, 1603. By noon, the *Bonne Renommée* was tugging at her anchor cable in the roadstead under the high mountains, through which the Saguenay poured its spring floods into the St. Lawrence. In the afternoon Pontgravé and Champlain were rowed ashore to pay their respects to the Great Chief, Ana-da-bi-jou, in his village of Tadoussac. With them went the two Montagnai Indians whom the foresighted Pontgravé had taken back to France on his previous voyage, to be trained as interpreters and to be awed by Paris.

Ana-da-bi-jou made the two Frenchmen welcome, and with great ceremony conducted them to the Council House, where were gathered eighty of the chiefs and principal men of three Algonquin Nations. It was Frenchmen's luck that on May 27, 1603, Ana-da-bi-jou was feasting the warriors of the Etchemins of the Bay of Fundy, the Ottawas of the Ottawa River, and his own Montagnais of the Lower St. Lawrence, just returned from a war party, bringing with them a hundred Iroquois heads. It had been one of the rare Algonquin successes against the Iroquois warriors, usually more numerous and always more aggressive. Bes-ou-at, proud War Chief of the Ottawas, had led a combined force of a thousand warriors to the River of the Iroquois (Riche-lieu River), which brings the water of Lake Champlain into the St. Lawrence. Near the mouth of the river, Bes-ou-at had made an ambush, but because of unfavorable dreams and omens the Etchemins and Montagnais demurred, as was their right under the Confederation. A war party of one hundred Mohawk Iroquois fell into Bes-ou-at's trap, and the five hundred Ottawas killed all of them.

The embassy of Pontgravé and Champlain, to offer an alliance in peace and aid in war, was fortunate to find three of the strongest Algonquin Nations in one place, celebrating a lucky one-sided victory over a perennial enemy whom they feared and dreaded. The French offer of an alliance could not have been made at a more propitious time.

When all was ready in the Council House, one of the two interpreters rose to deliver his prepared oration, translating into the musical Algonquin tongue, and embellishing with the beautiful imagery of the Indian, the staccato Biscayne French of Pontgravé and Champlain. The man spoke at length, as was the custom in Indian oratory at the Council Fire. Not only did he translate the Frenchmen's words, but he interspersed these with descriptions of those splendors of France which old Pontgravé had been at such pains to show him. A handsome, bearded King Henry in his gilded armor grew in stature in the telling, impressing the Great Chiefs of the Algonquins, blanketed though they were in the skins of black marten, soft grey squirrel, or the rare silver fox from the barren Arctic lands. And what was a war party of a thousand painted Indians, when the armored cavalry of Henry's French Nation rode by on mooselike horses, followed by a host of pikemen and musketeers, controlling the lightning with their thunder?

At last, when the interpreter's account of France led impressively to King Henry's message, it was accepted with dignity by the chiefs, and all the Algonquin people rejoiced in their new ally, the French.

Pipes were smoked in ceremonial sealing of the treaty, and gifts were exchanged between the chiefs and the Great King's ambassadors: metal objects from Europe in exchange for the finest furs of North America. In the feast which followed, the excitement of the Algonquins, already aroused by their victory over the Iroquois, was increased by anticipation of new and greater triumphs over their old enemy. Watching the feast, the Frenchmen exulted in the thought of the great fur-trading empire which they had gained by a single stroke. A battle or two with the primitive Iroquois meant nothing to men who, under the white plume of Henry of Navarre, had fought across the fields of Europe.

After the meal had been devoured, there was dancing of a most sinister nature. It was a boasting dance to show each Indian's bravery in battle. In a net of vines on the back of every warrior was the head of a dead Iroquois, nodding and bouncing in ghastly accompaniment to the turning and stomping of the dancers. The beat for the dance was given by a rhythmic slapping of the thighs and a chanting through pursed lips.

Samuel de Champlain watched with something more than curiosity. As the military member of the expedition, he studied these strange allies of his Most Christian King against the day when they would be his companions in arms, fighting the unknown enemy in the forest to the south and west. As the first colonizer of North America to come from France, Champlain was studying out in his own mind a French colonial system. On his voyage to Spanish America he had observed and repudiated Spain's policy of exploitation to extinction of the natives in the new lands. As he watched, an honored guest at the feast at Tadoussac, Champlain envisaged for France a friendly co-existence with the Indians, who, in exchange for trading rights, would be made strong at home by education in agriculture, and whose boundaries would be extended with the help of France in fighting their border wars.

The Algonquins of the St. Lawrence River and the Maritime Peninsula came to be allies of France and objects of French colonial ambition because, in the reign of Francis I, the indomitable Jacques Cartier, by raising The Cross on the Gaspé Peninsula, had claimed all the Algonquin lands for France. Three-quarters of a century had passed before Samuel de Champlain took up Cartier's claim and bound himself and his country to the Algonquins by joining their war party.

For two long weeks the French guests sat out the interminable dancing, feasting, and orating of their Algonquin hosts. Nor did they stand apart; with proper ceremony,

Pontgravé and Champlain fired the cannon aboard the *Bonne Renommée*. The loud explosion echoed off the headland, and the huge fire-streaked puff of black smoke billowed across the waters of the river, filling the Indians with awe and fright. They crowded closely around their new allies for reassurance, and shouted their glee at the thought of Mohawk warriors consumed by the roar and smoke of the iron fire log.

The enforced stay at Tadoussac before setting off to explore the inland country gave Champlain an opportunity to observe the confederated Algonquin Nations. He recorded all his impressions in his journal and in the sketches that accompanied it.

He saw that the Algonquins possessed judgment, yet had vices that showed a lack of judgment. He admired the fine physical proportions of both men and women, and marveled at the lack of deformity among them. He had inquired of the Indians regarding their beliefs and their religion, and had been told their pretty story: that men and women alike sprang from the straight shafts of arrows, stuck into the earth by the God, Manitou, after he had made the land. To a Christian the four gods of the Algonquins seemed too many, and Champlain was shocked to be told that the Mother Goddess was worthless and "ate things up." He decided at once that, when the French came, they must bring priests to teach the Indians of the Trinity, and how to pray together, not each in his own heart as he desired. Priests, too, would teach the Indians to cover their unconcerned nakedness, preach chastity to the unmarried girls, and give laws to the people.

Blind revenge was an Indian quality that disturbed Champlain, the soldier. As he came to know the Algonquins he thought about the Iroquois, the objects of so much hatred, and he suspected much of the boasting and lying was rooted in fear.

At last, on June 11, Champlain was free to go exploring. He wanted to see the land of the Iroquois, but first he made a week's trip up the awful chasm of the Saguenay. Then, on June 18, he set out with Pontgravé for the Upper St. Lawrence. They traveled on the 12-ton shallop that had come out on the *Bonne Renommée*, and at the end of five days they reached the St. Charles River and the high bluffs above the narrow foreshore on the St. Lawrence side, where Cartier had wintered in 1535.

Westward from the Maurice River along the shore of Lake St. Pierre, the shallop quested into new country, which, in the spring, was a fertile and promising land. Pontgravé cautiously piloted the little barque among the islands at the lake's western end, where the interrupted waters again became a river, and almost at once the party reached the mouth of a swiftly moving river, flowing into the St. Lawrence from the south.

As the Frenchmen approached the inlet of this new river, they were hailed from the shore by a group of Indians. They approached warily until assured by their interpreter that these were friendly Indians and not the dread Iroquois. They proved to be a band of Ottawa Algonquins, several of whom Champlain recognized, returning home from the feast. The Frenchmen were made welcome to the camp, which was fortified after the Algonquin fashion. The fort was square, the sides facing inland made of small trees set into the ground on end and covered with bark, the two sides on the rivers left open. Champlain judged the walls of the fort to be useful only for delaying an enemy, and noted that the canoes which lined the water sides of the fort were ready for quick flight.

This caution, as Champlain learned, was reasonable, for the camp was on the very River of the Iroquois. On its shores Bes-ou-at's Ottawas had taken the hundred heads, and down its waters would come — or so the Algonquins feared — a vengeful, howling horde of Iroquois.

That evening Champlain learned more of the River of the Iroquois, and made his first discovery.

Sitting by the Indians' campfire, with the shallop riding to anchor, its bow on the swift spring current of the river, he questioned the Algonquins over the map they traced with sticks in the dry earth and the ashes of the fire. Impatiently, he sat and listened to the strange jargon he never was able to learn; eagerly, he hung on the translations made by his French-trained interpreters, as his searching questions led him up the River of the Iroquois.

The Indians said that the river was broken by falls (Chambly), but above the falls the waters became smooth again and passed around islands (Ile aux Noix and Ash Island), before the river took its beginning at the foot of the Lake of the Iroquois (Lake Champlain).

The lake extended southward for ninety miles as the Canada goose flies before the icy winds of fall, through mountains set on a high, marching skyline, from which countless brooks and small rivers led down across a rich, wide valley floor. The Indians said that the waters of the lake were blue and sweet, and the shoreline ran through marsh and confining mountain narrows, by wooded points of land and into deep bays. It ran past many islands, some of them lone gray rocks whitened with the chalk of seagulls, others wide and long with little mountains on them, like lands in miniature.

At the beginning of the seventeenth century all this was territory dominated by the Iroquois. At Ticonderoga, twenty miles north from the point where the lake ends at the foot of a domed mountain, the Mohawks had a great source of black flint. In temporary camps along the shores of the waterway they chipped their arrow points, while parties hunted in the surrounding mountains and went out in boats on the lake to fish.

From the Lake of the Iroquois, known to the Indians by the more descriptive name of "Ca-ni-a-de-re Quar-ant," ("The Lake That Is the Gate"), two ways led to the south. These roads separated at Ticonderoga.

The western path climbed up around the falls and rapids of a stream flowing out of another lake. This lake was the floor of a closed valley, and was a long, thin ribbon of island-studded water — water of the deepest blue, glimmering and clear. "An-di-a-ta-roc-te" was the name the Indians had given this narrow lake (Lake George), and to the big mountains on its shores they gave great thundering names such as "Aa-nuck-so-ho-ry" and "To-kagh-wan-ker-a-negh-ton." The lake's Indian name meant "Tail-of-the-Lake." It was a tail thirty-six miles long, and on its very tip was a big summer encampment of the Mohawk Iroquois, out of which a long portage wound through the mountains in a south-easterly direction.

From Ticonderoga, the eastern road was over Lake Champlain, continuing through a long reach of marshes to its end at South Bay. Where the marshes met the bay on the eastern shore, an arm of the lake extended through a cleft in the hills to a crystal-clear pool below a twenty-foot fall of water. This pool, and the marshy land to the north of it, during the spring freshets so teemed with long, mottled pike that the Indians scooped the fish from the surface of the water as they scooped up chunks of venison from a boiling stew. For this reason the place was known as "Kah-cho-qua-na," or the "Place-Where-One-Dips-Fish" (later

Skenesborough, now Whitehall, New York). Above the falls the water road continued up the northward-flowing Wood Creek.

Both at An-di-a-ta-roc-te and on Wood Creek, where the Indian war parties, returning Iroquois, or, in former times, southbound Algonquins, beached their canoes at the end of water navigation, tote trails led through ten miles of forest. These long portages ended on the shores of a wide southward-flowing river whose swift, smooth current, Champlain learned, would carry a canoe to the ocean within two days.

For Champlain this was a momentous discovery. He knew that the Atlantic coast stretched northeast to southwest from Newfoundland to Spanish Florida, and that it spanned some 25 degrees of latitude. Since leaving the fishing banks of St. John's, Newfoundland, the *Bonne Renommée* and the shallop had come through 20 degrees of latitude. But the course they had taken from Anticosti Island, at the mouth of the St. Lawrence, to the River of the Iroquois was parallel to the coast and nowhere, he calculated, were they more than three hundred miles from the Atlantic Ocean. This River of the Iroquois, therefore, was part of a water route to the ice-free southern waters.

Champlain begged Pontgravé to explore the river at once, but the old Saint-Malo seaman insisted that this was impossible. Not enough time remained in the sailing season, that year of 1603. As the *Bonne Renommée* had been delayed by ice floes in the Gulf of St. Lawrence until May 20, so she must be out of the river before the freeze, and back across the Atlantic to her native France before the autumn storms. Eventually, however, Pontgravé relented sufficiently to permit a short cruise of the shallop up the River of the Iroquois, but this proved disappointing. Fifteen miles upriver at St. Ours, the clumsy boat was halted by the swift current. With a skiff and a couple of sailors to row it for him, Champlain continued on for another five or six miles, but had to return to meet the shallop. For a long moment he stood in the stern of the little craft, gazing to the south up the far reaches of the river. At last he gave the order to turn back.

～～～～～～～

It was six years before Champlain returned to the River of the Iroquois. The Rouen ship of the 1603 expedition, while cruising in the Bay of Fundy, had heard — and be-lieved — an Indian story of a rich copper mine there. This promise of quick wealth for the taking turned French colo-nial efforts, including those of Champlain, away from the fur country of the St. Lawrence. In 1604, Champlain es-tablished his colony in Acadia. The copper mine proved a will-o'-the-wisp. The four summers and three winters that Samuel de Champlain lived and worked on the northeast coast of North America returned nothing to the expedition's backers in France but a store of experience for their lieuten-ant, Champlain.

During the summer months he sailed along the coast on voyages of exploration. Once, he rounded Cape Cod and was in a fair way to coming upon the Hudson River — the Atlantic end of the waterway to the St. Lawrence of which the Algonquins had told him. But he ran into hostile Indians, whom he fought in battle, and he also had to prepare winter quarters, so he was forced to turn back short of that dis-covery.

The winters were a grim struggle for survival against cold, starvation, and disease. That the French colony in Acadia was able to survive was due largely to the indomi-table will and the directing genius of Samuel de Champlain. But, finally, in the autumn of 1607, he returned to France.

Since his first voyage to Canada in 1603, Champlain had dreamed of a permanent French colony there for exploration, trade, and development far up the St. Lawrence. His experience in survival and exploration in the now abandoned Acadian settlement had only quickened his resolve to return to Canada and to continue up the River of the Iroquois.

It was for his dream that Champlain gave up the quiet, wonder-filled forests of North America; it was for his purpose that he accepted life in the morass of crooked streets that was Paris during the wet, dank months of winter in 1607–8, and waded through the bog of Court politics.

By January 7, 1608, Champlain was a lieutenant under the Sieur de Monts, who held the trade monopoly to the St. Lawrence Basin without which no expedition to Canada could finance itself. On April 13 of that year, Champlain sailed from Honfleur in his ship, the *Don de Dieu*, bound for Tadoussac. In addition to trade-goods, cattle, and supplies, he carried on board a 12-ton shallop in which he intended to sail up the River of the Iroquois, preferring this light sailing vessel to the birch-bark canoe. With him went a little band of artisans who would build the house in which he proposed to spend the winter, far up the St. Lawrence.

On their arrival, this house was built on the site which Champlain chose for his *habitation:* the narrow foreshore below the cliffs where the St. Charles River meets the St. Lawrence — Quebec. The *habitation* consisted of three dwellings, a storehouse, and a dove tower, all behind a moat and palisade, and was completed during the summer months.

The Algonquins were impatient at all these activities. Being themselves improvident, they could not understand Champlain's careful preparations for winter, which consumed the whole war season of 1608. Five summers had passed since the Algonquin Confederation had been promised French aid in its war against the Iroquois.

Champlain's foresight, however, carried Quebec City — and with it many of the starving Montagnais — through the first terrible winter. As it was, of the twenty-four Frenchmen sixteen died before the snows melted in early April 1609. The arrival of the relief ship from France in June found Champlain impatient to explore, and to join his allies in making war.

At the end of the month, he set out in the shallop bound for the River of the Iroquois. Except for the hundred severed heads at the Tadoussac feast, Champlain had never seen an Iroquois. His knowledge of the terrible Iroquois warrior was based on the tales that were told to him by overawed Montagnais, Ottawas, and Etchemins.

The Iroquois were an alien race to the primitive hunters of the Algonquins. They were nomadic tillers of the soil, who had come out of the setting sun in search of a promised land, which their god had told them they would recognize by the imprint of his hand upon the ground. This prophecy was fulfilled when the Iroquois came at last to the Finger Lakes region of what is now western New York State.

Five Nations — Senecas, Cayugas, Onandagas, Oneidas, and Mohawks — had settled down on the fertile land stretching from the mouth of the Mohawk River to the headwaters of the Ohio. All around them were the far-flung Algonquins, whose hunting ground they had so boldly appropriated. To preserve their island in the Algonquin forest-sea, the Iroquois had resolved their national differences in a league of peace. By the tenets of the League of the Long House, named for their communal dwellings, each Nation contributed to the strength of the whole, and the decisions agreed upon at the Great Council Fire were binding on the whole.

Of these Five Nations the most cruel, the most cunning,

the most savage was the Mohawk. Among their allies in
the Great Peace which the Iroquois League maintained
among its members, they were called the "Kanienga," the
"People possessed of flint." It was in their lands at the
easternmost end of the Long House where the quarries
in which was found flint for arrow heads and war axes were
located. "Mohawk" meant "cannibal" and was the name
given to the Kanienga by their enemies, the Algonquins.
The Mohawk warriors were proud of this opprobrious name
(which was not undeserved) and wore it like war paint to
keep terror alive in the hearts of the Algonquins.

The Mohawks had their principal village and their tribal
Council Fire at the junction of the Mohawk and Hudson
Rivers. Their contribution to the collective security of the
Iroquois League's five hearths was to act as keepers of the
eastern door of the Long House. During the hundred years
or more that the league had existed before Champlain arrived to challenge it, the Mohawks — always bold, aggressive, and warlike — had extended their dominions northward, making a warpath to the very doorway of their perennial enemies, the Algonquins of the St. Lawrence.

There had been a sixth Nation of the wily Iroquois: the
Ochatequins. Becoming separated from the Five Nations
that settled and united around the Finger Lakes, they had
come to rest on the shores of Georgian Bay. This Nation's
name, "Huron," was derived from the French word *hure*,
meaning *head of a boar*, because of the stiff crest of hair
worn by their warriors. Completely surrounded by the
numerous Algonquins, the Hurons made crafty friendship
with their neighbors and even joined the loose Algonquin
Confederation against their distant kin. From their position
on Georgian Bay, between the tribes of the great fur country to the north and west and the Algonquin tribes to the
east, the Hurons became rich *entrepreneurs*, dominating

the source of furs, the trade route, and the merchant nations of the coast who sold to the European markets. In their cousins of the League of the Long House, the Hurons recognized potentials which could — and would — upset their trade empire. Until 1609, behind a buffer of Algonquin-Iroquois war, the Hurons had been successful in keeping the wonderful steel and hard iron out of the hands of the Iroquois and the European traders isolated at the mouth of the St. Lawrence.

While the Hurons viewed with mistrust the French penetration of Canada which might lead to their doing business with the Iroquois League, the Ottawas and Montagnais were eager to impress their Huron allies with the power of French weapons, which (they hoped) could exterminate the Five Nations. Skeptical but curious, the Huron warriors came down out of the north to join — if they were sufficiently impressed — an Algonquin-French war party against the Mohawks.

Champlain met the Hurons seventy miles above Quebec, on an island in the Batiscan River. Armored and plumed, he stepped proudly ashore from the shallop. With him were twenty swaggering Frenchmen, with the admiring Montagnai and Ottawa warriors. The Frenchmen were prepared for war, not for trade, and Champlain stalked boldly in among the painted savages. No Huron then remembered the talk against the French!

But Champlain was not yet free to begin his explorations. First, the Hurons must be properly impressed with the might of France. From the Batiscan River, Champlain led the whole convocation of Nations, three hundred warriors with their women and children, back to Quebec, so that the Hurons might see his wonderful house and hear the cannons roar. Still no one made a move to attack the enemy up the

River of the Iroquois, and again Champlain's explorations had to be postponed, while the long ceremony of the War Dance was performed.

At long last, all appeared to be in readiness for the departure of the great war party; but there remained one final ceremony. Champlain and his companions were standing off-shore in the shallop, when from the Indian huts there came the sound of singing, which swelled until every voice in the camp was included. Then from out of the huts and wigwams came the Indians: men, women, and children stark naked, with not an ornament on their brown bodies. Singing and dancing, they cavorted across the shore to the beached canoes, where the warriors embarked. The women helped to push the light craft out into the water. Then, as the canoes moved out from the shore, the women followed, swimming alongside — not mournfully, holding the men back, but joyfully, splashing, teasing, and promising a warm welcome on the warriors' return with scalps and glory. It was a mock battle in the water, a play of hesitant departure, and promised incentive and inducement to return.

Once away, the party moved swiftly to the entrance to the River of the Iroquois, and Champlain with his twenty Frenchmen hurried on, rowing the shallop up the river until the way was blocked by the falls at Chambly. Here, at the threshold of the Mohawk country, the bravery of Frenchman and Indian alike wavered. The French found an excuse for not going on in the fact that the shallop could go no further. The Indians, whose fear of the Mohawks grew as time and distance dulled the ardor of their departure, found their excuse for not going on in the reluctance of the French.

But Samuel de Champlain would not be denied. He persuaded two of the Frenchmen to accompany him, and a proportionate sixty of the Indians consented to go with them.

These Indians were drawn from the three tribes: Hurons, Montagnais, and Ottawas. The reduced war party portaged twenty-four canoes around the Chambly falls, and at the relaunching place Champlain gingerly took his seat in the bottom of a frail birch-bark canoe.

The Algonquin canoe was well made, light, handy, and strong, in contrast to the crude dug-out log boats of the Five Nations, whose attempt to copy the Algonquin birch-bark canoe produced only a rough, heavy vessel of stiff elm bark. To hunt, and to travel along the big rivers and great lakes of their homeland, the otherwise backward Algonquins had developed the birch-bark canoe into a sturdy craft, graceful and fast.

The twenty-four canoes of Champlain's war party were small, designed to carry warriors traveling light and fast, close along a shore. They were but eight or nine feet long, with a width not exceeding eighteen inches, but with a safe-carrying capacity of a thousand pounds.

The three Frenchmen sat with legs extended, their armor and weapons piled around their feet. In addition to his arquebus and bandolier, each had with him his sword, tassets, breast plate, back plate, gorget, and plumed helmet. Champlain's astrolabe was always close beside him. In the heat of the July day, the heavy leather arming doublets and high leather boots were stored in the bottom of the canoes with the panoply of arms. The Frenchmen traveled light, progressively modifying their fashionable European dress until they rode as bare as Indians and, burned by the hot sun, as brown. Only their long hair, which they soon learned to tie back, and their untrimmed beards set them apart from their barefaced and high-crested Indian allies.

For two days the party was on the river, paddling upstream in fair weather. At nightfall on July 3, Champlain arrived at the foot of the lake. The light had gone from the land and the water. In the last faint glow of the long summer twilight still brightening the rim of the western sky, the land was flat and black beyond a wide pavement of dark water. The lake seemed silently to beckon; there was promise to the south over the big water.

Champlain explored the lake for twenty-six long days. His canoe skirted the many islands, and he went back and forth again to look into deep bays and journey up new rivers. He marveled at the beauty of the distant mountains that showed themselves when once he was on the lake and could see over the tree-lined shores. Often, as the canoes slipped around a rocky point of land they surprised deer at the water's edge. The deer did not run away, but only stared back at the wondering Frenchmen.

To the camps which they built among the trees, the hunters of the party brought venison, and the anglers brought fish of many species. Once, the Indians brought Champlain the head of an enormous pike which they said was a gift for King Henry of France, and Champlain solemnly accepted it on behalf of the monarch. The Algonquin guides were eager to show Champlain the lake, but they seemed less eager to find the Iroquois; nor was Champlain himself impatient for war.

On the idyllic journey around the lake, Champlain, as a soldier and an armed ally, had studied the Indians' method of advancing, making camp, and preparing for battle. Nine Indians, in three canoes, went ahead as scouts. Cautiously they paddled up the lake, landing frequently to climb some headland, or a tall pine tree, from which they would have a broad view of the lake beyond the next point of land. Before camping at night, and in the morning before breaking camp, the scouts roamed the woods looking for signs of the enemy.

Behind the scouts, the main party followed openly and

carelessly, paddling in silence to the next place selected for a camp. There they built the inevitable stockade of logs and bark, always following the same pattern: three, or sometimes two, sides of logs, the water side always left open for the quick launching of the canoes. It horrified Champlain that the Indians never posted sentries while they slept. They had complete faith in the report of the scouts.

Following behind came those told off as hunters for the day. They arrived in camp in the evening, after the two-hour job of building the stockade had been completed by the main party. All shared in the evening meal of deer meat or fish, speared in the shallows, which was mixed with the dried corn each warrior carried as cold rations.

In this military drill Champlain and his two French companions took no active part. They rode in their canoes as tourists, honored and feted guests in the camp. It was only when Champlain insisted that the party press on up the lake in search of the enemy that he found out the true cause of hesitancy on the part of the Indians to attack. Ever superstitious, ever seeking signs and omens, they were waiting for some such auspicious omen to be given to them by the Frenchman.

Obligingly, that very night Champlain dreamed of Iroquois drowning in the lake, and to the Hurons, Montagnais, and Ottawas this was a very good omen. Their confidence restored, the Indians went over to the attack. All pretense was gone. The Great War Chief took omnipotent command. Carefully, he prepared his plan of action and gave out his order of battle. He did this by placing in the ground, in the desired array, sticks equal in number to the warriors present. Each warrior was told which of the sticks represented him, and the whole party lined up, each in his appointed place, to walk through the subsequent maneuvers. Patiently and painstakingly, the exercise was repeated until both the Indians and the skeptical Frenchmen had learned the formation.

Now the war party traveled at night, hiding during the day in fireless camps. Scouts went ahead to spy out any parties of Mohawks heedlessly traveling the lake by day. The lake was empty. No smoke betrayed an Iroquois fishing camp along the shore. The party passed through the narrows, hugging the high west shore.

On the night of July 29, they put the bows of their canoes into the narrow ribbon of water above Crown Point, driving swiftly for Ticonderoga. The Algonquins would go to An-di-a-ta-roc-te, if necessary, to see their enemies drowning in the lake. The twenty-four canoes plunged on. With each strong stroke of the paddles, the water lapped up from the curved bows to race down the dappled sides. The night was dark, and the only sound was the swishing of the paddles, sliding edgewise through the water on the silent recovery of the Indians.

About ten o'clock, the Ticonderoga Peninsula seemed to bar the way ahead. High black mountains filled the sky beyond and to Champlain's right. He felt the canoe swerve to the left, and turned quickly to look forward. On the lake ahead, he saw a dark blob — then another — another — and many more. The dark objects took shape as canoes, many canoes — Iroquois canoes. The Algonquins broke the silence, calling excitedly to each other. In the stern of Champlain's canoe, the Montagnai War Chief let out a long, howling whoop ending in a series of gargling notes. From the strange canoes in the distance an answering, chilling cry went up. Champlain reached forward for his firearm carefully so as not to tip the canoe.

Nothing happened, out there in the darkness on the lake. Gradually the Algonquin canoes drifted together, like insects rafting in a stagnant pool. The canoes of the Iroquois were over toward the west shore, against the black shadows of the trees. Across the water came the sound of chopping; then a tree crashed in the forest, close to the water's edge. There were other sounds on the shore, and Champlain's interpreter whispered that the Iroquois were building a stockade.

For two hours Champlain waited, motionless and alert, in his canoe on the oily black waters of the lake. As the Iroquois prepared to fight on shore, the Algonquins prepared to fight on the lake, where their better craft gave them an advantage. With poles and paddles, the twenty-four canoes were lashed together into a platform which was stationed the length of an arrow shot from the west shore.

When all was in readiness, two Iroquois canoes came out to parley. They asked if the Algonquins wished to fight, and were assured that it was for battle that the Algonquins had come. But it was too dark to tell friend from foe, so both sides agreed to wait until morning. Then the Algonquins would come ashore and the Iroquois would come out of their stockade, to meet in battle on the open land between the water and the forest.

The plans for the contest having been agreed upon, each side withdrew to spend the remaining hours of darkness in hurling threats and invective at each other, in loud reassurance of their own courage.

Samuel de Champlain was alone with his thoughts.

At false dawn, Champlain and his two French comrades buckled on the various pieces of their armor and returned to their seats as the canoes were unlashed. They sat low in the craft, hiding themselves from view, and got ashore unobserved.

It had been agreed that the battle would begin at dawn.

Precisely as the sun rose, the two hundred Iroquois left their stockade and took up defensive positions outside. The Algonquins lined up in prearranged groups. Champlain was behind the massed warriors in the main body. The other two Frenchmen, with a few Indians, had gone off in a flanking movement through the woods.

At a shout from the Great War Chief the Algonquins ran toward their enemy, howling and brandishing their war clubs and steel tomahawks. In armor, Champlain labored along as best he could behind his naked allies. At thirty paces the Algonquins stopped short. Quickly, the force split, leaving a narrow avenue in the center. Through this lane now stalked the shining figure of Samuel de Champlain, a cloud of ostrich feathers nodding from the top of his helmet. On he strode, toward the silent and awestruck enemy. Immediately, he recognized the three War Chiefs of the Iroquois, who had been described to him. They wore high plumes, and, as befitted leaders, they marched together in the front and center of their men.

The effect of surprise was only momentary, for the Iroquois were a trained fighting race. Champlain, staring thirty paces ahead, saw a movement in the ranks of the enemy as arrows were notched to bowstrings. The moment had come. He raised his arquebus and leveled it at one of the chiefs. The wheel rasped on the flint. A puff of acrid powdered smoke burst before his face; then he felt the kick of the butt against his shoulder plate. He was enveloped in a great roar. Two of the chiefs were down and another Iroquois was rolling in agony on the ground. Three of the four round bullets with which Champlain had loaded his piece had found their mark.

A shout of glee went up from his Algonquin allies, and they loosed a flight of arrows over Champlain's head. The Iroquois immediately retaliated. As Champlain calmly went through the complicated motions of reloading his arquebus, a shot came from one of the Frenchmen on his left, and the third of the Iroquois chiefs was dead.

The second French shot burst the hoop of discipline and tradition. Casting down their weapons and their shields, the Iroquois fled, with the Algonquin warriors in pursuit — Hurons, Montagnais, Ottawas, Frenchmen, all in a joyous race through the forest. The battle of Ticonderoga was won.

With nothing further to keep them on Lake Champlain, the Indians paddled quickly northward, bearing with them Champlain and his two French companions. At Chambly Rapids the allies separated, the Hurons and the Algonquins of the Ottawa traveling westward to Montreal and the Montagnais proceeding to Tadoussac, taking the Frenchmen with them for the long Victory Feast.

New France Expands

In 1609, Champlain had traveled a long way up the lake to which he gave his name; and with his sworn allies, the Algonquins, he had gone a long way down a road that would turn back on the French and their Indian friends. Never would there be a lasting French peace with the Iroquois, who would find their own allies in the European enemies of France. Champlain himself was to fight the Iroquois on many occasions, but the war he started at Ticonderoga on July 30, 1609, would be fought out bitterly by Frenchmen yet unborn. For a hundred and fifty years Lake Champlain would bear the southward traffic of French war parties, but never would they go in victory through to the ice-free sea. Always, there were the Iroquois, especially the Mohawks who guarded the eastern door.

The Iroquois soon recovered from their defeat by Champlain and his two musketeers. The searing flash of panic that had sent the Mohawk warriors flying from Ticonderoga was quickly cooled by the wise heads at the Council Fire of the League of the Long House. The collective wisdom of the chiefs of the Five Nations recognized at once that a new concept had entered the old border war — a war that had degenerated into perennial spring raids, with contest-like battles between purposeless war parties.

To meet the new conditions of war and survival, the Iroquois had to rearm with steel weapons, even with muskets.

But these wonderful things could only be had by the exchange of furs with white-skinned traders, whose markets were set up deep in Algonquin-held territory.

Luck, however, hung in the smoke over the solemn Council Fire of the League. Within a matter of weeks after the crushing defeat at Ticonderoga, Henry Hudson arrived in the land of the Mohawks, the flag of the Dutch East India Company flying from the stern of his white-winged ship. Five years later there was a Dutch trading post at the eastern door of the Long House; and soon after that the English, supplanting the Dutch, came to stay.

Ever quick to learn, the Iroquois saw the old European alignment of French against English, even as their own League rivaled the Algonquin Confederation. So, to please their English customers, the Five Nations craftily opposed the French, forever holding them to blame for the unprovoked intervention and crushing defeat by Champlain on July 30, 1609.

While the Mohawks kept Lake Champlain closed to any French advance, the newly found and acute business sense of the League of the Long House sought to disrupt the French trade route through the Algonquin lands, and to divert the western furs to its own market outlet at Albany. The fierce warriors of the Iroquois ranged far to the north and to the west, terrorizing and imposing treaties as they went. But during all the long trade war, with its pitched battles, raids, ambushes, and drawn-out tortures, the powerful Nations of the Finger Lakes were not themselves averse to turning a gainful beaver skin with those French traders who had sufficient temerity to enter the Long House. French soldiers and Algonquin war parties were stopped far down Lake Champlain, and priests like Father Isaac Jogues, who in 1642 was the first white man to see Lake George, were tolerated only so long as their influence did not touch upon matters of policy and trade. But the advance of the eager merchant from Quebec, or from the new city of Montreal, was condoned in the villages along the Mohawk River so long as he matched trade goods with the English on the Hudson.

As colonies developed at the two trade outlets — French on the St. Lawrence, British on the Mohawk and the Hudson — these rivers took on the aspect of an extension of European political borders. Lake Champlain, which lay between, became a battleground for European wars.

It had never been a tranquil lake; Champlain had only given a new direction to a hundred years of Indian wars.

Champlain had established New France in Canada; his life as an explorer, a colonizer, and a servant of his King was fulfilled. The colony prospered. With the belligerent Mohawks on the Hudson, Lake Champlain and the River of the Iroquois was an arrow, the point of which was ever at the throat of New France. As the colony grew, successive governors, reinforced by French soldiers and an increasing number of *habitants*, as the colonists from France were called, sought to dull the Iroquois arrow and turn it around so that the waterway would become a French arrow, notched on the St. Lawrence and pointed toward the enemy on the Hudson, be he Indian or Englishman.

In 1642, the French started to build the shaft of their arrow. In that year Fort Richelieu was built at the mouth of the Richelieu River. To voice their claim, the French did away with the old Indian names for the waterway. The River of the Iroquois became the Richelieu River, named for the Cardinal Minister of Louis XIII; the lake was called Lake Champlain; and An-di-a-ta-roc-te, "The Tail of the Lake," later to be named Lake George, was given the French name of Lac du St. Sacrement, the name first applied to it by its French discoverer, Father Jogues.

Fort Richelieu did not long survive. In the fall of 1645, it was abandoned, and the ever-present Mohawks burned it before it could be reoccupied by the French the following spring. Twenty years later it was rebuilt, and in that same year Fort St. Louis and Fort Ste. Thérèse were built at opposite ends of the St.Jean-Chambly portage. In a long step southward, the French also surveyed a fort on Ile LaMotte, on Lake Champlain itself.

In that year (1665) a new governor came out to New France, and with him he brought the French regiment of Carignan-Sallières. It was a good regiment, of twenty companies. Raised in 1644 by the Prince de Carignan, it had fought well on many European battlefields. When its colonel, the Marquis de Sallières, brought it to New France, its ranks were filled with hardened, durable men led by bold, adventurous officers. No regiment served Canada better. For more than twenty years it fought for, and garrisoned, New France, and when at last it sailed for home, it left Canada peopled with stout-hearted men from its ranks.

On arrival, the new governor and the new regiment immediately took the offensive. In the dead of winter, they struck at the Mohawk towns. Three hundred men and officers of the regiment, with two hundred *habitants*, set out from Fort Ste. Thérèse on January 9, 1666. Like the lowest soldier of the line, Governor Daniel de Courcelles carried a thirty-pound pack. On down the ice he led his five hundred men. Everyone had to wear snowshoes, for with the bitter cold of that year had come deep snow. To the soldiers, newly arrived from France, the round, cumbersome snowshoes of the Indians were a trial. But they were undaunted, and before they had gone far they had picked up the plodding, shuffling gait that eats up the white miles.

On the lake, the wind lashed at the long tails of their brown coats and whipped at the blue and yellow ribbons on the points of the officers' shoulders. Luckily, their wide-brimmed beaver hats had been replaced by Canadian caps of fur or wool. They wore bright yellow scarves, pulled up over the mouth and nose against the searing cold. These grew white with beads of frost as the men labored through the swirling tails of dry, cold snow on the unprotected lake. To leave the open lake at Crown Point for the protection of the mountains seemed at first a blessing; but in the mountains the snow was four feet deep.

The guides lost their way in the valleys west of Lake Champlain, and instead of falling on the unsuspecting villages of the Mohawks, Courcelles found himself near the English settlement at Schenectady. There the French met the Mohawks in an inconclusive battle, after which they fell back on Albany, where for three days they received succor from the English.

The homeward march began on February 13, and was dogged as far as the lake by vengeful Mohawks. When the Indian wolves turned back to their warm lodges, the trail of the French army was picked up by the lean-jawed Beast of Hunger and the numbing talons of the Owl of Cold. Sixty men fell behind on that march, dropping off to sleep till death in the soft snow beside the deep-grooved snowshoe trail.

Courcelles and his regiment were not deterred from their purpose by their nearly disastrous winter venture. When spring came that same year of 1666, they returned with a will to Lake Champlain. On Ile LaMotte, Fort Ste. Anne was built and garrisoned by the Carignan-Sallières. When two officers of the regiment were taken prisoner near the new fort, Captain Sorel followed with three hundred men in European boats and Indian canoes, pursuing the Iroquois war party to the Mohawk villages, where the release of the prisoners was secured.

Sorel brought back from the Mohawks intelligence that went into the plans of M. de Courcelles, who was preparing to mount an expedition against the Mohawk towns in the autumn. Pressure from France was bearing hard on the governor to bring an end to the Indian Wars, which were beginning to show diminishing profits to the Court and to the Crown. To help the governor, Louis — now the resplendent XIV of that name — sent the formidable old Lieutenant General the Marquis de Tracy. With cold logic, the two commanders reasoned that when the storehouses of the enemy were filled they would burn all the better, and the wake of their destruction would bring starvation and death during the winter to follow.

The six hundred regular troops gathered at Ile LaMotte were now forest-worthy, after a year in this wild land of the lakes, at the very end of known civilization. On the mainland, just across LaMotte Passage, six hundred Canadian volunteers were encamped. The young *habitants*, in their gay colored sashes, were from river-bank farms close by a tall-steepled church: they were going against a heathen, cabin-burning enemy; broad-shouldered *voyageurs*, when the trade routes were open again, would paddle westward in their brigades to bring back furs; and there were half-wild, half-outlaw French *coureurs de bois*, whose Algonquin squaws made camp for them, not among their countrymen but with their Indian relatives, from whom they were indistinguishable.

With the Marquis de Tracy and Governor Courcelles, there were a hundred warriors from the Hurons and the Ottawas. The governor, with an advance party of four hundred, left Fort Ste. Anne on October 1 and, paddling swiftly in their birch-bark canoes, were soon out of sight around Cumberland Head. Old as he was, General Tracy himself led out the main body of the army on October 3, followed on October 7 by the rear guard.

On Lake Champlain and Lake George the expedition met head winds. In the deep-troughed waves of the persistent autumnal south wind, a canoe would disappear as though gobbled up. In the sweep of an onrushing crest, the heavy-laden, flat-bottomed, low-sided bateaux, which the French introduced as the work horse of the American waterways, would swamp, founder, and go down. Only on those gem-bright, mild days of a northern fall could Courcelles and Tracy order their flotilla out on the lakes in their southward march to the Mohawk. The last steady flow of the upper Hudson before the binding grip of winter carried the expedition quickly to its objective.

On the Mohawk, the French regiment did its work well. With drums beating and flags flying, the soldiers of the Carignan-Sallières dashed about, joyously putting the torch to the long houses and full granaries of the Mohawks. The Algonquins and *coureurs de bois* scouted the woods and reported back to the generals, waiting under the lily banner of France planted firmly in the center of the dead ashes of the Council House: the Iroquois had gone. All believed that the Mohawk Nation had been crushed.

The return journey found Lake Champlain's mood a petulant one, as though resenting its new master who would harness it with strange craft of sawed boards and forged nails. An autumn storm caught the French armada in open water and scattered its boats far and wide. The lake took its toll: two boats and the lives of eight men. At the drying-fires that night, *voyageurs* and *coureurs de bois* told of the invisible people who lived in palaces at the bottom of Lake Champlain. Many of the young men listened, and when the expedition was water-borne again and the priest was not nearby, they surreptitiously beat out the full bowls of their unsmoked pipes against the sides of their bateaux. Those who knew had said that a gift of tobacco ensured the good will of the invisible people.

The fifty-three-day expedition of 1666, up the lake to the Mohawk towns, brought a quasi-peace that lasted for more than twenty years. The Iroquois seemingly were cowed by the Frenchmen who had taken their lakes and their river; but it was the truce of the red fox, waiting patiently at the edge of the clearing.

There was no abrupt ending to the Franco-Iroquois "peace" imposed by the Marquis de Tracy and by Cour-celles. It was merely shouted down by the cries of the Iro-quois as the decade of the 1680's moved toward a close. And the war cry of the Indians was but the echo of the wails of a baby prince, lying new-born in the royal cradle of England.

Catholic James II had a son and a male heir. Mary, his eldest daughter and his heiress, had lost her pretensions. Wil-liam of Orange, Mary's husband and the most militant Prot-estant in all Europe, implacable foe of his father-in-law's *alter ego*, Louis XIV of France, was forced to rescue Eng-land and his wife's heritage from Catholicism. The unpopu-lar King James fled before the invasion of William of Orange and its resulting revolution in England. Together, the Dutch William and Mary Stuart mounted the English throne. Louis of France was left with two refugees — the abdicated King and the infant Pretender — and with the monarchs of Europe banded against him in a league which was the creation of William of Orange and of England. The upheavals in Europe came to Lake Champlain, as two un-friendly European powers faced each other with only the empty blue waters of the lake between them.

It had been French colonial policy to contain the several

British colonies on the strip of land lying east of the Allegheny Mountains. France envisaged a trading empire with a buffer fringe of Indians who were friendly to France, unfriendly to England.

English colonial policy, on the other hand, was that of the dissenter colonist who came to the Atlantic seaboard to settle and to make his home, and who crowded out the aboriginal inhabitants; the colonist had come to establish, under the British Crown, his own individual way of thought. Most of the English in America in the seventeenth century were rabid anti-papists who welcomed the Protestant William and Mary. With a crusading zeal, and the suspicion of a merchant for his competitor, the Englishman hated the French — whether at home or in New France. In the New York Colony, particularly, the royal Anglo-Dutch marriage was hailed with enthusiasm. There, the English rule was only a veneer over the earlier settlement of the Dutch, whose knack in trade had cracked the Alleghenies through their only pass: the valleys of the Mohawk and Lake Champlain. In the last years of James II, the League of the Long House had become the ally of the English, and Albany had become a settlement among the Mohawks. No longer was it an isolated trading post that could — or wished to — give warmth and food and friendship to a punitive raiding party from Canada, as it had done for Courcelles in January 1666.

The Iroquois of the Long House, always politically astute, read the changing times in the smoke from their stone pipes. They saw thousands of Englishmen on the seacoast, and a few hundred French traders scattering out from the two cities of warehouses at Montreal and Quebec. In the smoke, the Iroquois saw the sunset of New France and a final revenge upon their old enemy. The terrible strength of the Iroquois warriors was joined to the British.

In the new warfare, the French struck first. A plan put
forward in 1689 to seize New York City by an invasion
southward through Lake Champlain and down the Hudson
River, thus cutting the English colonies in two, was not
attempted until the following year. Then the ambitious plan
had dwindled to a winter raid that fell on Schenectady.

The leadership of this expedition was divided between
an impetuously bold Lieutenant de Mantet and the Sieur de
Ste. Helene, one of the ten fabulous brothers Le Moyne.
They set out with a force of three hundred men, divided
almost equally between Frenchmen and baptized Indians.
For fifty of this hardy band, the sub-zero weather of a late
February cold snap proved too much. After toiling for five
days on the Richelieu River from Montreal to St. Jean,
they gave up. The rest of the party moved on up the river
and, dragging their laden sledges, started the long trek up
Lake Champlain. The cold gave place to a thaw. Sweat
started on the brows of the men as they dragged the heavy
sledges through the wet slush. Each step was a gamble:
would the crust under the wet top-snow sustain the pressure
of a moccasined foot? Would the foot fall knee deep . . .
thigh deep . . . on the hard ice of the lake below? For eight
days they plodded up the lake, one labored step after another. When they reached the Hudson River, the bitter cold
returned.

On such a night of zero cold, Mantet and Ste. Helene
dashed through open gates where only ludicrous snowmen
stood guard, to massacre and fire the town of Schenectady.

At dawn, the French were off for Montreal. The return
journey was a more rapid one due to the horses they had
captured at Schenectady, which pulled the sleds and provided food for the men on the march. So it was that they
were able to outdistance their pursuers, fifty young men
from Albany, who gave up the chase at Crown Point, and

a hundred and fifty Mohawks who kept on into Canada.

The Schenectady massacre alarmed the settlers on the upper Hudson. Within six weeks the English, who were the first to make use of its military potentials, had a watch post at Crown Point. And Captain Abram Schuyler, of the family that even then was leading the settlers at Albany, set a guard at the Otter River while he raided as far north as Chambly, killing two Frenchmen and bringing a third home as prisoner.

Though the French attack had been timed to profit by the administrative confusion of the interregnum of England's government, it alarmed the royal governors of Massachusetts, Connecticut, and New York into co-operating in their own attack on Canada. Hastily organized for the summer of 1690, one part of the expedition went by sea, its destination Quebec; the other, with Montreal as a goal, went via Lake Champlain. The latter force was commanded by Fitz-John Winthrop, son of the governor of Connecticut and an old soldier under Cromwell. He got his sixteen hundred men to Wood Creek, where the hastiness of the organization became evident. There were no canoes or bateaux to carry the men over the lake, so Winthrop took his soldiers home again. Only another Captain Schuyler, John this time, refused to return without an attempt on the enemy — an enemy so very real to an Albany man. Accompanied by twenty-nine Englishmen and one hundred and twenty Mohawks, Schuyler raided down the lake and through the woods to despoil La Prairie, across the St. Lawrence from Montreal itself. He then returned safely home.

For eighteen years, 1691–1709, raid followed raid, and the valley of Lake Champlain carried the war parties to and fro.

In June of 1691, Major Philip Schuyler, the brother of

John, passed over the lake in canoes with his men to a second battle at La Prairie. His force of four hundred and fifty men killed or wounded some two hundred Frenchmen on that occasion.

The French preferred to travel in winter, when the water on the lake was frozen. In January 1693 the great governor of New France, Frontenac himself, led a raid against the Mohawk villages west of Schenectady. Major Philip Schuyler led the pursuit, which ended in a snowstorm that severely tried both French and English, and left each of the two forces groping in retreat before the weather.

In 1704 a large war party of French and Indians skated up Lake Champlain as far as the Winooski River, which they followed into the Green Mountains to the White River. This, in turn, guided them down to its junction with the Connecticut. Leaving their women and sleds at the mouth of the West River, two hundred Frenchmen and a hundred and forty Indians dropped down to Deerfield in Massachusetts, which was their planned destination. They struck at night when all were sleeping, and left in the morning with a hundred and eleven prisoners. In Deerfield only two houses remained standing, and forty-eight dead lay scalped in the white snow. The raiders got safely back to Lake Champlain and home to Canada. Some of the prisoners died on the journey; others were killed by the Indians. Some stayed with their Indian captors, though most were ransomed home. John Williams, the parson of Deerfield, was taken captive, having been sought out particularly and preserved as a prisoner to be exchanged for a Canadian of equal importance. Little Eunice Williams, the parson's seven-year-old daughter, remained with the Indians, though Governor de Vaudreuil tried to buy her from her captors, one of whom she later married.

Another big war party, following the same route out of

the Champlain Valley, repeated on the town of Haverhill the horrors of Deerfield.

To these raids out of Lake Champlain, and to other raids eastward into Maine and the Maritimes, the British retaliated with plans for a major attack for the conquest of Canada in 1709. As in 1690, a colonial force would approach Montreal via the Lake Champlain Pass, concerting its attack with a sea-borne invasion of Quebec by the Royal Navy, with five regiments of British regulars from England, and a contingent of Massachusetts colonials.

For the attack on Montreal, Colonel Francis Nicholson, with an army of fifteen hundred men, cut his way through the woods, widening to a road the old Iroquois trail from the Great Carrying Place on the Hudson (Fort Edward, New York) to Wood Creek. There Nicholson waited for word of the attack of the British fleet on Quebec. For months, eight hundred New Yorkers, a hundred and fifty Pennsylvanians, two hundred men from New Jersey, and three hundred Connecticut men sat in the woods beside the sluggish stream, slapped mosquitoes "big as swallows," and grumbled. Fifteen hundred Frenchmen came against them, but lost themselves in the woods east of Crown Point and turned back. The soldiers from the four separate colonies grew bitter toward one another; their only unity lay in their collective mistrust of their Indian allies. In September, Colonel Nicholson marched his men home again, and at Albany he carefully stored away all his military supplies against another try.

Two years later, Nicholson issued the arms and equipment to another army, this time four thousand strong. Again he moved to Wood Creek and waited. The time before, the English had had no fleet to support them; now, Nicholson knew that ships with sixty-four hundred souls aboard were on the way to Quebec. Nicholson's boats and canoes lined the banks of the stream, ready for the dash down Lake Champlain. His men were not so fractious, and reasonable hopes of success kept their morale high. But when word finally came from the fleet, it was to tell of disaster: it had wrecked itself near Anticosti Island. For Nicholson to go on alone would have been futile and foolish. Frustrated a second time, he had reached the limit of his patience. Carefully, he removed his hat and handed it to an aide. Then, with equal deliberation he removed his wig and threw it on the ground where, to the accompaniment of his own oaths, he trampled on it in a furious dance. His men gathered round to stare in wonder and approval. Then they all went back to Albany.

The Treaty of Utrecht brought peace to Europe in 1713, and with it peace came to North America. Safe travel became possible on Lake Champlain, and trade prospered.

A young man named John Henry Lydius moved up from Albany, and at the Great Carrying Place built himself a strong house of logs, cut with loopholes. Nicholson's old road still was clear, and Lydius kept canoes on Wood Creek and at the Falls-Where-One-Dips-Fish. From there, in summer, it was a pleasant paddle through the marshes, alive with duck and shore birds, past the promontory of Ticonderoga to the long, flat point where the narrow part of Lake Champlain comes to an end.

At this place (Crown Point) in 1731, the French built a fort for thirty men which they named Fort St. Frédéric, in honor of King Louis's secretary of state, Frédéric de Maurepas. Three years later it was enlarged to accommodate one hundred and twenty soldiers, and by 1742, it was a strong stone fort with a solid tower at the water's edge. Around this stronghold a village grew up, and across the lake farm clearings widened and met in a community of neighbors. Around their stone chimneys the *habitants* built their houses of boards, set vertically on frames. Among neighbors, work was exchanged for a cutting from a fruit tree, and soon orchards were started. An enterprising *habitant* at the north end of the lake built a ship which he called *La Vigilante*, rigged as a square-sail schooner. Through the ice-free months she sailed between the wooden fort and storehouses at St. Jean and Fort St. Frédéric in a regular carrying trade. Her first trip in the spring was eagerly awaited at Crown Point. Beyond there she dared not go; her captain-owner saw no reason to risk the only vessel on all Lake Champlain to the uncharted waters which led only to uninhabited Ticonderoga and the falls of Wood Creek; beside which, he was busy enough fulfilling his government contract. Thus the waters south of Crown Point remained undisturbed, and Lac du St. Sacrement lay quietly between its tall mountains. Few passed over the lake; those who did remarked upon its beauty, unchanged since time itself began.

The major war which erupted in Europe in 1740 and ended in 1748 scarcely troubled the waters of the northern lake. The mistrust bred on far-off battlefields ended the neighborly visits between John Henry Lydius and the now-augmented garrison at Fort St. Frédéric. Brush grew up on the portage road that was the stile over the divide between the southward-flowing Hudson River and Wood Creek, draining northward into the St. Lawrence. Lydius moved back to Albany. His caution was wisdom, for out of the woods one sunny day came Marin, the laughing partisan leader from Quebec, who cheerfully burned the abandoned house to the ground before continuing down the river to sack the English settlement at Saratoga.

Throughout the eight years of the war, the colonial governors screamed "Encroachment!" but London paid them little heed. Only in Massachusetts was there taken a vigorous and successful counter action: the Bay Colony's governor captured Louisbourg on Cape Breton. Word of the signed peace reached New York in time to end the bickering among the New York colonial councilors over their plans for an attack designed to drive the French from Fort St. Frédéric. This delay in committee postponed for seven years the military career of the expedition's designated commander, a remarkable young man named William Johnson.

II

England Triumphs

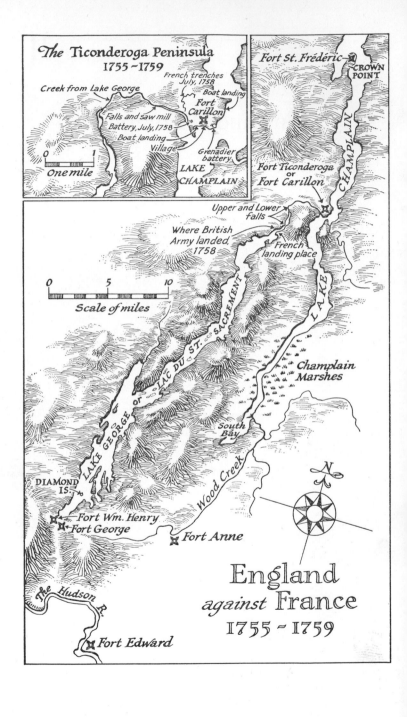

The Ticonderoga Peninsula
1755~1759

Creek from Lake George

French trenches July, 1758

Boat landing

Fort Carillon

Falls and saw mill

Battery, July, 1758

Boat landing

Village

Grenadier battery

LAKE CHAMPLAIN

0   1
One mile

Fort St. Frédéric

CROWN POINT

CHAMPLAIN

Fort Ticonderoga or Fort Carillon

Upper and Lower falls

Where British Army landed, 1758

French landing place

LAKE

0   5   10
Scale of miles

LAC DU ST. SACREMENT

Champlain Marshes

South Bay

LAKE GEORGE or

Wood Creek

N

DIAMOND IS.

Fort Wm. Henry

Fort George

Fort Anne

The Hudson R.

Fort Edward

England
against France
1755 ~ 1759

William Johnson Moves North

William Shirley, captain general and governor of the Massachusetts Bay colony, considered himself a military man and had a major general's commission to prove it. In William Pepperel, Shirley had a lieutenant who, in 1745, had demonstrated his strategic acumen by taking the great French fortress at Louisbourg. Pepperel had received a baronetcy for this impressive victory of colonial arms, principally those of Massachusetts Bay. In the early days of 1755, quite contrary to his intention, William Shirley paved the way for a second and last knighthood granted to an American.

William Johnson was now forty years of age, estate manager for his uncle, Admiral Sir Peter Warren. By his "good neighbor policy" Johnson had gained such control over the Iroquois Indians, among whom he lived in Pashanate splendor, that he was a power to be reckoned with on the road which Shirley wished to take to greater glory.

Shirley wanted to march his new uniformed regiment, the 50th Foot, with the 51st (called "Pepperel's," as the 50th was called "Shirley's") up the Mohawk River and lengthwise through the League of the Long House to the French fort at Oswego, on Lake Ontario's south shore. With that fort in his hands, he could claim a share of the glory expected to fall upon General Edward Braddock, just out from England with two veteran regiments of the line. Braddock was to attack Fort Duquesne in the main British effort against

New France for the 1755 campaign. The capture of Duquesne would cut the long line of French posts encircling the British Atlantic colonies from the mouth of the St. Lawrence to the delta of the Mississippi. The fall of Oswego would be another blow at the body of New France.

To deal with William Johnson, farmer, without divesting himself of any part of his own glory, Shirley proposed a diversion. He asked Governor-General DeLancey of New York to appoint Johnson to command an expedition against Fort St. Frédéric, at Crown Point — a fort which the French, so impertinently, and contrary to the English interpretation of the Treaty of 1713, had placed on English land and waters. Governor DeLancey willingly complied, and in exchange for a commission of Lieutenant General in the provincial troops, William Johnson assured the Massachusetts men of the co-operation of the Long House. Immediately, he went to work with that indomitable will which was to bring him a baronetcy.

Governor DeLancey's letter of instruction to General Johnson is dated April 16, 1755. From a friendly informant in London, too, a letter had come to Johnson, telling him what was expected of him there, at the fountainhead of tangible praise in terms of pounds sterling and hereditary preferment.

But the expedition itself had to be put on the road. Johnson considered the road: it was mostly water, up the Hudson to the farmhouse of Lydius, the Dutchman, at The Falls (Hudson Falls, New York). There, on the property belonging to Mr. Lydius, whose house might or might not be standing at the moment, Johnson would build a fort. The status of the house depended on Dutch perseverance and on the whim of marauding Indians.

From Fort Edward, as this fort was to be named, it was a twenty-mile carry to South Bay, on Lake Champlain. A small fort would have to be built there to protect the boat-landing. Perhaps Johnson would build a schooner at the head of South Bay, below the big round mountain that his Mo-hawks told him about; or perhaps he would carry the pre-pared ships timbers and planks up to the peninsula of Ticon-deroga, where he would build a third fort, to oppose Fort St. Frédéric on Crown Point and contain the French until he was ready to force them out. The French, who had a schooner on Lake Champlain, never sailed it below Fort St. Frédéric. Perhaps the channel was not deep enough?

While he must consider the eventual building of a navy on Lake Champlain, now, in Albany and at his own home on the Mohawk River, William Johnson had more immedi-ate problems for his pen and his desk, his secretaries and his bookkeepers. More urgently than a proud schooner to be assembled on Lake Champlain, he needed other boats; he needed cannon; and he needed men.

To secure cannon was never a simple matter of requisi-tion. Cannon were guarded jealously by those who had them, and they were cloaked in ancient mysteries presided over by artillerists, whose patroness is St. Barbara.

General Braddock sent to Johnson as an artilleryman, Captain William Eyre, who was also to act as chief engineer and quartermaster. Captain Eyre found another guild mem-ber at liberty, and persuaded him to join the expedition. The fact that Captain Doyle had but one arm was no hin-drance to him in his duties with the guns, and his Irish tem-perament was of help in the training of mattrosses and bom-bardiers, recruited from the New Englanders and Yorkers of the colonial army.

With the aid and knowledge of these two veteran gun-ners, Johnson was able to assemble an artillery arm far stronger than that planned for in his original table of organi-zation. By June, the expedition's artillery park consisted of twenty-two cannons and five large mortars for lobbing shells over the walls of Fort St. Frédéric, as well as six small mortars of the royal and coehorn type, which Johnson personally had requested from the governor of New York. It was not an inconsiderable array of guns. The largest cannon (and there were two of these) threw a shell weighing 32 pounds, though the pride of the siege train was a 13-inch brass mortar.

But the increase in the artillery was not without its debit on the logistics side of the staff ledger. It meant that more drovers must be hired, more teams of horses found, and more carriages and carts built to take the guns and their stores over the long carry. As the road to Crown Point was for the most part a water road, more boats would be required on the approach leg of the journey up the Hudson to Fort Edward, and still others, of a special nature, for the attack march from South Bay to Crown Point.

It would take one hundred ordinary bateaux to move the siege train to Fort St. Frédéric, in addition to which Johnson figured on building six special boats, large enough to carry the 18-pounders in firing position and strong enough to absorb the shock of recoil if the big cannon were fired from on board. Johnson's treasurer told him that these six boats would cost £10 apiece, while the remainder of the artillery boats could be had for £5 8s each. An artillery train comes high on a military budget!

The naval situation worried the general. In May, Johnson already had changed his thinking from a prefabricated schooner to be assembled at South Bay to a completely built row galley, ready to sail and fight when launched on Lake Champlain. Immediate naval domination of the lake was of primary importance to the whole success of his amphibious campaign. The row galley would provide this from the moment of its arrival at the bridgehead with the main body of the army. Its 40-ton burden, its 2-pounders, and its two swivel guns could out-gun anything that the French might send against it. With the row galley, Johnson could protect the embarkation at South Bay, guard the convoy of bateaux north to Crown Point, and without delay begin the blockade of Fort St. Frédéric, preventing help from coming to it up the lake. Later, when a schooner had been assembled, launched, and fitted out, she would reinforce the row galley.

The naval vessels, however, were but a small part of the fleet that Johnson's army would require, once it got to Lake Champlain. If one bateau were estimated to carry every five men, eight hundred bateaux would be needed for the expedition. To build such a large number of boats at Albany, where the army was to rendezvous, would draw attention to its destination before Johnson wished to give up the element of surprise. To the well-informed French, the troops gathering at Albany could mean reinforcements for Shirley's Oswego-bound regiments; but taken together, troops *and* bateaux could only mean a thrust down the Lake Champlain water route toward the throat and head of Canada — the arterial St. Lawrence, with its cities of Montreal and Quebec.

With secrecy in mind, contracts were let out far from the rendezvous, and builders in New York City, on Long Island, and in the bays and inlets of Connecticut and Rhode Island made good money putting together these basic carriers. The bateaux of the lakes and waterways of North America were, in general, standard in design, though varying in length. They were flat-bottomed for shallow water, sharp at both ends, and had a low freeboard amidship. There were seats for rowers, and a stumpy mast for a sail, which more often than not was a makeshift one. The oarsmen found the bateau obstinate when laden, and when empty, like a rooster weathervane in a squall.

Men to row and men to fight when the time came — this was to be William Johnson's constant worry. He was promised forty-seven hundred men, not including his own Indians: eight hundred New Yorkers, a thousand from Connecticut, fifteen hundred Massachusetts men, four hundred Rhode Islanders (some of whom were to be sailors for the Lake Champlain fleet), and five hundred men each from New Hampshire and New Jersey. In the end he got somewhat less than this quota, as the promises of the colonial governors exceeded their capability to recruit. And somewhere along the line of march, or at the assembly point, the entire five hundred of the New Jersey contingent paraded off west with "General" William Shirley. This was a blow to Johnson, as the "Jersey Blues" were well trained and well equipped, a regiment fit to be on the regular British Army establishment. "The Blues" were under the command of a member of the Schuyler family of Albany, albeit he lived in Peterborough, New Jersey.

With the troops came their colonels, their lieutenant colonels, and their majors. Each could claim to be heard in a Council of War, as he had been heard in a Town Council back home, or in the private closet of a royal governor, where the Inner Circle would gather for port, picquet, and plums. They were good men, on the whole, brave in battle and wise in their leadership of local troops. That the old colonial jealousies showed themselves was not surprising. The religious schisms that founded Connecticut and Rhode Island were still evident in doctrinal disputes, and the old Puritan godliness of Massachusetts called forth from Colonel Ephraim Williams the observation that the army, "present company excepted," was "wicked and profane . . . especially the Rhode Island and New York troops." When this remark was made, the troops from Episcopalian New Hampshire had not yet arrived in camp!

In the interest of harmony and military discipline, General Johnson published, in his standing orders: "No rum in camp; no bad women in camp," and, presumably for the benefit of the sinners from New York and Rhode Island, Albany was put off limits. The men's wives were considered as a part of the army, and were put on their decent behavior and adjured to wash and mend, as well as to eschew any immorality, under pain of chastisement.

Phineas Lyman was sent to Johnson as his second-in-command. Lyman came to Albany with his own 1st Connecticut Regiment, which was only slightly under full strength. He assumed the appointment of major general, and on July 17, 1755, took the advance guard to Lydius's house and set his men to work building the fort.

Johnson was housed in Albany when Lyman went north. He was still trying to meet the problems of command: leaking bateaux, capital offense courts-martial, the placation of Colonel Williams for having taken twenty of his men to crew a new artillery boat, and similar problems, when word came of Braddock's defeat. At first, the news was discounted; then, as messenger succeeded messenger and detail piled on detail, the enormity of the disaster took hold on the imagination alike of royal governor, soldier, and civilian. Two regiments of British regulars had been ambushed, defeated, and utterly routed, within a day's march of their goal at Fort Duquesne! It hardly seemed credible, but it was true. Its main chance obliterated, the whole military plan for 1755 was on the verge of collapse, as the British commander in chief in North America had collapsed under a bullet from out the forest. The plan would die from numbing shock, as Braddock had died from his wounds, unless leadership could find the herb from which to make the cure. It was found as an anti-body already present in the hearts of the colonials, and in the body politic of their leaders. The

North American stock had been born in the forest clearing, in the fertile valley near the community church, and in the seacoast town. Its spirit had shown itself in Massachusetts men at Louisbourg, ten years before. The Schuylers of Albany, Captain John and Major Philip, had tested it on Lake Champlain. When all the reports of disaster to Braddock and his British regulars were in, they showed that massacre and total destruction had been averted by the Virginia Americans. Under their commander, Colonel George Washington, they had stood off the Canadians and their Indians among the trees of an American forest while the British regulars made their retreat.

In the hastily summoned Councils of War, convened in Albany to consider the fate of the Crown Point expedition in the light of the collapse of the major effort of the year's campaigns, the colonial composition of General Johnson's army must have been apparent. Brash young confidence permeated the councils, and the Johnson campaign went forward.

William Johnson himself must have had misgivings. He had been chosen as leader because of his tight control over the League of the Iroquois. But word had now come to him out of the forest that the Senecas, most distant of the Iroquois, had sent warriors to fight with the French against Braddock. Young Seneca bucks were wearing red coats faced with buff and yellow, not gifts from a Father-King in London, but pulled from the lifeless bodies of soldiers of that king. Though Hi-o-ka-to, the Seneca Chief, came to Mount Johnson and renewed his pledge of four hundred of his Nation's warriors, the warriors did not come, and Johnson was left with only six hundred of the thousand Indians he had promised to Governor DeLancey and the five other governors whose expedition he was leading to the north.

The Johnson expedition, however, did not run the course

that had been planned for it; the events of July and August effected a change. With French reinforcements, released by the removal of Braddock's threat, now moving into the Champlain Valley; with the Iroquois inactive behind their protestations of good faith; and with the immense logistic and recruitment problem eating into the days and weeks of the campaign season — a new plan of advance was adopted. This took into consideration a second and limited objective to the expedition originally directed only to the capture of Crown Point.

Instead of striking north from the head of navigation on the Hudson to the foot of the water road on Lake Champlain, Johnson's army would carry its bateaux overland to Lake George, and from a base camp at the southern end of the lake, float down to a short carry which would take British arms and boats into Lake Champlain at Ticonderoga. This route bypassed the uncertain channels of the long marsh that chokes out Lake Champlain between South Bay and the open water that begins again a few miles south of the Ticonderoga Peninsula.

The change of direction was completely defensible on every practical consideration: twelve miles of road to be built instead of twenty, and the navigation of Lake Champlain below Crown Point was believed to be impossible for any but boats of the most shallow draught. The change of route was wrong only on the basis of something General Johnson and his officers did not know. It would be a year before the French themselves would dare to venture their single schooner to the lake below Crown Point, and twenty years before the Americans would build a fleet at Wood Creek, which *does* have a channel deep enough even for a full-rigged ship. But what Johnson did not know or consider was what the French, even then, were surveying: a great fortress to be built on the Ticonderoga Peninsula. Had

William Johnson seized his "Ti-en-on-de-ro-go" with a bold stroke of calculated military risk, he would have secured a base on Lake Champlain. There the British and American genius for shipbuilding might have shown itself in 1756 in a fleet (such as was built later) that could have claimed the whole water gate for Britain, and poised a strong hand at the St. Lawrence to choke out at its throat the very life of French Canada. But Johnson did not act — probably he could not have acted — and the French built their great stone fortress, which for four years denied Lake Champlain to the British at the point where they would have entered it with the waters from Lake George.

With these decisions made — to go on in spite of Braddock's defeat, and to go the sure way, via Lake George — Johnson and his army moved north with renewed determination. Of the forty-seven hundred soldiers originally pledged, there were mustered less than three thousand, and without the Senecas there would be only six hundred Iroquois. Nevertheless, the whole army was lighthearted when it set out early in August 1755.

Johnson had had to write hurriedly to Governor Benning Wentworth of New Hampshire, whose regiment was coming overland. Colonel Joseph Blanchard had consulted with his soldiers from the back-country behind Portsmouth, who chose the long trek through woods and mountains in preference to a sea voyage to New York and up the Hudson. Joe Blanchard had told General Johnson that he would meet him before the walls of Fort St. Frédéric with a fit and rugged regiment, instead of a wretched mob of seasick woodsmen! The course of the New Hampshire regiment was diverted, and, true to Blanchard's word, the men came striding up the forest road to the new rendezvous at Fort Edward, led by their ranger company and by Blanchard himself, all fighting fit.

Curiously, during all this preparation for war on Lake Champlain and at Oswego, and at the time of Braddock's battle, continental England and France were not officially at war. The "Seven Years' War" of Europe would not begin until 1756, though in America, where the struggle was to be called by the English the "French and Indian War," the fighting began in 1754. The war itself was considered inevitable by the terms of the peace treaty of the preceding war, signed in 1748 at Aix-la-Chapelle. Louisbourg, which had been won by the colonies, had been handed back to France, and the swelling body of French Canada was pressing too heavily on its North American bedfellow. The colonists were heaving out while sleep consumed the British Cabinet. It would take a Pitt to wake the lion, and in 1755, William Pitt was just taking in his hands the sticks of the reveille drum of empire. In June 1755 had come the diplomatic break.

Meanwhile, William Johnson wrote his several gubernatorial bosses that the road to Lac du St. Sacrement was being made, and although it was August 29 when he arrived, he proposed to build there a magazine and a fort to which he could return, for, even at that late date, he planned to go on. Incidentally, he changed the name of the "Lake of the Holy Sacrament," and called it, instead, "Lake George," in honor of the English King. This placated the New England men, so conditioned to mistrust of all things papist that they hesitated to risk their lives on a lake bearing such a Roman-ish name as "St. Sacrement."

General Johnson's hopes were high as his army gathered around him in the fortified camp on Lake George, while the "Haws" of the drivers and the squeal of iron brakes on iron-shod wheels echoed in the valley as the long convoys of loaded wagons came slowly down the last steep hill of the portage road.

In the woods were Johnson's Indians, not including those dancing and boasting in their own camp to the south. King Hendricks, the venerable Chief of the Mohawks, was the Great War Chief of the Iroquois contingent, and to Johnson he was worth the four hundred Senecas who were not there. Johnson felt an honest admiration for the fat old warrior "King," and he was proud to think of him as an uncle, which he was by Indian marriage. The old "King's" warriors would keep the woods around the camp and the carrying road clear of French Indians; and from their cousins, Christianized by the French and now living in their village at Caughnawaga, near the St. Lawrence, Johnson expected to obtain valuable intelligence of Fort St. Frédéric and the French reinforcements.

One little storm blew up in camp: the wagoners were deserting the army. They had been hired, not enlisted, and they demanded more soldier guards to protect them and their valuable teams on the road from Fort Edward to Lake George. General Johnson had not completely resolved that question on the morning of September 8, 1755.

With General Johnson's army moving against him up Hudson's river, it was time for Pierre François de Rigaud, Marquis de Vaudreuil, Governor of Canada, to react.

Made aware of the English plans through a document picked up haphazardly near one of the overturned carts of Braddock's defeated army, Vaudreuil had prepared his counterattack before Johnson reached Lake George. The French victory on the Monongahela had left Shirley's two regiments at Oswego as ineffectual as a hammer without an anvil. The French reinforcements on their way to defend Canada in the west must be called back to defend the water gate to the south, which already France recognized as vital to Canada.

All the French regiments in Canada were under the command of the German Baron Dieskau, whom Vaudreuil now sent hurrying to Fort St. Frédéric. Dieskau did not loiter in this defensible position. The great Marshal Saxe had taught him to attack. Dieskau left in their familiar ramparts the twelve hundred men he found at the fort, and with his reinforcements still in momentum, he pushed them on up the lake, following after the war canoes of his seven hundred Indians and three hundred *voyageurs*.

At Ticonderoga Dieskau left off a detachment, more as a guard to the engineers surveying the site for the stone fort than as a rear link. The true rear link he left at the defile of the two rocks, ten miles further south on Lake Champlain. It was the eight platoons of the Regiment de Languedoc who gratefully dropped their packs there by the lake, and watched the last of Dicskau's force, still at their paddles and oars, disappear through the marsh grasses that bordered the water like a field of yellow grain.

From the southern end of Lake Champlain it was a high trail that brought Dieskau to a position overlooking a stretch of the new, raw road that Johnson had built from the Hudson to Lake George. From this position, he saw that he could attack one terminus or the other of the portage road. He chose Johnson's most recently established camp on Lake George. Though new to North America, Dieskau made a sound appraisal of the motives and military capabilities of the Indians, when — with a cunning which they appreciated — he had adjured them against taking scalps *during* battle. They understood the logic of his simile, in which he likened a battle to the harvesting of a field of maize; the shucking of the ears came at leisure, *after* the battle. In deciding which post to attack, Dieskau was influenced by another Indian characteristic, one which would also apply to his force of Canadian militia. Neither Indians nor raw troops could face cannon fire, and he estimated that the camp at Lake George would not yet have cannon.

Later, Dieskau would blame his Caughnawaga Indians for the loss of complete surprise, but his screen of Indians made it possible to prepare the ambush that, on the morning of September 8, 1755, was to give him the initial success of the day.

Word of Dieskau's force reached Johnson in his field tent, and to gain time for the preparation of his main defenses, he sent Colonel Ephraim Williams, with a thousand men, to delay and contain Baron Dieskau at a distance from the camp. Williams dashed back down the portage road into a three-sided box of French and Indians.

Fat old King Hendricks fell from his pony at the first volley, to be butchered later by the Algonquin women. Williams, who had stood heroically upon a great boulder after his horse had been shot from under him, tried to rally his men from panic. He was too good a target to survive for long. When their colonel died, the survivors fled back to the barricades that had been hastily thrown up during their absence.

Dieskau pursued, now moving up into the van of his army the eight platoons of the Queen of France's own fine regiment and the tall grenadiers of Languedoc. The French regulars attacked; Johnson answered the assault with well-served cannon which he had brought up. The French regulars stopped, the fire withered their ranks, and they sank down, firing back to the very last and keeping, in death, their formation that had so delighted the Queen of France.

Dieskau, wounded and in danger of being bayoneted where he lay, had been right about his Indians and militia.

They heard the English cannon, and the Indians remembered the harvest of scalps to be gathered at the scene of the morning's battle. There, the remnant of Dieskau's army was surprised between a pursuing force from the now victorious army at Lake George and a relieving force from Fort Edward. Those who were not killed fled into the woods. The contemptuous American soldiers threw the bodies of their enemies into a little pond nearby, a nameless little pond known thereafter as "Bloody Pond."

The American provincial soldiers were drunk with their victory over the French. The capture of Fort St. Frédéric? A simple matter!

But in the Indian camp, the red fillets with which the Iroquois had bound their heads as a British uniform had quietly been put aside. Mourning streaked the old war paint. Four great Iroquois Chiefs were dead, including King Hendricks himself. William Johnson, whom the Indians called "War-rac-ji-ja-gey" (He-who-does-much-business), lay painfully wounded in the tent which he shared with the half-killed Baron Dieskau. There was not an Indian who, had he been able, would not have finished slowly the killing of the French general who had ended the long life of King Hendricks, Johnson's uncle. It was strange business. As far as the Indians were concerned, the war party was over.

Major General Lyman, flushed and confident with the afternoon's victory, his by acclaim, led the war faction. General Johnson, still weak from dysentery, had to reassume the leadership of his expedition, taken from him by the French bullet that had crashed into his leg at the very first fire of the Regiment La Reine. That he dominated the Council of War, prevailed on it to give over the offensive (which in truth it never had held), and sent the men back to their homes rejoicing in a battle won, as though it had been a victorious campaign, was in fact a great personal triumph.

With that triumph, Johnson quit the game of soldier. His was the only messenger of victory who went to the Court of St. James in London during that whole year of 1755. In due course, the messenger returned with Johnson's personal reward: a baronetcy.

While the Johnson expedition did not go forward, it did not fall back. Before Sir William left his army for his triumphs in Albany and New York, he laid out an ambitious work plan which would consolidate his gains in ground. The fortified landing at the falls of the Hudson River, which all summer had been known as Fort Lyman in honor of his second-in-command, Johnson now completed and neatly named Fort Edward, for his monarch's second son. At the head of Lake George, which would be the launching point for the next campaign against the French, plans for a great fort were made, and work begun. This fort Johnson named for two other of the King's sons, William and Henry. He considered building a third fort, at South Bay, but gave up the idea. One long portage was enough to maintain and protect.

Any future expedition would stay out of the deep woods — the woods that had swallowed Braddock, stopped Shirley, and on the morning of September 8, had cost Johnson so dear in soldiers and friends. The problem of an invasion of Canada had a water solution. General Johnson found that solution when he established his two forts, dominating the watershed between the south-flowing Hudson and the north-flowing lakes. From the head of Lake George, all water flowed downward into Lake Champlain, into the St. Lawrence, and onward to the French warehouses and government palaces at Montreal and Quebec.

Any future invasion would be carried by a water-borne army, drifting, rowing, sailing down into Canada. To protect this floating army, a navy would be needed. The sloop that Johnson had envisaged, and the big bateaux — each of which cost £10 and carried a cannon — would do for Lake Champlain. The particular conditions on Lake George called for a floating island of cannon, a spiny porcupine around which a brood of bateaux could gather when fast French war canoes attacked in packs, and which could cover a landing with cannon fire.

In his files, Johnson had the plan for just such a boat as he now needed. The previous August, with an order of "oakem," two "barrils of pitch," and some caulking irons, there had come a letter from one John Dies, suggesting that Johnson build a raft of heavy timbers, like the flat platform used by ships' carpenters in careening large vessels, adding to its sides breastworks pierced for cannon, muskets, and oars. William Johnson needed to read no further.

He called in a man named Stephen Webster, gave him a copy of Dies's letter with all the constructional details, assigned him thirty-six carpenters "from Colonel Bagley's regiment," and told him to build two floating batteries. Webster had his troubles. The carpenters refused to work and stand guard as well. Everywhere at Fort William Henry it was the same. A lieutenant would be lucky to find ten or twelve workmen of a party of fifty, and the five hundred men assigned to build the fort and the hundred men constructing boats were dilatory if present, and deserters if unaccounted for. The army was ready to go home.

General Johnson, too, wanted to follow his distinguished prisoner, Baron Dieskau, to Albany. Dieskau had written to him, asking to be removed from the kind care of Johnson's sister, Mrs. Farrell, who had been a saint and angel to the sorely wounded Baron. The prisoner had just learned that Matthew Farrell, killed at the ambush on Lake George, was the husband of his gentle nurse. "Consider the feelings," wrote the Baron, "realize the pain to this kind lady, who nurses the soldier who killed her husband . . ." Johnson had indeed been thoughtless.

When the orders had been given and the great captains had departed, the camps at Fort Edward and Fort William Henry subsided into places as docile as their sheepfolds, where a thousand sheep placidly ground their cuds. Winter set in.

At the forts, men stayed indoors. Frenchmen at Crown Point thought of Montreal; Englishmen on the watershed thought of Albany and of home; only one man was curious.

Rangers over the Lakes

Robert Rogers was a big man, and from the fringe of Governor Benning Wentworth's "Court" at Portsmouth, New Hampshire, he had stepped out of the forest onto the Lake Champlain frontier, captain of the Ranger company of Colonel Blanchard's New Hampshire regiment. The size of his footprints was to measure the valleys during the next four years and to leave their mark; and always they would lead outward and show themselves where Frenchmen were.

As a captain, Rogers had shown his worth to his general. After the battle at Lake George in September, of the many scouts sent north to spy upon the enemy, he had been the one to bring back true reports and accurate estimates of what he had seen. As scouts, the Indians had failed William Johnson, and the Ranger company captains who had gone out had brought back worthless information. Only Rogers, it seemed, had gone where he was sent, observed what he found there, and reported the whole truth.

When the generals had departed and the lethargy of life in winter quarters had set in, Rogers emerged from his chrysalis as a captain of Rangers and showed himself as a *leader* of Rangers — a white devil of a moth that flitted everywhere around the dying flame of New France, a moth with the claws of an eagle.

On October 9, 1755, Robert Rogers fought his first Ranger battle and drew his first French blood. It was a little affair. Rogers with five men waylaid an enemy patrol of nine Indians and a French officer in their canoe, as they passed by the point (near Hague, on Lake George) where the Rangers were hidden.

Rogers was the first to fire; the slowest of his men fired only a second later. In the big French canoe, a wave of panic all but overturned the craft as hit men tumbled and whole men ducked. With a shout, the Rangers rushed their own canoe out from behind its screen of bright autumnal leaves and down to the water's edge. The French officer was beginning to get hold of his party. By the time the Rangers were water-borne, the enemy, too, was under way. Though Rogers counted but four paddlers left in the big canoe, and though he increased his pace, he could not close the gap. Scared men are hard to catch. Neither could Rogers bring fire to bear from his position, tandem behind the bow paddler in his own precariously balanced craft. Far down the lake, near the great shelving rock that one day would bear his name, Rogers saw two canoes break out from the shadow of the shore onto the sunlit surface of the water. It was time to end the chase. The stern man held his stroke, and twisted forward and outward with his paddle. The Ranger canoe swung in a tight arc, and again the men picked up the rhythm of the stroke that bore them quickly back to Fort William Henry, thirty miles up the English lake.

Within a month, Robert Rogers had induced his second naval battle; this, too, was down at the far end of Lake George. The November 4 scouting party went out prepared to fight on the water. Instead of the usual canoes, Rogers embarked his force of thirty Rangers in four bateaux, each of which had a swivel-mounted wall gun in the bow and at the stern. Thus, in pursuit or in retreat, there was a gun to bear, capable of sinking a bark canoe with a single shot.

Rogers knew that the French had an outpost at the foot of Lake George. On arriving there, with two of his bateaux as bait, Rogers enticed two big war canoes, with thirty French and Indians aboard, to give him chase. Maneuvering his own vessels like an admiral of the fleet, Rogers drew on the enemy canoes. When they were precisely in the position he wanted them to be, between his own two boats and a party of Rangers hidden onshore with the other two bateaux, Rogers mounted the wall guns and, at a hundred leaking and filled with inert dead and thrashing wounded, the survivors tried to escape to safety ashore. Their efforts succeeded only in bringing them under fire from the wall guns and muskets of the Ranger shore party. At the last moment of hope, a strong sortie from the French camp arrived to cover the landing of their sorely beset comrades. Outnumbered, the Rangers took to their bateaux and, with yards, raked them with galling fire. Beaten, their two canoes a few strong pulls at the oars, joined Rogers out on the lake where the English, in their four armed bateaux, ruled supreme.

Never one to miss an opportunity to strike or to taunt, Rogers paraded his little fleet down the shore, firing their wall guns into the forest. Then, with a last broadside at the post itself, where two hundred Frenchmen were forming ranks, he turned back to Fort William Henry.

Lake George was Rogers's playground during that autumn and early winter, but his intent was to carry the war onto Lake Champlain. There was a French fort at Crown Point, and he had observed and reported the building activity on the Ticonderoga Peninsula. By November 12, he had been to Ticonderoga and had counted eighty French bateaux hauled up on the shore.

But all thoughts of boat action were halted by the freeze. The shallow southern end of Lake Champlain froze over first, then Lake George. On January 14, 1756, the ice would hold a man the size of Rogers, and he was away again, sixteen Rangers at his back, skate blades flashing. Their bearskin sleeping-robes strapped to their backs, they gave the appearance to those left on shore at Fort William Henry of hairy goblins scurrying back to a white hell, for so they were pictured in the Bible of an Albany Dutchman.

Three days later they were back — Rogers, his sixteen Rangers, and two prisoners.

The tale the Rangers told in the huts of the provincial soldiers was of a swift passage over the black ice of Lake George, a cold supper at the upper falls, and a night march which ended in the setting of an ambush in a clump of evergreens on the east shore overlooking the ice of Lake Champlain. It was somewhere between Ticonderoga and Champlain that a word of caution came from the lookout, as he held up two fingers and mouthed the word: "Sleds!" The waiting Rangers suddenly felt warm again. At Rogers's order, they leapt down onto the ice and, screeching like banshees, went toward the sleds. Muffled to the eyes in toques and scarves and blanket-coats, the drivers went stumbling off, with four laughing Rangers after them. Ensign Noah Johnson hit a piece of glare ice and went down, legs and arms flying. Someone got to a horse's head and held it, while another Ranger felled it with a hard blow from a hatchet. The poor beast staggered back into the traces and dropped. Someone killed the other horse. Meanwhile, the prisoners had been stripped down for marching. A signal from Rogers, and the whole party followed his deceptively slow, lumbering walk, going westward over the snow carpet in a wide arc around Ticonderoga to Lake George, where they took to their skates again.

So it was that Robert Rogers took the initiative. He sought out the French, he found them, he attacked them. He used the mountain tops to spy on the Frenchman and his works; from under the walls of the forts he gathered in prisoners for interrogation; and always, he harassed "Monsieur Puff" on his line of communication — frozen Lake Champlain.

In May 1756, Rogers received his first reward. The Rangers were created "An Independent Corps" on the establishment of the British army, and Robert Rogers's commission as their captain came from the King. It was high recognition for a colonial to be admitted as a regular officer of the British army. As succeeding generals took command in North America, they more and more called on the services of Rogers' Rangers. Eventually, he commanded several companies, with the rank of major, and his leadership and the training methods he devised and supervised during the winter of 1755–56 remained the standard in the "Corps" for the rest of the war.

Few Rangers, however, were as durable as their leader, who kept up the pace, winter and summer, for five long years. If the enemy didn't get you, the frost did. The Rangers were constantly recruiting. Regulars, young officers from good homes in English shires (if they were intelligent), made good Rangers. Sergeants and privates from the highlands of Scotland or the border mountains of Wales made good Rangers, if they would work under orders. A British general of imagination scouted with Robert Rogers. But mostly the Ranger was an American, familiar with the North American woods. Like Lieutenant John Stark, he might be a former captive of the French Indians, or a half-breed, as was Sergeant Philips. But for the most part he was an American boy, who felt himself qualified or inspired to " 'list into the work," which was army slang for joining the Rangers.

Having carried the war to the French on Lake Champlain, Rogers sought out new techniques of attack. He needed a vehicle for transporting his men and equipment. Skates and towed light sleds served well on the lakes when they were covered with snow and ice. But a bark canoe was too light and fragile for attack, as had been proved in the October battle on Lake George. The bateau, which at the French post in November had proved its worth as a heavy gun carrier, was too hard to row and too slow to maneuver; and on a portage, a bateau required a cleared road and a wheeled cart. Rogers was looking over the eastern mountains of Lake George to Lake Champlain, and already he had decided on the most likely pass for the boats he would have there. In his canoe he had his race horse, and the bateau was a fine pack animal. He had to find a boat with the characteristics of a hunter: a fast, easy gait, the ability to surmount obstacles, and the strength to carry a heavy rider first to the kill. He decided to go after the French schooner, *La Vigilante*, which for ten years had sailed under the command of her builder-owner-master, between St. Jean at the first falls of the Richelieu and Fort St. Frédéric.

To hunt the whale, the men of New England launched whaleboats. Rogers would have whaleboats for his Rangers! These boats rowed easily, and the spoon bow tended to lift with forward speed, offering a good shot to the swivel gunner, his piece secured to the bow beam, made strong and high to brace a harpooner's knee and to snub a running line. The sturdy construction and flaring sides of a whaleboat gave her shallow draught and a dry inside, roomy enough for three Rangers on every seat, if need be. A rudder at the stern made a whaler responsive, and she was steady in a sea or tied to a wounded whale in a "Nantucket sleighride." Keel boats, they sailed well in case Rogers wanted to go all the way up to St. Jean itself.

In June 1756, six whaleboats were delivered to the Rangers at Fort William Henry. Five of them left Lake George before the month was out, going the hard way: over the mountain. It took the fifty Rangers of the party five days to carry the boats up through the pass and down across the flats to a marshy bay on Lake Champlain, where on July 3, 1756, Britain launched her first flotilla against the enemy. There was no thought of ceremony, except perhaps a drink of rum all 'round while the officers and sergeants checked the stores and the pickets were called in.

The cruise lasted for five days. All travel was at night, the days being spent in watching and gauging the French bateau travel. On one occasion the Rangers were almost discovered in their hidden bivouac by seven enemy boats, intent on landing to prepare a meal. At the last minute, however, the French officer chose a spot 150 yards above the alerted Rangers, where, all unsuspecting, the Frenchmen cooked and ate their dinner before moving on.

Rogers heard the French sentinels exchanging watchwords as he led his flotilla, with thole pins wrapped and greased, under the high cliff of Ticonderoga. The night he chose to pass through the narrow channel between Fort St. Frédéric and "Chimney Point" was too bright, but the following night all five whaleboats safely ran the dangerous passage. Now Rogers was in the lane plied by *La Vigilante*.

At noon on July 7 the French schooner was sighted by the lookout posted on a high cliff on the west side of the narrows. She was running north, a bone in her teeth. When the southeast wind dropped about 3 p.m., Rogers's hope of overtaking her that night increased. As soon as it was dark, the whaleboats set out along the west shore. A mile from the mouth of the Bouquet River, Rogers stopped his advance until a scout could go forward to see if *La Vigilante* was in that safe anchorage for the night. She was there, and Rogers prepared to board her.

But luck turned against the Rangers, in the dark shape of two blundering French lighters. Rogers was forced to pursue and intercept. He tried to do the job quietly, not to frighten the big game nearby, but the French boatmen fired first, and the Rangers replied with a volley before boarding with the hatchet. It was short work with the lighters: four of the twelve men aboard killed, one man wounded, and the rest so frightened that they told, in the truth of terror, that five hundred men were in a convoy, coming close behind. With this intelligence, Rogers was forced to give up his intent against *La Vigilante*. Nothing was left but to sink the lighters and their cargo (reserving only some casks of brandy to cache in the woods against next winter's cold), and make off to the south and home. At first light the Rangers landed on the west shore, where they carried their whaleboats in behind a low ridge. Hiding the boats in a windfall, they made all haste inland.

The schooner, *La Vigilante*, variously reported by the British as of 40- or 60-ton burden, had seen some twenty years of service on the St. Jean–Crown Point run when Rogers made his first attempt to board her. Never had business been better for her aging captain-owner than in the summer of 1756. With the building of the new fort at Ticonderoga and the reinforcing of the army there and at Crown Point, every trip south found a rich cargo filling the hold and overflowing onto the deck. And every trip, that summer, carried some distinguished guest, military or civil. To them, the captain played congenial host, pointing out the beauties of distant mountains, or the plaintive honking of a gaggle of geese, scrawling their uneven "V" across a tumbling white cloud. In return, these passengers, usually elegant, often elderly, were vociferous in their thanks to the garrulous captain, whose vessel saved them from remembering their voyage on Lake Champlain as a long, agonizing cramp, flashing through the numbness of legs outstretched in a flimsy bark canoe.

But the captain-host of *La Vigilante* had named his vessel for opportunities of trade, not for the vigilance required of a ship of war. Precipitously, in the pre-dawn hours of July 8, 1756, she had continued her scheduled trip north, flinging voluble warnings to the southbound convoy as it passed. It was never French naval policy to engage at once. A French navy co-ordinates and regulates its policy according to the military requirements and conditions ashore. Thus it was that the only schooner on the lake left the convoy unescorted, and hurried north with the terrible news that the British were on Lake Champlain.

The official French reaction was slow. It would be three years before armed sailing ships would be built for Lake Champlain. Until then, convoys on the lake — whether bateaux or sleds — depended on guards of soldiers, or defensive French and Canadian officer-led Indian patrols in the woods. To watch over the schooner, the crew of *La Vigilante* was increased from twelve to thirty men, but the eighteen "marines" merely crowded the deck, hampering the sailors, cutting down the pay load, and keeping all on board in a state of alarm by their eager talk of repelling "boarders."

Rogers gave the schooner cause to watch the shadows. By the end of August 1756 he was back at his hidden whaleboats. Two of the boats were carried down to the water and launched from a shingle beach. Rogers himself commanded the first boat, and the second was in command of Lieutenant Stark. Again the whaleboats cruised north together, and again the Rangers were unlucky. The schooner passed in the opposite direction, running fast, all sail set. Pursuit was useless, and as *La Vigilante* had not seen him, Rogers continued north. The whaleboats proved their qualities that night, covering twenty miles in spite of the waves, and in spite of an added cargo of eight Mohawk Indians who were useless with oars in their hands, and whom Rogers, ever suspicious of Indians in general and of Johnson's Mohawks in particular, was glad to see depart about their own business the following day.

An ambush on "a point" (which might have been Cumberland Head) the day of August 27, drew a blank. Still eager to board *La Vigilante*, Rogers cruised back to Crown Point in search of her. There he took a prisoner, Monsieur Vaisac de Guienne, who knew, and described in such detail, the French plans and order of battle, that Rogers abandoned two of his precious whaleboats to certain capture, deeming them a fair price to pay for getting the Frenchman and his story quickly back to Fort William Henry.

The primary mission of Robert Rogers and his Rangers was the gathering of intelligence. They were the eyes, the ears, and the probing, inquisitive finger of the British army. They stole the Frenchman's brandy from his supply sleigh; they watched Monsieur while he drilled, or fished, tended his cattle, or built a great stone fortress. And they marched French prisoners such as M. Vaisac all the way back, to tell their own stories in the field tents of the British generals.

But as Rogers's reputation as an officer came to be recognized, his own participation in these small-party intelligence scouts and on the "nuisance raids" was soon to end. Increasingly, his qualities won appreciation and his responsibilities grew, until his command of a single Ranger company had expanded into that of six companies or more. By that time he had been commissioned major, as well as having been made principal training officer for British regulars, who now showed interest in this new concept of war — informal, personal, and total.

In the fall of 1756, however, Rogers was still carrying out

his own war against the French on and about Lake Champlain. The high command and the British army were occupied on other frontiers, and concerned Rogers not at all — until young James Abercromby came to the forts.

To Rogers fell the duty of showing the enemy to the captain from England. The necessity for this lay in the fact that Captain Abercromby was aide-de-camp, nephew, and namesake of the commander in chief! The tour was a whaleboat ride down Lake George to the French post at the northern end of the lake for a distant look, followed by a prudent withdrawal, during all of which the lurking dangers were not minimized. On their return, Captain Abercromby entertained the scouting party, remarked on the "romantic and noble scenery" through which he had been conducted, and went back to his place at the elbow of his avuncular major general. He took with him a pretty shrewd appraisal of the Rangers' service and of the latent potentials of their extraordinary commander, Robert Rogers.

Unhappily, Rogers's next foray onto Lake Champlain met with near disaster. His activities had called forth from Canada more Indians, to counter his Rangers and to capture or kill Rogers, on whose scalp rode an extra bounty.

On January 21, 1757, Rogers made an ambush of the ice road between Crown Point and Ticonderoga. His party of seventy-four (he had been forced to send back eighteen sick or lame Rangers during the approach march) was divided into the three classic groups of an ambush: the stop party ahead, the cut-off party behind, and the main party, whose role was that of making the actual attack. A sled approached from Ticonderoga, its horse trotting along the road marked by evergreen branches. At the moment when Lieutenant Stark was about to leave his concealment with twenty men to head off the sled, Rogers, with the cut-off party, saw ten more sleds coming up, hidden from Stark's view around a low point of land. It was too late to warn Stark to let the single sled go through. Shouting for a melee, Rogers led his party out onto the ice to attack the ten sleds.

There was no volley of aimed musket fire to break the silence, and no confusion of drivers and horses. It was raining; the powder was wet and useless in the muskets. That the Rangers caught three sleds and six horses was a creditable showing; and that seven Frenchmen submitted themselves prisoners only proved that it was not a day on which one wished to fight.

From the prisoners, Rogers learned that at Ticonderoga a French force was ready to go out, and once the eight sleds returned, that force would go out against him.

In anticipation of a battle, Rogers hurried his men back to the place, three miles from the lake, where they had left their fires of the previous night. There they dried out their muskets and reloaded with dry powder from their horns. They then continued their retreat, and had gone scarcely half a mile before they were attacked. It was then two o'clock in the afternoon, and though severely mauled by the first fire at close range, they fell back on their own rear. There, in a good defensive position, they held off the two hundred and fifty French and Indians until dark, when — the whole and the wounded — like mist, they slipped silently away.

Fourteen Rangers had been killed, six taken prisoner, and six wounded. Rogers was among the latter, and had sacrificed his queue, stuffing it into the hole in his wrist in a successful effort to stop the flow of blood. His wound sent Rogers back to Albany for medical attention, and while there, in March, he had the smallpox.

By April the army had sent him to Halifax, Nova Scotia, with three companies of his Rangers, for the proposed Louisbourg expedition. This "expedition" stayed in Halifax, where the Rangers were set to cutting hay in the meadows. Kept away from his "Happy Hunting Ground" for a whole year, Robert Rogers was paying the price for his fame as a Ranger. High commanders wanted him near them, and it was not until 1759 that a general with imagination would know how to make use of Rogers's qualities and would give full rein to his instinct for leadership of men and encourage his lurid imagination for destruction.

Meanwhile there was activity on the lakes, though Rogers himself was not there to participate in it. There was, for instance, the St. Patrick's Day raid on Fort William Henry. Quite logically, the French deduced that the Irishmen who garrisoned the fort would still be drunk, or would be badly hung-over, and planned an attack on March 17. Unfortunately for the Frenchmen, John Stark, who commanded the company of Rangers in the fort, had the ability to think like a Frenchman and outsmart an Irishman. On March 16, he ordered the sutler to close the bar and not to sell a drink to any Ranger without a written order signed by John Stark. During the rest of that day, Stark was seen by every man in the fort, his right arm heavily bandaged. At dawn on St. Patrick's Day, the Rangers beat off an attack on Fort William Henry.

Themselves now a little drunk with victory taken in the warm room of battle, the Rangers stood in the frozen slush on the battlements and watched, helpless, as the Canadians and their Indians spent their venom on the piles of upturned bateaux on the frozen shore. The evergreen boughs that had covered and protected the boats sent high columns of flames and sparks into the clear dry air. The sloops burned briskly through all one night, but when the huts where the Rangers lived were discovered, this was too much. The men begged

Stark to lead them out in a sally to save their precious treas-
ures, but he forbade this, and warned that mutiny would
be put down immediately by his own strong right hand.
So the Rangers could only watch, and finally saw the last
of Louis Philippe de Rigaud's Canadians disappear down
the lake, five days after they had come.

Rigaud's full name was Rigaud de Vaudreuil, and he was
brother to the governor of Canada. His troops were Canadians, and his St. Patrick's Day raid on Fort William Henry
was an affair of internal Canadian politics, more than a military operation. By the success of his brother's expedition,
Governor de Vaudreuil sought to emphasize his own military independence and acumen, to the discomfort of Montcalm, the general sent out from France.

Louis Joseph, Marquis de Montcalm, was the last great
leader to rally the devoted to the cause of France's Canada.
It was a cause in which even the king and his mistress,
Madame Pompadour, were losing interest. Montcalm succeeded Baron Dieskau as commander of French troops and
led his seven fine regiments in a series of victories that sustained the French in Canada until 1759. For a time, his flame
ignited even the jealous Vaudreuil, who could not understand it. François Bigot, the intendant and the evil strangler
of New France, could not quench his fire. The French Indians, never political fools, drew to Montcalm as they would to
the last great pine tree of the Canadian forest, and followed
his leadership — until it was time to loot.

In 1756, Montcalm established the French right on the
Great Lakes, and the following year he turned south to
drive the British from their encroachment on the Champlain
watershed. There, he recognized, lay the vital threat to Canada. The English commanders were away, ineffectually investing Louisbourg from distant Halifax, and the water route
from Fort Carillon (Ticonderoga) to Fort William Henry

lay open to his boats. He flooded the woods on either side of Lake George with his Indians and rode up the lake with his regulars on the bateaux of his artillery train.

Colonel Monroe's defenses of Fort William Henry was foredoomed, as the French artillery shells fell into the fort from above and the saps were dug closer from the west. From the east, where there was another British force at Fort Edward, came encouraging messages from the cowed General Webb, but no reinforcements. A dignified capitulation was arranged.

Then the Indians broke loose. Montcalm himself could not hold them, and the Canadian officers, cadets, and interpreters were not inclined to do so. The sick and wounded in the hospital died first, and their scalps were borne out triumphantly, dripping blood and vengeful smallpox germs. Then the new graves were opened and the smallpox dead were scalped, among them the corpse of Robert Rogers's brother. Finally the paroled prisoners were looted, to be killed if they resisted this wild sack of Fort William Henry. Sated, all the Indians then disappeared into the woods, trailing their loot and bearing to their villages, as far away as the great central plains beyond Lake Superior, the germs for an epidemic of the dread smallpox.

As Sir William Johnson had been turned back from his purpose when his Indians left him, so Montcalm turned back, for the same reason: he was eyeless in the forest. Montcalm left Johnson's fort a smoldering ruin, hoping that the flames would burn out the horrible memory of the ghastly orgy. They never did.

Victories and Defeats

Robert Rogers was back on the Champlain frontier on December 17, 1757. He kicked around the ashes and charred bits that were all that remained of Fort William Henry and stood for a moment on the spot where he thought his brother's grave might have been. Then he set off down the west shore of Lake George, his hundred and twenty-three Rangers, dragging their light sleds, following behind him. Rogers found it was good to be at large on the lakes again, in that safe area beyond the outposts, where generals did not go and where a man could deal directly, conclusively, and finally with his enemies.

When he saw the French fort at Ticonderoga again after so many months, the change in the frontier must have held misgivings for him. The days of the bold little scouts of five or ten Rangers were buried in the snows of other years, buried with the good men he had lost.

From the lookout on Mt. Defiance, he ordered his scout to the French outpost on Lake George, which was found to be abandoned for the winter. Chance showed him where the French had stored their boats. They had been neatly sunk in rows offshore, where the ice could not crush them in nor fire destroy them, as the British bateaux had been destroyed the previous winter. It was cold work, but they did it: the best swimmers among the Rangers plunged down into the icy water to secure ropes to ring-bolts and rudder-posts, while Rangers on shore heaved on the lines, shaking the French boats and tearing them to pieces where they lay anchored with stones to the bottom of the lake. It was a slight revenge for the burned-out huts of the Ranger camp, the lost clothes, the charred keepsakes.

By June 1758 the big British expedition, aimed at Ticonderoga and the lake road to Canada, was on the move. The youthful brigadier, Lord Howe, whose ability was in such marked contrast to that of the imperious and custom-bound British commander in chief, General James Abercromby, had ordered Rogers to bring back to him a plan of the French works at the north end of Lake George; of the ground between that place and the fort; of the whole French fortress called "Carillon"; and a plan of the three miles to the north of the fortress.

On June 12 Rogers loaded whaleboats onto wagons, and left Fort Edward by Johnson's road to Lake George. That night he had these favorite craft launched in the lake.

When he returned to Lord Howe with the plans, and with another skirmish under his belt, Howe, with three thousand troops, was making camp on the ruins of Fort William Henry. General Abercromby himself came up on June 28, and with the momentum of its number kept in motion by a Regular Army staff and command, the army of fifteen thousand was ready to embark by early morning of July 5.

It was a relief for everyone to climb into the bateaux and rest on the baggage and barrels, which the troops had loaded with so much sweat, toil, and bad temper. It was even a joy for each soldier to take his turn at the rough handles of the long oars, and with shouts and calls, slowly to find his exact place in the regular columns making up on the cool waters of this lake.

The roll and rattle of drums beating the march sounded over the lake and was heard in every one of the seven hundred boats making up the vast armada. At the sound, men leaned into their oars, poising the blades above the water, waiting and listening for their boatmaster to give the stroke that would set them off for Ticonderoga. The army was in four columns. The two center columns, fifty yards apart, were comprised of the regiments of British regulars — Scotsmen and Irishmen, Welshmen and Englishmen, far, far from home. Two hundred yards out on each flank, rowing easily and naturally, were the regiments from the colonies. Leading the whole were the whaleboats of the Rangers and the light infantrymen seconded from their regiments. Down Lake George advanced the army, keeping their dressing as though on the parade square. Only at the very rear, where followed the hospital, the commissary, and the sutlers' boats, did military precision become ragged.

Late in the afternoon, the lead boats of the four columns broke out from the myriad islands of the narrows into the open northern third of Lake George. Two miles further on, at Sabbath Day Point, a halt was called to rest and reform for the night approach, which would bring the army to the invasion beaches. Morning brought the whole force to the landing, and its omnipotent momentum carried it ashore intact and unopposed. Quickly the regiments formed up and, following Rogers and his Rangers, they plunged out of the light of the lake into the shadows of the forest. There, in the deserted wilderness of trees, Abercromby's army received the shocking wound from which it could not recover.

George Augustus, Brigadier General Viscount Howe was shot dead from his saddle, as he spurred his horse forward into a chance encounter between his advanace guard and a retiring French detachment, lost in the woods. His brilliant young second-in-command was dead on the eve of battle, and Major General James Abercromby now found the responsibility for all command decisions resting squarely on his own shoulders. For advice, he could only turn to his own official family of aides, nicely mannered, keen young officers from England, dutiful but as yet untried. Abercromby had no other contact with his army. As commander in chief of all the British troops in North America, he had remained aloof and distant. His splendid position was the reward of a long, pedestrian military career, and he was shielded by a second-in-command so enterprising for a British regular officer as even to see worth in the usually despised provincial soldiers, with their new concept of warfare. Thus, as Abercromby sifted the intelligence reports that came to his headquarters, the only grains that assayed true to him were those brought in by his small staff of Englishmen. Major General Abercromby might have been tenting in Windsor Great Park, for all the inspiration and influence he drew from his command as he stood, deeply committed to battle, in the virgin forests of North America.

Abercromby knew that the French forces against him numbered but thirty-five hundred men, and their general, the Marquis de Montcalm, was only a youngster. His staff engineer had told him that, recklessly, the young French commander had left his fort to meet the English attack at a flimsy barricade of logs, hastily built to the west of the citadel. To corroborate his engineer's report on the field works of the marquis, General Abercromby had the solemn word of Sir William Johnson's Mohawk scouts. The close connection of these savages with one who, though a colonial, had achieved a baronetcy, gave credence to their report. As a matter of fact, however, the Mohawks themselves had never seen the works in question. Both the Indians and the general eagerly awaited the arrival of the fabulous Sir William, who was expected to come from Albany to army headquarters, now set up at the French sawmill a mile distant from Montcalm's works.

On these inaccurate reports of the French position, and at the optimistic urging of his aides, Abercromby gave the order to his regiments to assault with the bayonet; the artillery to remain in the boats; the attack to go in, when the troops were formed up, on July 8, 1757.

The thirty-five hundred French were confident out of all proportion to their numbers. They took their strength from their commanders: the gallant Montcalm, the dependable Bourlamaque, and the beloved Gaston François de Lévis. The latter officer, Montcalm's right hand and his successor, had arrived only just in time for the battle of Carillon. He had come at dawn by canoe, with a small reinforcement. It was typical of the man that his Indians had awakened him from his nest of blankets at the bottom of the canoe, so that he might see the sun rise, and the effect of the dawn light on Fort Carillon's new walls of gray stone and yellow logs. The arrival of Lévis raised the French spirits to the highest notch, and his enthusiastic pleasure in the dawn of the day spread rapidly through the regiments, hard at work.

The battle of July 8 was a signal victory for Montcalm and a disgraceful defeat for Abercromby, though the latter's regiments gained a measure of the immortality which bravery often brings to badly led and defeated soldiers. The British, provincials, and Rangers hurled themselves, not at the breastwork of logs which Abercromby had prepared them for, but against a strongly entrenched position. English boats had been carried over from Lake George and launched in the pool below the falls, at the French sawmill. With these boats, Abercromby intended to encircle the Ticonderoga Peninsula and cut off Montcalm's retreat by water. In anticipation of this move, Montcalm had stationed Canadian volunteers and a company of grenadiers on the low ground of his left wing, where he also put a field gun.

When Lévis arrived, the picket of the Royal Rossillon Regiment was added to the guard at the water's edge, and the artillery commander in the fort itself was directed to train his guns so as to command the mouth of the river from Lake George. As soon as they emerged onto Lake Champlain, the British whaleboats were met by this gunfire, and promptly withdrew. Thus ended the British campaign on Lake Champlain for 1758.

On August 28, 1758, a victory was celebrated by the subdued regiments at Fort William Henry. Word had just been received of the capture of Louisbourg on July 27 by Amherst. Admiral Boscawen's fleet had brought him there, and James Wolfe had led the troops ashore. Heartened by a victory *somewhere*, the men gave three rousing cheers for General Amherst, and all the muskets were fired in succession from the right so that a wave of sound swept from one end of the line to the other — a *feu-de-joie*.

General Abercromby's main British army was back at Fort William Henry, having fled up Lake George in panic after the battle of July 8. The neat, orderly columns of boats that had made such an inspiring picture of the advance down the blue waters between the high green mountains presented in retreat a stereoptican of disaster. The boats moved forward jerkily under the strokes of bent-backed men in whom there was now no gaiety. In daylight, the mountains smoked from campfires hastily left, and the boats near the shore could hear the terrifying roar as a giant spruce or hemlock took fire all at once. By night, the end of the column kept to the middle of the lake, away from the burning mountains and clear of the smoldering islands.

At Fort William Henry order had been re-established. General Abercromby, whose bewildering commands had precipitated the flight from Carillon, had disappeared down-country "like a rower, advancing backward." At Lake George, the camp put itself into a state of defense, ready for another year, another commander, and another expedition to Lake Champlain.

All through the hot days of summer, the British army clung to its forts on the portage between the Hudson River and Lake George — preparing, watching, waiting . . . The unpredictable Frenchman at Ticonderoga might do anything. Montcalm might even attack with his still numerically inferior force. To observe South Bay and Wood Creek, the direction from which Baron Dieskau had come, Robert Rogers spread a network of patrols through the woods and set up watch posts on mountain overlooks. He himself took out the whaleboats, scouting through the narrows to the northern end of Lake George. British sloops sailed the wide lake near the British camp in defensive patrols, supplying and changing the strong picket guards standing to on the nearby islands.

There had been a change in command of the fleet on Lake George. Lieutenant Colonel John Bradstreet, deputy quartermaster and transport officer to General Abercromby, had gone west to capture Fort Frontenac, on the Upper St. Lawrence. Joshua Loring of Hingham, Massachusetts, an experienced seaman and a captain in the Royal Navy, became boatmaster, and was to earn and enjoy the title of Commodore of the Lakes. He was an able man, and had *sailors* to help him on board his land-locked navy. As a quartermaster, Colonel Bradstreet's principal interest had been in carrying an army and its supplies along the waterways of the wilderness. As a means to this end, he had created his regiment of versatile bateaumen who could — and did — leave their bateaux on an enemy shore, to assault with the infantry. As a mariner, Captain Loring set out to build, maintain, and fight a separate service on the lakes, while accepting, of course, the traditional navy role of overwater carrier to the army.

On taking command, Captain Loring's first act was to make things shipshape: "A place for everything, and everything in its place." His demand for hard work and discipline invited mutiny, which, when it came, he put down firmly and conclusively. One court-martial was enough to establish Loring firmly in his command.

In all departments on the Hudson-Champlain frontier, discipline and morale were being restored to regiments gone slack and sullen in the aftermath of defeat and flight. Under regimental surgeons, the physical health of the men, too, was being restored. Green vegetables and vinegar were issued to the scorbutic; evening exercises were ordered for the weak and convalescent; camp sanitation was strictly enforced, and, ever mindful of the plague, the surgeons ordered new earth to be spread on the old, plundered smallpox cemetery near the burned-out ruins of Fort William Henry. A little war was started against nits and lice, and under adjutants' inspection, the men were turned out washed and combed, with clean underwear twice a week — an order which kept the washerwomen at the lakeshore and out of mischief.

A military training program took the individual man, restored him to the human race, and made him again a part of his company team. Exercises took the form of charging and reforming in the woods, and of learning the woodcraft which the men should have known long since and which they would need so often in the future. Under the strict regime the men "got moving," until company by company the army reported itself able. Even the French were quiet.

In September 1758, Sir Jeffrey Amherst became commander in chief in North America. At forty-one, he had staff experience in five campaigns and was the choice of William Pitt to carry out the "Great Commoner's" plan for the conquest of Canada. Pitt's ability to pick military commanders who would carry out his policy to the letter was shown to perfection by his choice of military leaders for North America. For the specific capture of Quebec, he chose the brilliant, impatient, flashing James Wolfe, and sent with him a wily old sailor, Admiral Charles Saunders, who had begun his career afloat the same year that Wolfe was born. For the general conquest of Canada, Pitt needed a staff officer, and in Jeffrey Amherst he made his customary good choice. France lost even her ancient Indian allies to Amherst, who showed them that the cause of "O-non-thi-o," at Versailles, or of "Peru Louis," was lost. Eventually, all of French Canada was annexed to England so conclusively that, when put to the test fifteen years later, Canada would remain loyal to the British Crown.

For the campaign of 1759, Amherst took immediate command of his strategical center. Wolfe would be at Quebec; General John Prideux would take Niagara, and cut Canada from Louisiana; Amherst himself would end four years of mismanagement and loitering at Lake George, and would take Lake Champlain.

Amherst put life into the army. The officers at Fort Edward and at Fort George, building to replace the ruined Fort William Henry, had anticipated the "new broom" and had cleaned house. They were ready to welcome the three new regiments of regulars to their frontier. If the provincials came straggling in, they smartened up as they came within sight of the new camp. They approved, as did Rogers and his Rangers, of the cut of the uniforms worn by the newly formed light infantry companies of the regiments.

Here was a short-skirted coat and a small round hat that wouldn't hamper a man in a cedar tangle, or hinder him at an oar. There were new arms, too, short "carbines," over seven hundred of them, for the light companies of the regulars. Gage's light infantry turned in their old long muskets (520) and drew carbines in their stead. Officers carried fusees, as well as swords or short hangers, and grateful sergeants left their halberts in stores, and like the men and the officers, for this campaign fought with a firelock.

Captain Loring was busy on the lakeshore. A great number of new bateaux had come up from Albany and lower on the Hudson, to replace the broken and battered ones left over from the Abercromby expedition. The pine boards in the flat bottoms had a tendency to dry out and to be beyond caulking after a winter on shore. The bateaux had come at the last minute, and needed countless minor repairs after the long pole up the rapids of the Hudson and the carting over the rough road of the long portage. A convoy of nearly four hundred wagons had brought them to Lake George. It had been a long day's work unloading them.

By dredging out a channel, Loring had brought the sloop *Halifax* up to the wharf. The ark *Invincible* was launched without ceremony on July 17, and on July 18–19 the artillery was loaded aboard her. Pork and flour were loaded all day on July 20, and the following day tents and baggage were put on board and the men climbed after them.

Major General Jeffrey Amherst's army was off to take "Boges," which was the name they gave to Fort Carillon.

At dawn on Sunday morning, the army landed, unopposed, at the northern end of Lake George. The provincial regiments set to work unloading the bateaux and the ark, and getting forward the artillery. "Boges" was in sight, and in Captain David Holmes's company of Colonel Eleazer Fitch's 4th Connecticut Regiment, all were "brave and hearty, all but our Company clerke," or so opined Private Robert Webster.

For five days General Amherst made his siege preparations and the men toiled.

Behind the high walls of Carillon, four hundred men of the Regiment La Reine under Le Sieur de Bourlamaque were having a soldiers' field day: they were wrecking the fort. With Montcalm heavily engaged at Quebec, Fort Niagara falling — or fallen — to Prideaux without any hope for reinforcement, Ticonderoga with its small garrison was not important strategically and would be better abandoned than cut off. In a final rampage of destruction, therefore, the soldiers of the Queen of France made ready to evacuate before Amherst's siege guns battered them into submission, or British troops encircled them, cutting them off from Montreal, where an anxious governor was calling them back.

A tentative plan of wide encirclement had been suggested to Amherst by Colonel Montresor. Three thousand men, including five hundred carpenters, were to go overland to Otter Creek, on the east shore of Lake Champlain. There they would build boats, and command the French supply line where the lake narrowed, twelve miles north of Crown Point. From his field headquarters in the siege lines at Ticonderoga, however, Amherst needed only a closer encirclement in order to capture the French garrison with the fort.

To complete that encirclement, Amherst called Robert Rogers out of the line and gave him his orders: that night (July 26/27), Rogers would cut the log boom maintained by the French across Lake Champlain from the battery at the extremity of the Ticonderoga Peninsula to the east shore of the lake. There was a certain justice, even humor, in giving this difficult mission to Major Rogers. The barrier boom had been put in place to prevent free passage to

Rogers's own whaleboat excursions. Now that the boom hampered the general's plan completely to encircle the Ticonderoga Peninsula, it was only fitting that Rogers himself should remove the obstacle. There was urgency in the general's order. Reports indicated that Fort St. Frédéric would not be disputed, which meant that, once drawn from Fort Ti, the French would run for it.

Rogers took the first sixty Rangers he could find and led them back of the lines to the pool below the lower falls, where quite a fleet of boats already had been assembled. Only the day before, a hundred horses had arrived from Lake George with their harness, carts and drivers, and were making easy work of getting the English boats over to Lake Champlain. Leaving the Rangers at the pool, Rogers went up the falls to the sawmill. Despite the lateness of the hour, he found Captain Loring tinkering with the mill, while assigning work on cogs and cradles and whips to a group of Gaelic-speaking Highlanders who carried carpenters' tools. Rogers signed out his boats with the "Commodore," bent on building his Lake Champlain fleet at once. He selected two whaleboats and a large, flat-bottomed "English" boat armed with a 3-pound cannon, and had his party waterborne by eight o'clock that night.

It was a quiet operation, as there still remained a sting in the dying fortress. At nine o'clock, Rogers was in the shadow of the mountain on the east shore, approaching the boom. In the bow of the flat-bottomed boat, the saw men were ready.

Suddenly the whole peninsula lit up and the Rangers stopped, open-mouthed and staring, while the roar of a giant explosion swept over them. Rogers yelled "Down!" and the sixty men sought what scant cover they could find in the bottom of the boats. In this position they seemed to drift for hours, listening to the splash of debris as it fell into the lake after the first great explosion, and the lesser ones that followed. Cowed, they would have stayed even longer, had not Rogers got them back to their places and driving for the boom. They had to get over this boom and on down the lake, where they now knew that the French boats were retreated from the burning pyre of Fort Carillon.

Although the night was dark, the three British boats got among the French flotilla and broke up its formation. Despite the fact that they were armed only with muskets and one puny cannon, the Rangers succeeded in driving ashore ten bateaux, which next morning were found to be heavily loaded with baggage and military stores. The French soldiers made good their escape.

Once again, Robert Rogers had led the British onto Lake Champlain. His beloved whaleboats were water-borne and operational, but now there was a difference. There was no more hiding them in the bushes; nor, when they were discovered, was there any long line of replacements over the hills from Lake George. Instead, horse-drawn wagons would bring the boats down the short portage from the lake, and they would rest openly, under guard, on the shore at Ticonderoga and Crown Point. Their graceful lines resembled bullets in the breech of a rifle. Lake Champlain was the rifle's long, slim barrel. It pointed, now, at the heart of New France.

"Success to General Amherst"

Captain Loring was wasting no time when Robert Rogers drew the boats from him on the evening before the French blew up their Fort Carillon. General Amherst wanted to dominate the lake, and Loring had promised him a fleet of ships to outmatch any that the French could send against it. With this in mind, Loring's first concern was to get the saw-mill working again.

The army had been combed over for carpenters and ship-wrights, who were placed under command of the Royal Navy captain for as long a time as he could find employment for them. The supply line through Lake George to the Hudson was the responsibility of the deputy quarter-master general, Colonel Bradstreet, who was bringing up the naval stores that had been stock-piled down the long line of communication.

Loring had planned his ships some time before the assembling of the Amherst expedition. Indeed, a Lake Champlain navy had been in the British plan of things ever since 1755, when Governor Shirley first looked to the Lake Champlain water route to Canada. Now this navy was to be born on the shores of the Ticonderoga Peninsula, in the few weeks that remained of the summer of 1759.

There were to be two ships. The larger one would carry a battery of eighteen guns: six 6-pounders and twelve 4-pounders. Her crew would be made up of seventy seamen to sail her and man her guns, and sixty marines for the twenty swivel guns that ringed her bulwarks and for landing parties on the shore — ever a naval consideration on the narrow lake. The other ship, only slightly smaller, was cut with ports for sixteen guns: four 6-pounders and twelve 4-pounders. There would be room in her to mount twenty-two swivels. Her complement would be sixty sailors and fifty marines.

By the end of August, a deserter to the French was able to report to them that the English had launched a sloop of eighteen guns, and that two others were building. In this he was both right and wrong.

The sloop, the *Duke of Cumberland*, had been launched with fitting ceremony, and was named by Amherst for his old commander in chief, William August, third son of George II, whom the Scots called "Butcher." But when the time came a second mast would be stepped and the *Duke* would be brigantine-rigged.

The sixteen-gun vessel would be launched in September. Her masts and spars, already cut from the straight and clean pines that grew everywhere along the dockyard, correctly indicated to the deserter, as he walked among the laid-out poles and gaff and boom and yards, that she would be a sloop with square topsails, and that she would carry a long bowsprit.

The third "sloup" of which their informer told the French was too new-laid-down for him to ascertain her type, so he guessed her to be another sloop. Actually, she was the radeau *Ligonier*, an afterthought, added to the British fleet when Amherst had received positive information about the French fleet against which he must sail.

In the time left to him, Captain Loring could not build another sloop or brig. The individual pairs of knee-braces that gave a sailing ship her lines must be selected for shape from a living hardwood tree, before the adzemen could get to work on them for the final shaping and fitting into the keel. A radeau, on the other hand, was an easy thing, whose timbered floor and planked sides could be turned out in a couple of weeks by the big vertical saw at the mill. When she was launched and christened by Loring on September 29, 1759, the *Ligonier*'s high sides were cut with ports for six big iron 24-pounders. She was eighty-four feet long and twenty feet wide, and it was hoped that when the two big square sails were set to the two stumpy masts, they would carry her before the wind. Otherwise, the *Ligonier* was to be propelled by long sweeps, or oars, manned by gunners of the Royal Artillery, who furnished her full complement.

The British knew of the old schooner, *La Vigilante*, which Rogers twice had attempted to board. Now, it seemed that the French had been building a navy! Two sloops had been built, and at least one other was on the ways at Ile aux Noix, and would be completed in time to meet Loring's flotilla unless something was done about it. A Sergeant Hopkins tried to burn her on the night of September 11, ten days after her launching, but his attempt failed. Shortly afterward, she was able to join her two sister ships on patrol in Lake Champlain.

Like the British, the French had imported a sailor to take command on the lake—one who was resourceful and imaginative in the way that one would expect of a Mediterranean Corsair. He was Monsieur de La Bras, captain of a French man-o'-war, and probably more at home in a sea than on an ocean. Though the English were expected to build a navy if, or when, they gained a foothold on Lake Champlain, La Bras made no plans to meet it in a yardarm-to-yardarm gun fight, which was the English way. Instead, the Frenchman approached the problem with an eye to a fast patrol boat which could defend herself against boarders, and even invite them, while having enough gun power and range to cause havoc in a whaleboat or bateaux convoy. The French vessels, therefore, were built on the lines of the xebec (the craft favored by Mediterranean pirates), which was relatively long in proportion to its breadth. La Bras, however, chose to rig his xebecs as sloops, rather than with the characteristic lateen sail on a short mast.

To carry out the Corsair role envisioned for them, the first two vessels to be launched were named *La Musquelonguy* and *La Brochette*. The third had to be content with the name of *L'Esturgeon*, not a hunting killer, as is the muskellunge and the great northern pike, but the bane of the fishermen's nets.

Each of the three carried eight guns, and as many swivel guns as place could be found for along the rails. Captain La Bras, who chose *La Musquelonguy* as his flagship, had two brass 12-pounders for long-range work, and respectable broadsides were built up by six iron 6-pound cannon. The other two vessels carried only 6- and 4-pounders. A man-o'-war officer named Rigal was second-in-command to La Bras, and captained *La Brochette*.

These two sloop-rigged xebecs, with the 60-ton *La Vigilante*, her sides now pierced for ten guns, 6-pounders and 4-pounders, left Carillon for the last time on July 7, and moved into the open lake above Split Rock. There the French fleet cruised, in a constant nervous watch for the coming of the British.

Robert Rogers had to go through this picket line on his epic raid to the Indian town of St. Francis. He slipped through in the dark of the moon, his Rangers paddling the big whaleboats without the scrape of a shaft against a gunwale, or the gurgle of a blade pulled too hard against the water. The hundred and forty-two Rangers in the boats afterward agreed that they had held their breath for "longer than it takes to skin a moose." During all that interminable hour their only terror was the slight creak of running gear, as one of the French vessels nearby in the darkness lifted to her anchor cable in the gentle swell. Avoiding any encounter on the lake, the Rangers came safely to their destination at the far corner of Missisquoi Bay, where they abandoned their boats to the French and struck out overland to St. Francis.

Rogers was wary of these new French vessels. Sergeant Hopkins had brought back details of the Corsair tricks which had made the sloop such an invitation to arson, but such a beehive when aroused. So Rogers avoided the three French fish and never hunted them, or *La Vigilante* again. He left them to Captain Loring's proud sails and trained gun crews. Rogers himself had business up ahead, two hundred miles beyond Amherst's army, where six hundred English scalps, unavenged, hung rotting from the lodgepoles of St. Francis.

With the chips flying and the hammers ringing on the anvils at Captain Loring's shipyard, General Amherst had to wait. His soldiers gladly would have waited with him, in delightful slothfulness under the shade trees by the shore, but Amherst and the whole conspiracy of officers and sergeants of the army found work for the troops.

At Ticonderoga, five provincial regiments were put to work patching up the fort and building a strong new wall, for a heavy battery to command the lake to the south, facing Britain's own Atlantic colonies.

Crown Point, which the army occupied on August 5, without a contest, caught Amherst's eye as a defensive position not to be overlooked. As Fort St. Frédéric was a cracked and crumbling pile of stones, and small in size, all hands were set to building a system of earth and log forts to dominate the point, and to command the channel on the east and the anchorage in Bullwagga Bay to the west.

Even the Rangers were not excused the building fatigue. Two hundred of them were put to hacking out a road across the Green Mountains to the Connecticut River beyond — a road which would give Massachusetts and New Hampshire direct access to the northern frontier.

By these forts and roads, General Amherst made the English base, built on the Ticonderoga–Crown Point axis, a formidable position. To command the lake, he waited only for the ships that Loring had promised him.

At the end of September, with the season closing in, Amherst lacked only the sixteen-gun sloop. Work on her was hurried forward, and she was launched *Boscawen*, in honor of the admiral who had brought Amherst to Louisbourg. This was a pretty compliment to the Royal Navy on the inland waters of North America. Lieutenant Grant, of Montgomery's Highlanders, was given command. With a new ship and a new crew, he set out around the tip of the Ticonderoga Peninsula on the morning of September 11.

Grant had his ship in hand by the time he came in sight of the raw earth walls of Fort Amherst. His arrival was none too soon, as the army was forming up the bateaux ready to move out. In the midst of all the activity squatted the boxlike *Ligonier*, flagship not only for the transports but also for the escort fleet of four row galleys, each of which was armed with a captured 18-pounder, the flatbottomed boat carrying a 6-pounder, and four bay boats mounting swivel guns. In the distance rode the *Duke of Cumberland*, her jib holding her, while aloft her top men were making ready her sails, as she waited for her consort *Boscawen*, to be off on their mission.

At four o'clock, with his orders in his hand, Grant fell in on Loring's stern, in line ahead, on a course north-northeast for the narrows, eleven miles away. Their mission was to find and engage all the French ships: the three sloops and the schooner. Under no circumstances must these get through the British battle line of two vessels, and in among the boats of the army.

A red signal flag broke out from the mainmast of the *Ligonier*. The dull thump of a saluting gun from the fort came downwind, enveloped the two warships for a moment of time, and passed over them toward the barrier mountain.

For a week, Amherst had no true word of the fleet.

At noon on October 12, Major Gladwin of Gage's light infantry, who was marching on shore as a scout, sent back word that at first light he had seen vessels engaged. This was true, but his messengers were not specific. Major Reid of the Highlanders shamefacedly brought back to Amherst the alarming details of Gladwin's "naval engagement." During the night of October 11, Reid, with his division of bateaux, had followed as best he could the mast-light of the brig, instead of the radeau. When day broke, Reid found himself among the French sloops, Loring's mast-light nowhere in sight. He had been fired upon, had lost one bateau, with Lieutenant M'Koy and twenty men, and had retired in all haste. He had not been pursued.

So the three French sloops were now between the battle squadron and the army transport flotilla. The navy had sailed ahead, proudly and stupidly, passing by the French fleet which had anchored for the night in the shelter of Les Quatres Vents (now called the Four Brothers) islands.

While he was ruminating upon the navy in general and

Captain Loring in particular, Amherst's attention was drawn to the change of the wind. It had veered twice during the last hour, and his pilot now pointed to the north, where a squall-line of dark water divided the lake. It was a wind that could bring the French sloops driving into the mass of English boats while the men were fully occupied at the oars and their powder wet with cold spray. General Amherst gave the order for the whole army to land.

The storm raged all during the next five days and nights. The army huddled on the west shore of Lake Champlain and wished for the sheltering walls of the forts and barracks they had built so grudgingly through the hot and sultry days of summer. During the night of October 15, the puddles of water froze. It was the worst night since the beginning of the storm, when whaleboats had been sent out to look for Loring but had been forced back by the north wind. No British boats ventured on to the lake, nor did the French sloops come in sight.

Meanwhile, Captain Loring was on his quarter-deck before daybreak on October 12, in a position that he estimated as forty-five miles north of Crown Point, approaching the passage between Grande Ile and Cumberland Head. Gradually, the dawn light came, and with it a hail from the foremast lookout. The schooner *La Vigilante* was dead ahead! Up went the signal "to chase," and the deck crew leapt for the shrouds to make more sail.

The *Duke* and the *Boscawen* pursued up the channel reaching to the west shore, in an attempt to force *La Vigilante* in toward the lee of Grande Ile. They seemed to be succeeding in this, and overtaking as they did so; two small islands were ahead of the Frenchman, and on the *Duke's* deck there was speculation as to whether the schooner would pass them to la'board, or go inside. At the last moment, *La Vigilante* took the latter course, and the English boats

turned inshore on a course that would cut in obliquely to
La Vigilante's wake, as she fled behind the first of the two
small islands.

As soon as his bottom scraped the hidden shoals, Loring
realized that he had been maneuvered into this ridiculous
position by a very lake-wise captain. He was fast aground,
his bow high and his sails flapping. Grant, close on Loring's
tailboard, gave the *Boscawen* hard left rudder, spilled the
wind from all her sails, and by her own momentum she was
carried on a half-cable length in a wide arc toward the island.
With a gentle bump and a shudder, the *Boscawen* found
and struck her own shoal.

La Vigilante continued on, picking her way through the
shoal water which her pilot knew so well.

Commodore Loring and Captain Grant rowed around
their stranded vessels and were shamefaced and polite to
each other. Neither was stuck fast, and by shifting the bow
guns aft and using the sweeps as poles, while the jolly boats
pulled at the stern, first one British vessel was freed and
then the other.

It was now late afternoon of October 12, and the squalls
that further up the lake were driving the army to shelter
ashore had settled into a northeaster. White mares' tails
flicked along the top of the rising waves. Thus, the white
sails of La Bras's three sloops, beating north against the
blow, were not immediately spotted either by Loring or
by Grant, nor could the French captain pick out the bare
poles of the British against the islands to the north of him.
Neither commander expected the other to have slipped
between him and his base. When recognition dawned, the
hour was late and the reactions were instinctive. The British
with the weather gauge made all sail for the sloops. La Bras,
seeking a position more advantageous than the open lake,
turned and accepted pursuit, leading the heavier British

vessels into the setting sun and the approaching night. The Frenchman hoped to find a sheltered anchorage behind a protective island or headland where he could fight his guns defensively from steady decks or hide successfully while Loring sailed by him in the darkness.

Neither hope was fulfilled. Though the French gained a position in a bay near the west shore, slightly protected by an island (Crab Island), the British found them and lay to for the night, watching and waiting for the morning to begin their bombardment. La Bras called a conference of officers aboard *La Musquelonguy*, where it was decided to scuttle. This was done in the dark of the stormy night, La Bras, Rigal, and the sailors tending to the details, while white-coated soldiers of the regiments Languedoc, Bearn, and La Sarre ferried themselves back to the shore. There they waited on firm ground for the man-o'-war's men to finish their work and allow the retreat on St. Jean to begin.

The morning of October 13 — the morning on which Loring expected battle — showed a French fleet sunk and abandoned, two of the vessels in five fathoms and the third canted on a reef, guns spiked and mast cut away, but capable of being refloated.

Leaving Grant to get the Frenchman off the reef, Loring turned north in the *Duke of Cumberland* to search out *La Vigilante* and to take revenge on France's last vessel on the lake. He did not find her, and when Amherst came up on October 18, with a fair south wind at his back and clear skies overhead, he found his fleet with their salvaged prize between them, and *Amherst* painted over the French name on her counter.

Now Amherst had to make a command decision: either to go on and invest Ile aux Noix in the narrow Richelieu River, where Bourlamaque awaited him with twenty-three hundred soldiers, or to fall back until spring on his new fort

at Crown Point. Remembering the freezing temperature of
two nights before, and the autumn storms, which if repeated
(almost a certainty in these latitudes) would slash his supply
line for days, Amherst chose to go into winter quarters.
Strategically, too, this decision was a logical one. On October 16, Amherst had received news of the capture of Quebec
and the death, not only of Wolfe but of Montcalm, an
enemy general to be respected with caution. English arms
had been successful in the west. Without the stimulus of a
success at Ile aux Noix, should the unseasonable siege of the
island fortress fail, New France would be weakened by a
winter of dread anticipation. Though Amherst could expect
one counterattack by Montcalm's lieutenants, the campaign
of 1760 would be a triumphal closing of the ring of British
armies that now encircled Montreal — though at a distance.

The bateaux and artillery boats, therefore, turned back
up Lake Champlain. Lieutenant Grant and the *Boscawen*,
with the *Amherst,* stayed behind to complete salvage operations and to make an attempt, within the next few days, to
raise the two sunken French sloops.

Commodore Loring sailed north aboard the *Duke of
Cumberland*, with two hundred men in whaleboats, to cruise
at the mouth of the Richelieu River. Loring remained there
"on station," until the insistence of the oncoming winter
forced him back to shelter in the shipyards at the British
forts. He had hoped to intercept the elusive *Vigilante*, if
she was still in the open lake; he never saw her again. But
Loring's final cruise of 1759 kept Bourlamaque on an alert
defensive behind the walls of his fort on Ile aux Noix, and
in that sesquicentennial year of the discovery of the lake by
Samuel de Champlain, the Englishman denied the waters of
the whole lake to every Frenchman.

The campaign which put the English firmly on Lake
Champlain was ended. Now Robert Webster could go home

to Connecticut. "Thursday, the 25 October. All hands at work on the Fort," he wrote on his last evening with the army, in the diary he had kept faithfully ever since he set out from home on April 5. A sergeant in charge of thirty-six men, he left the fort on October 26 to return to Connecticut by way of "Number 4" (Charleston, New Hampshire), building bridges along the new road as he went. Each night Webster made an entry in his little calf-bound notebook. On Sunday, November 18, Sergeant Webster was given a pass, and 2 shillings 8 pence traveling money. This item was duly entered in his journal, as were the events of each successive day, until at last he was able to write ". . . and got home in the evening very tired. Robert Webster."

He had never looked back.

Five Years' Work Is Done

While the provincial regiments of the British colonies and the militia of French Canada were recruited only for the campaign season, the professional soldiers had to be housed, fed, and paid all during the dismal winter months. The lucky men went into billets in the cities and towns along the St. Lawrence and Hudson Rivers and found places for themselves around family firesides. Less fortunate regiments garrisoned the isolated forts.

By the time the first ice came to the shallows and marshes of Lake Champlain, all had to be in readiness for the great cold and deep snow to be expected with Christmas and the New Year. Bateaux and whaleboats had to be pulled ashore, overturned, piled, and covered with evergreen branches, or sunk in the lake to lie beneath the ice until spring. The large vessels must be winched up in cradles onto the shingle, or penned in by piles driven into the mud, and the ice inside kept clear of the hulls every morning. Down by the camps of the few Indians who would winter at the forts, bark canoes would be sunk in order to keep their tender skins from drying and cracking. The parade ground (or Place d'Armes), where squads and platoons had drilled under big-voiced corporals, now mustered rank upon rank of wood stacks, and somewhere, handy to the stalls and folds, would be haystacks for the waiting sheep and beef cattle who would not live to see the new grass.

The soldiers stayed indoors, drew their rations, kept their fires, and cursed their duties. Snow had to be cleared from the bastions, and drifts that built themselves against outside walls like scaling ramps must be cut back. Then there were the interminable rounds of sentry-go, which grew more frequent for the healthy as the chorus of night coughing spread through the close barrack rooms; daily more and more sick moved their blankets to the hospital.

The duty officer sat in his little guardroom, glad, perhaps, to be away for one whole day from the too familiar faces and mannerisms of the anteroom. With the turning of the hourglass on his table, he sent the relieving sentries out into the cold night, himself dreading "rounds," when he would have to bundle up and visit his posts.

In every direction was whiteness and the gray boles of hardwood trees, relieved only by the dark, dark green of the cedars and pines. The lake was only a flat whiteness between the molded contours of the land, and north from Fort Amherst far away to the French fort on Ile aux Noix the white surface lay unbroken. There was little winter travel. Scouts of the British Rangers or French Indians kept to the ridges overlooking the lake, and only an occasional sleigh passed on the snow road behind the forts.

One of these occasional travelers was Major Robert Rogers, returning to Crown Point where two companies of his Rangers were stationed. He had been in New York City, to wait upon General Amherst and to give his intelligence reports to the planning staff, who were preparing the 1760 campaign.

Rogers spent the night of February 12 at Fort Ticonderoga. In the morning he set out with sleighs and thirteen recruits, along the ice road to Crown Point — the same road that he had ambushed with such relish in former years. Then he had had his old Rangers with him; now so many of them were gone. Rogers himself had been wounded in the head after the last sleigh ambush, when Captain Spikeman and Lieutenant Hobbs had been killed, with the young ensign, Caleb Page, from Rogers's home town in New Hampshire, and seventeen other men he knew. Now, on a cold winter's day he must wear his fur hat, or the two-year-old-scar on his skull would throb painfully. He put his hand to his head.

Suddenly, the French sprang their ambush and Rogers was caught, sitting in his sleigh. Old instincts leapt over the windfalls of memories in his brain, and he reacted as does a trained and experienced officer. He estimated his position as hopeless, but saw at once the one weak spot in the attacking force of — he put the number at sixty men. Gathering together those Rangers near him who were not too shocked into surprise, Rogers counterattacked through the French weak spot, and, herding his recruits (now only four) before him, reached a picket guard from Fort Amherst.

Robert Rogers was back! He never seemed to arrive quietly, even at a listless winter cantonment. Frenchmen were attracted to him as though he gave off the smell of their hate, and if they were not attracted by his scent he waved it close by their forts and camps. The ice and snow and water, and the thick leaves of trees, held the tantalizing perfume and lured the Frenchmen out.

The French called Rogers lucky, to explain their own failure to catch him; but their Indians called him "Wo-bi-Ma-da-on-do" (White Devil), and treated him with a great awe and fear.

For Rogers, personally, the ambush of 1760 was most unlucky. When he led the picket back to the site of the ambush, there were five scalped bodies lying dark against the snow, and though he looked through his scattered baggage, and looked again, his money-box was gone. He had lost £1196 in York currency, of which £396 was his own.

And, worse than this, four of his men had been led prisoner up the broad trail of the Indian retreat. For Rogers' Rangers, that meant torture.

Together with the Rangers he had left at Fort Amherst he could pursue, overtake, and recover his men and his money, and he could avenge the five bodies now lying under blankets thrown over them by the staring picket guard. But Colonel William Haviland would not let the Rangers go. His men were winter-sick; he had no clear picture of the French and Indian party outside the walls, of whom the sixty men might have been but a small part; and not being an officer who led his own men in battle, but an Amherst-trained staff officer, he prided himself on seeing the whole campaign without rancor.

The final conquest of New France depended on the continuation of the Amherst plan, which in its second year called for three British armies to converge on Montreal from the three posts seized from the French in 1759. General Amherst himself would lead the main force down the St. Lawrence from Fort Oswego. Brigadier General James Murray, who had succeeded to Wolfe's command at Quebec City, would march up the St. Lawrence. From his advance base at Crown Point, Colonel Haviland would advance by water to the Richelieu River, reducing the posts he found there, and by marching along the road from the Richelieu to La Prairie, would appear on the south side of the St. Lawrence opposite Montreal, at the same time as the two general officers coming from the west and the east.

To Colonel Haviland, expecting promotion to brigadier general and entrusted with a major role in the 1760 campaign, the maintenance through the winter of the forts at the southern end of Lake Champlain was the pivot of his whole plan and career. No matter what the temptation, nor how much his Major of Rangers importuned him, he must keep on a tight defensive until Amherst, according to the strategical timetable, gave him orders to move out. Aside from this, Haviland was not easy in his fort at Crown Point, with his ships frozen in and Lévis still operational with an army of winter-wise Canadians and veteran French regiments. Though the French counterattack against Quebec and the sea lane to France was expected, Lévis was a bold commander, capable of bringing off with flashing success the illogical and the unexpected. Recognizing Lévis's qualities of generalship (which were to bring him a maréchal's baton and a dukedom), Haviland could not take any chances with his fort.

In late April, Lévis attacked Quebec, but a British fleet arrived to relieve the closely besieged Murray, and on May 16 Lévis retired to Montreal, to make what defense he could in that sprawling river-bank city.

The British armies prepared to move. On Lake Champlain, Robert Rogers opened the campaign with a hell-raising expedition to the Richelieu River, ordered by Amherst for the purpose of drawing off the French troops besieging Quebec. The expedition was tailor-made for the Rangers, and though it did not leave Crown Point until a fortnight after the French had lifted the siege, Rogers had no way of knowing this. No scout from Murray had come out of the woods with the news, nor could word have traveled the long sea lane around the Maritime Provinces and New England and up the Hudson River and the lakes to where the Rangers were busily loading their whaleboats on to the four vessels which were to carry them to the northern end of Lake Champlain.

The ships were commanded by Captain Grant, the Highlander sailor. With Rogers and his amphibious Rangers,

Grant worked out a combined land and water operation that quickened the spirit of all on board the four vessels, standing down the lake with a fair wind. They sailed first deep into Missisquoi Bay, where Lieutenant Holmes and fifty men of the light infantry were put ashore on a separate task of destruction down the little river Wigwam Martinic, which flows into the St. Lawrence between the Richelieu and St. Francis Rivers. At the same time, four Rangers shouldered their packs and struck out through the swamps and forests, bearing messages from Amherst to Murray. Grant left one of his sloops cruising in the bay, to take off Holmes's party on its return, while the remainder of his fleet sailed for the mouth of the Richelieu.

The whaleboats were put overside on June 4, and two hundred Rangers took their places at the familiar oars. Under cover of the darkness, they rowed to the west shore of Lake Champlain, where they landed. Concealing their whaleboats behind the marginal verge of new-leafed bushes, they sat down to wait while the navy played out a diversion.

At dawn, in spite of a drizzling rain that dampened the wind, Captain Grant managed to coax his three vessels into the Richelieu itself. He did not stay long in the narrow waters, but when he left for the safer breadth of lake south of Windmill Point, he drew the French watch boats with him — as was his intent.

Watching from the shore, Rogers saw the French boats, like orphaned puppies mindful of their manners, follow the three British warships south to Ile LaMotte.

The following morning, June 6, Rogers was ready to begin the detour march through the woods which would bring him, undetected, to the French towns above the fort on Ile aux Noix. The Rangers were drawing the damp powder from their rifles and rolling their sodden blankets at the impatient urging of the sergeants, when the advance scouts came in with discouraging news. The presence of the Rangers was known to the French, who were themselves landing a force on the west shore. The scouts had waited long enough to count three hundred and fifty Frenchmen being ferried from the island.

The Ranger position was attacked at eleven-thirty that morning. The attack was met with a determination and a counterattack that drove off the French force with forty casualties, including its commander. But for Robert Rogers it was an empty victory. His intent was now known to the enemy, and there were seventeen of his Rangers dead and ten wounded to be cared for. In addition, the soft June rain had come on again and had spoiled enough of the Rangers' provisions to make the intended bold strike inland appear foolhardy.

Rogers's successes, and indeed, his whole long life in a dangerous service, rested on his quick recognition of blank folly. Now, without hesitating in his decision, he recalled his pursuing Rangers, and embarking his whole force — quick, wounded, and dead — he fell back on the fleet.

When the whaleboats came back, Grant was lying off the southeast corner of Ile LaMotte, where it was agreed that he would be. With Grant, it was now Rogers's duty to restore the lost momentum to the expedition that General Amherst had ordered against the river towns.

Short of supplies, Grant sent a sloop to fetch more from Crown Point, while Rogers attended to the morale of his men, who had been snatched back from joyous pursuit, to sit in the whaleboats with the covered bodies of their own stiffening dead. Rogers selected a small island nearby (Cloak Island) and paraded his men there. With the ships arrayed off shore, the Ranger dead were buried in solemn ceremony calculated to breed renewed determination in the living.

By midnight of June 9, Robert Rogers was away again.

This time he landed well behind his fleet, at the mouth of the Chazy River. Grant had taken the fleet down to Windmill Point, to be discovered there at dawn. For three days, Grant made tentative attempts at what the French lookouts took to be the landing of a party. Then he sailed down the east shore, drawing the French attention after him, while Rogers led the Rangers in a wide circle well back from the western shore. Grant was careful not to fall too far up the lake. He made Ile LaMotte his southern reach, as he must be ready to go in and bring the Rangers off the enemy shore at their signal. After a few days, Grant gave up his watch on the west shore, south from the site of the battle of June 6. Rogers would return that way only if he were driven back before he could get by the French soldiers at Ile aux Noix. Now, as the days dragged out, Grant edged more and more to the east, and put the signal watch to give closer and closer attention to the shore below Windmill Point. Thus they saw the very first puff of smoke above the trees, and heard the three spaced volleys, while the bows of the vessels were swinging toward the beach. The whaleboat crews prepared to launch their boats the moment the ships' captains hove to.

Sails came down and anchors dropped, to drag jerkily along the bottom before the momentum of the driving vessels could be checked and the flukes take hold. The boats got away, and gun crews ran out their cannon ready to support the embarkation, but no support was needed as the green- or gray-clad figures filed quickly out of the woods into the boats and were water-borne. Within minutes the French appeared, eight hundred of them, and were left stranded on the shore as the English fleet, reunited with its soldiers, sailed away in safety and in triumph.

Regrettably for Captain Grant of the Lake Champlain Flotilla, and for Major Rogers of the Independent Companies of Rangers, never again did they go off together to harry "Monsieur"; time was running out on Robert Rogers's war for Lake Champlain. The water gate was ready to be swung open, and New France lingered on at Montreal only in the bombast of an ineffectual governor, and on the bayonets of all that remained of seven fine regiments, serving under a resourceful general.

To Gaston François de Lévis, major general since the great French victory over Abercromby at Fort Carillon in 1758, fell the onus of making the last French stand in Canada. Cast off and already forgotten by the Court at Versailles — with the corrupt civil authorities of New France wrangling and gloating over their stolen hoards while a foolish governor clung to the last vestige of his rank; with the Indian allies gone, and the *habitants* losing all care as to who governed them — Lévis prepared to take his stand.

All he could hope to do was to delay one or more of the three British armies which were converging on Montreal from such widely separate bases; and then, with his staunch regulars, to give battle to those British who *did* pass through the road blocks. It was hard for a devoted soldier to realize that he had been abandoned by a puissant monarch. Lévis and his soldiers clung fast to their loyalty and hoped that if they could hold out another winter, court politics at Versailles would change and help would be sent to them in New France.

East and west, up and down the St. Lawrence, brave captains held their posts, while on the Richelieu Lévis stationed the brilliant young Colonel Bougainville, whose name is remembered by a flower and an island in faraway Melanesia.

To meet Haviland, Louis Antoine de Bougainville had on Ile aux Noix and at St. Jean four hundred and fifty troops of the marine (Canadians hired, paid, and maintained by the Ministry of Marine, which controlled French colonial affairs) and two hundred and fifty soldiers. The militia under his control was unreliable. In the river near Ile aux Noix, he stationed a radeau and three armed boats as river guard. Montreal was only twenty miles away, along a single forest road down which he could not look for reinforcements. Bougainville could look only to Lake Champlain and to the enemy that he knew was coming.

On August 16, 1760, a week after General Amherst had set out from Oswego for Montreal, Colonel Haviland left Crown Point for the same goal. Robert Rogers led in his whaleboats, with six hundred Rangers and seventy Indians. Half a mile behind rode Colonel Haviland in his flagship, Grant (Haviland's commodore) on the quarter-deck beside him. Within hailing distance to port and starboard were the light infantry and grenadiers of regiments under Colonel Darby. These were Haviland's shock troops. Behind this advance guard followed Brigadier Timothy Ruggles, second-in-command to Haviland (though only a provincial by birth and in rank), with six regiments in three columns. The bateaux of the 17th and 27th Foot kept the center column, while on the flank rowed New England men. Four radeaux abreast transported the artillery and its stores, under a major of the Royal Artillery, while behind them trailed the storeboats and sutlers, shepherded by the busy sloops.

It was not an easy sail, and the men were hard pressed to keep formation in the strong wind of August 16. Next day a hard north wind kept the bateaux on shore, while the vessels and radeaux tugged uneasily at their anchor chains. Though the wind veered again on August 18, it was strong, and the boats groaned as they lurched under a following wave. One of the whaleboats split open and ten Rangers were drowned. But that day the flotilla won through to Ile LaMotte, and Haviland designated August 19 as a day of rest. He did not wish to bring a fatigued and seasick army to the siege he planned for Ile aux Noix. It was five miles from the northern end of Ile LaMotte to Windmill Point, and twelve miles down that stream to Ile aux Noix. Haviland and his army made the journey in a day, and arrived in sight of the French position while there was still enough light to land and dispose the troops, and to bring the unwieldy radeaux to their unloading beachheads.

On August 21, the siege of Ile aux Noix began.

For Haviland, with a rendezvous to keep at Montreal, a siege and artillery duel only played into the hands of Bougainville. Colonel Darby, with the assault troops, undertook to break the siege by an attack from the land on the French vessels, anchored in the deep east channel. Darby took under command four companies of Rangers, two companies of his own troops, and the Indians. With the men dragging two light howitzers and a 6-pounder, he forced his way through the thick woods and heavy brush to a good position, which provided a commanding field of fire for his lone gun, and a nice pitch into the high-sided French radeau for his howitzers. He need not have been so meticulous. The first shot from the 6-pounder cut the radeau's cable, and an obliging northwest wind blew the awkward craft to the shore. There, waiting Rangers swarmed up the high rampart sides, stepping on the ineffectual cannon barrels, and from behind loaded muskets grinned down at the French gunners, caged in their floating castle.

Threatened on the flank by cannon, and with only a forest wall into which to fire blindly, the three remaining French vessels weighed anchor for St. Jean. The decision was a desperate one, stemming from panic caused by the sight of the heavy-gunned radeau, aground and helpless as jetsam, swarming with the dreaded Rangers, who for so many long years had prowled on the wide lake in search of the French fleet. In the face of this old enemy, so close on the shore of the narrow river, with the cannon shells plopping into the water as they fell out of range, even the uncertainty of the channel and the bluff face of a contrary wind which would blow them toward the hostile east shore seemed preferable to a gallant stand and ringing immortality.

Out of the oar ports slid the long sweeps, reaching frantically for the water even before the anchors broke water, to dangle unsecured at the bows as the winch crews hurried to help at the oars. "*Sauve qui peut!*" Downriver was safety, and perhaps a man-o'-war to take them to the deep sea where shores were distant.

Rogers, too, had memories of French vessels slipping by his whaleboats in the dark, or sailing wide of the point where his ambush was laid. Now, in the last ten miles of navigable water in Lake Champlain, he had the French ships — scared, running, and only yards away. The radeau was taken. Perhaps, if he followed the retreating vessels, an opportunity to do them mischief would present itself.

He called in the Rangers at hand, and with Darby's blessing set off at a lope down the east shore, for the long reach of the river beyond the marsh islands, and the indistinct eastern shore of the channel behind Ile aux Noix. The marsh was the delta of a river (South River), and, where Rogers struck, it was thirty yards wide. There was no time to waste in trying to discover a ford. Slowly the first Rangers felt their way across, riling up the mud bottom, their balance precarious, with hands holding the all-important rifle high above their heads. Safely over, wet and covered with stinking ooze, they turned on the far shore to catch the cartridge pouches and belts, swung over to them by their comrades, still dry and clean. Robert Rogers roamed the shore, harrying the men and casting about in his mind for the quick way after the vessels. Before the last Ranger had found his belt and pouch, Rogers was off inland for the tall timber and hard ground.

From a tree, he saw the French boats just entering the long reach, making hard going against the wind. He set his course to intercept.

The next time he dared to look through the foliage on the river edge, he was abreast of the vessels, which now were racing each other, seemingly without attempt to keep in disciplined line. Rogers turned from his contemplation of the French boats to a consideration of the river. A long mile to the north, a little point stuck out like a nipple from the east shore. It marked the beginning of the shallows where the channel narrowed into a defile which might be within reach of aimed fire. With a little luck, a steersman might blunder, and the boat veer on to a mud bank.

The Rangers' luck was in.

From their new hide-out on the point, they watched the approaching vessels, long oars dipping in unison, masts upstretched and awkward like the necks of wading herons. Two were well out in the stream, the third waddling along behind. As the Rangers watched, wondering at their chances for a shot, in the first two boats the rhythm of the rowing broke, and in a splashing of oars the dark hulls were swung by the wind across the stream and into the current, which gently pushed and held the big ships against the mud bank they had run upon. The tall masts slowly tilted and stopped. Below water, the mud swirled and eddied around the stranded bottoms, building up a firm grip which the frantic shoving on oars by the French crews could not overcome. The third vessel turned east to find the channel, her oarsmen quickening their beat to flee more rapidly from the fate of her sisters. On the east side of the channel she met her own fate on another mud bank, this one within easy reach of the riflemen ashore.

For Rogers, after so many years and so many fruitless attempts, it was now so easy. Dividing the Rangers into two parties, he sent one to find firing positions to their liking along the shore, and with their ramrods and powder horns, their shot bags or cartridge pouches arranged beside them, the men settled themselves comfortably while awaiting the order to begin the shoot. The other party stripped themselves to the buff or breechclout, and taking only their tomahawks, lined up behind their officer at the water's edge, but modestly behind a screen of leaves, where the pink whiteness of their naked bodies would not stand out against the green shore.

The swimming party could hear the French sailors jabbering aboard their stranded vessel, while each rifleman, his bronzed and bearded face purposely streaked with mud and dirt, watched unabashedly the Frenchman selected by himself as a prime target. On the quarter-deck, a group was leading the jolly boat around to the lee side, probably to take on board the anchor in an attempt to winch her clear.

Rogers fired first. The other rifles spoke eagerly down the line, and the Rangers rolled on to their sides to load and fire again before all the Monsieurs could take cover. On board, the scramble grew quiet. A face appeared at a gun port, and six Rangers fired together; the face disappeared. Slowly now, the Rangers aimed their fire along the rails or at the gun ports. Not a French head showed. No one aboard dared grab for the line from the jolly boat, and it splashed into the water as the boat drifted out astern — a derelict.

A white arm waved up and over, pointing for an instant at the silent French vessel. Quietly and quickly, the naked men followed their officer into the warm water. On the bank, Robert Rogers had had a word for each man — encouragement, admonition, or a rough joke — as he counted them off. It helped him to suffer the disappointment of being a commander.

The route of the swimmers had been chosen so that their target ship hid their approach from the other two French vessels, aground on the opposite side of the river. Only their friends, giving covering fire, saw them gather at the bow of the doomed sailing ship. Hands grabbed the dangling anchors. From the shore came a last flurry of rifle fire. Then, in utter silence the boarders swarmed over the bow, tomahawks gripped between clenched teeth in faces that grimaced war whoops, suppressed to a rumbling growl as they rushed down in a torrent on the cowering sailors.

The French vessel fell without a fight.

Colonel Darby, meanwhile, had floated the radeau and brought her downriver to Rogers, where her big guns threatened the other two stranded vessels into submission. Sailors were sent down by Haviland to man the captured fleet, and by nightfall Ile aux Noix was cut off.

At midnight, Bougainville abandoned the island, leaving his sick and wounded to the care of Haviland, who found them on their pallets in the morning.

Major Robert Rogers, who had come the whole long English way, over the watershed and down the lakes a hundred bitter miles or more, wrote "Finis" to the French on Lake Champlain. He did it rather in the manner of a small boy, with the flinging of a handful of gravel and a wide swinging kick down the road.

Two days after the fall of Ile aux Noix, patrols found St. Jean in flames and Bougainville off for Montreal with his remnant army. Rogers pursued with his Rangers and Indian companies, fought briefly with the small rear guard, and returned to St. Jean, where the smooth waters of the lake broke in ripples and rapids down to the Sorel River, ten miles below.

Five years' work was done.

~~~~~~~~~~

Montreal capitulated to General Amherst on September 6, 1760. The inexorable march of the three British armies left the city no other choice. The last feeble cries of Governor Vaudreuil and General Lévis were merely the cracking of ice in a street puddle; the great floes had long since gone from the French rivers and lakes of North America. The water route to the heart of the continent was wide open to Englishmen.

Robert Rogers took this route with his whaleboats and his Rangers, and it led him to oblivion. Sir William Johnson saw the bright path made on the waters by the westward beckoning sun, and his commercial agents slithered along it, sending back tithes to the baronet on the Mohawk. The British soldiers rowed their bateaux up the streams and lakes to new Indian wars, far from the settlements on the coast and beside the tidal waters of the great rivers.

III

Independence Is Won

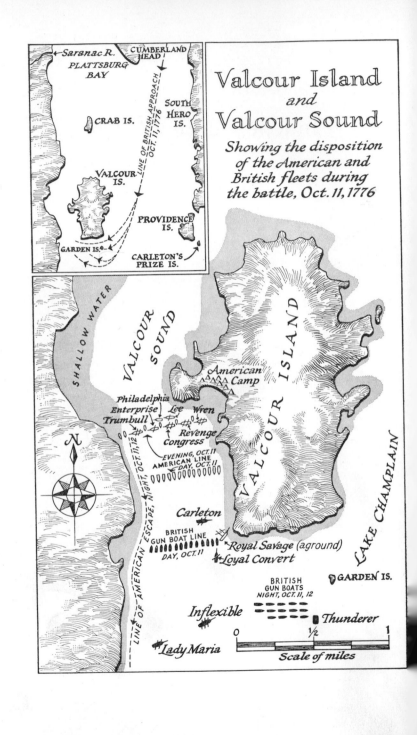

Valcour Island
and
Valcour Sound

Showing the disposition
of the American and
British fleets during
the battle, Oct. 11, 1776

Saranac R.
PLATTSBURG
BAY

CUMBERLAND
HEAD

SOUTH
HERO
IS.

CRAB IS.

VALCOUR
IS.

LINE OF BRITISH APPROACH
OCT. 11, 1776

PROVIDENCE
IS.

GARDEN IS.

CARLETON'S
PRIZE IS.

SHALLOW WATER

VALCOUR SOUND

American
Camp

Philadelphia
Enterprise
Trumbull

Lee

Wren

Revenge
Congress

EVENING, OCT. 11
AMERICAN LINE
DAY, OCT. 11

VALCOUR ISLAND

LAKE CHAMPLAIN

N

LINE OF AMERICAN ESCAPE, NIGHT, OCT. 11, 12

Carleton

BRITISH
GUN BOAT LINE
DAY, OCT. 11

Royal Savage (aground)
Loyal Convert

GARDEN IS.

BRITISH
GUN BOATS
NIGHT, OCT. 11, 12

Inflexible

Thunderer

Lady Maria

0   ½   1

Scale of miles

The Green Mountain Boys

The French-Canadians, who had hyphenated their national-
ity long before the façade of the Versailles government
crashed down at Montreal, remained on their farms after
the British victories but were apprehensive about the future
of their culture and their mode of living. Word had not
yet come from the parish priest in his pulpit. That word
did not come with the formal Treaty of Paris in 1763, when
England took the great square of Canada, which in the
chess game of kings secured the board to loyal Englishmen,
even to the vastness of Louisiana's river basins. Not until
1774 could the priest, robed for the Mass, preach a sermon
that would lull the anxiety of his parishioners. Then, going
into the fields and the wood lots, and to the rendezvous of
the wild *voyageurs*, the calm priests explained in detail the
Quebec Act, which guaranteed to the French Canadians
their religion, their language, their customs, and many of
their old *French* laws. To govern Canada came General
Guy Carleton, a veteran of Wolfe's victory at Quebec, with
a controlling hand as light, yet as firm, as that of the steersman at the stern paddle of a full-loaded canoe.

~~~~~~~~

Robert Webster, sometime sergeant in Colonel Fitch's 4th
Connecticut Regiment, was back home, leading his peaceful
communal life at the sides of his former comrades-in-arms,

on the adjoining farm, in the neighboring parish, or in other colonies along the Atlantic seaboard.

The English king's war against the old French enemy, as it now turned out for all the Robert Websters in British America, had been an important "local" war. With peace, the looming bulk of France had suddenly been lifted from the back lots of the colonies. Webster himself had helped to build a forest road, wide and well-bridged, from the menacing tip of the old French spear point on Lake Champlain to the Connecticut River, the back gate to New England. Formerly, the gate had been opened inward by French Indians, raiding the English colonies. Colonel Williams, of Deerfield, Massachusetts, had given his life in 1755, in an effort to close that back gate. Now, Webster realized, the gate was wide open and tied back. The road through it led outward from the old colonies, and there were no enemies to prevent his traveling freely along that road.

The Robert Websters, the Colonel Blanchards, and the General Lymans of the provincial colonies had come down another long road, and now stood at another gate. The defeat of France, and the pushing back of the Indian menace to the western and southwestern watersheds, was only the last clearing of brush from this road of the mind. During the decade and a half which spanned the years between the end of the old French wars and the year 1775, the gate stood out clearly for all to see.

Something had happened to the British provincial colonist, whether he knew it or not. He had seen the red and gold of an autumn, that he called "the fall"; he had heard a turkey gobbler calling his hens to roost in the glen; he had felled the great tree at the edge of his clearing, and had seen the new vista it opened from his cabin door. He had sawed his own boards, and from them he had built his own boat, to fish and to travel the running stream. He had shucked the husks from the red-tasseled corn — kissing the neighbor girl for each red ear of corn — and had eaten the golden kernels. He could never be English again.

The provincial really did not want to be English. He had lost some of the wonder, when he had soldiered with the omnipotent redcoat on the old frontiers.

Though they had shared the danger, the British regular had not shared the color of his coat. Blue or green, or a hunting shirt, was good enough for the uniform of a provincial. A provincial could achieve rank, even that of general, but his rank was below that of a British regular. A provincial was despised by the King's troops, and to make the mockery audible and musical, a British officer (and a mere army doctor, at that), on his way to the wars on Lake Champlain, had written a mocking song about the dull clods from the colonies. The song was all about "Yankee Doodle" and his awe and his fears in the camp of the regular British army. The provincial took the song for himself, and sang it from an expressionless mouth, and the redcoat did not see the turning mirth behind the Yankee's mask. Blue and green coats had gone up to the muzzles of French guns at the deep trenches before Carillon, and had been bloodied.

Through the 1760's and into the mounting tension of the next decade, horsemen rode back and forth among the thirteen Atlantic colonies, uniting them by a messenger service that made a common cause of each otherwise isolated act of perfidy perpetuated by the government in London.

Those who condoned the emanations from the foot of the throne were Tories; those who listened with indignation to the couriers' latest word of misrule were Whigs. The line of demarcation between the two zigzagged from farm to farm and through the side yards of closely packed city houses. Thus, the rich planter on the James River opposed, in thought, the baronet on the Mohawk who held his Iroquois loyal to the Crown.

Commodore Joshua Loring of Lake Champlain, living on half-pay in rabid Boston, continued to eat the King's bread as he had always done, while other officers of the King gave up their commissions and quietly became Americans. Horatio Gates, a brave major under Braddock, and handsome Richard Montgomery, adjutant of the 17th Foot with Haviland on the lakes, were but two of the latter.

While the thirteen Atlantic colonies (Canada was a potential fourteenth) were simmering before the boil, new lands were slowly being opened to settlers, who brought with them in their oxcarts the notions of Whig and Tory alike.

A few of the soldiers of the old French wars, no longer remembering the hardships of the campaigns along the northern lakes, settled on Lake Champlain.

Major Philip Skene, who had been with Abercromby and Amherst in 1758 and 1759, returned to Lake Champlain in 1765, with a grant from the King of many thousands of acres on the shores of South Bay. There, at the last falls of Wood Creek, at the northern terminus of a quick overland road to be constructed for heavy traffic, Skene built his mills, set up his tenants, and at Skenesborough erected his own great house, the head and heart of his demesne. He was a large, fine-looking Scot of affable mien, as befitted a laird, and with illusions of grandeur that, in his backwoods valley astride the Canadian-Colonial road, he had a fair prospect of putting into practice. In carrying out his duties as governor of the fortresses at Ticonderoga and Crown Point, he traveled the lake in a regal barge rowed by a picked crew of Negro slaves. There also was his private schooner, half-cargo vessel, half-lordly yacht, in which he could cruise with his family to urban Montreal. While giving himself pomp and importance, Philip Skene was ever loyal to the Crown, where lay the fulfillment of his ambition.

Other settlers in the wide, fertile, timber-rich valley were no less ambitious, though of less pretense than the magnificent major. They were the small men and women, owners-in-fee to the Onion River Company, whose unshakable determination to hold their own threw up a granite crag, gigantic as their leader. This leader was Ethan Allen, president of the Onion River Company, with assets in 1775 of 60,829 acres, worth $297,408.50. With such a large investment to protect, and ambitions so unconventional and flexible as to be either Whig or Tory, or neither, Allen's booming big voice rallied an army, and from the echo out of the hills of Vermont, the Green Mountain Boys were mustered.

While the colonists and colonizers were exploiting the newly opened valley in the restless throes of naissance, the lake itself remained the untroubled highway between the Atlantic colonies and the St. Lawrence, gullet of Canada. Settlers used it as a road-in-lieu-of-a-road, for no highway need be laid out up and down its shores as long as sturdy boats were built, and Committees of Safety and Correspondence passed their couriers down the lake with messages couched in terms calculated to inflame Canada to rebellion. The old question as to jurisdiction over the lake became redundant with the expulsion of France. The royal governors of New York and New Hampshire, however, had recourse to law over the ownership of the east shore, while Philip Skene thought in terms of a new Crown colony, and Ethan Allen dreamed of Green Mountains. The British military thought in terms of the old administrative border, the watershed between the Hudson River and the fort at the head of Lake George. Command, supply, and relief came to the garrisons at St. Jean, Crown Point, and Ticonderoga, from headquarters in Montreal, as in French times. And at the old forts the soldiers sat out their long enlistments and made the best of it, as old soldiers must do.

By the spring of 1775, the 26th Foot had replaced the 44th, and an elderly captain commanded the caretaker detachment at Fort Ticonderoga. Captain Delaplace lived with his wife in comfortable quarters at the fort. In his care were one hundred cannon and many military stores, and in his private locker were ninety gallons of his own rum. Until April he had but thirty men, some with their wives and a parcel of children belonging to them, to guard the moldering fortress.

Signs of growing discontent in the Hampshire Grants had caused him to request reinforcements from Canada. The first of these came as a boat's crew for Major Dunbar, with whom Delaplace and his wife had spent a pleasant evening before the major was forwarded down-country, where, if rumor were to be believed, trouble was brewing. At the end of the month, Lieutenant Feltham came up from Canada with the rest of the reinforcements, bringing the good news that Mr. Wadman and his wife were soon to follow, and take up residence in the fort.

On the night of May 9, Lieutenant Feltham went early to bed, having felt unwell for three or four days. Captain and Mrs. Delaplace also retired. Candles went out in the barrack rooms, and the one sentry took shelter in the covered way, eased his black felt hat onto the back of his head, and waited on his relief. In turbulent Boston, soldiers had been putting down the mob. But here at Ticonderoga, one hundred miles from tranquil Montreal, where could one find a mob? However, the fidgety old fuss of a captain wanted a sentry, so it was the lot of the poor bloody privates to stand the go.

Ethan Allen, too, had posted a sentry that fair spring

night of May 9. The Green Mountain Boy selected for the duty crouched on a small point of land from which he could watch the British fort at Ticonderoga, less than a mile away across the lake. Unlike his opposite number at the open entrance to the fort, the American sentry was alert and eager. He had been told to watch for two things: signs of unusual activity in the English fort and the approach of a boat from Skenesborough which would be sneaking along the shadows of the east shore. In either case, he was to slip back to the cove behind his watch point and tell Ethan, who waited there with an army ready to attack across the lake.

In the role of military commander, Ethan Allen was all that his wild Green Mountain youths could ask for: epaulets, a sword, a green uniform coat, and a roaring, bragging voice that could topple a tall grenadier or blast a breach through stone walls as thick as those of "Old Ti." Even the "Hard Money Men," who had come up from the Connecticut Committee of Safety with (and to watch over) a war chest of £300, accepted Allen as commander for the logical reason that the Green Mountain Boys would follow no other leader, while the surprise attack on the well-stocked English fort would not wait on the arrival of a more amenable army of disciplined soldiers.

In the interest of seizing the two forts on southern Lake Champlain, Ethan Allen's motives were accepted along with his men. In Allen's breast, patriotism burst into flame at the first word of the resistance to tyranny by the Massachusetts Minutemen. Patriotism was to be found and nurtured in the New Hampshire Grants, as well as in Boston, and tyranny was nesting in the barrack beds at Fort Ti. No need to send the Green Mountain Boys down-country while the redcoats were so close at hand. At Ticonderoga, tyranny was on the very doorstep of the Onion River Company (Ethan Allen, President). Capture the forts and patriotism would be served, or so it appeared to the owners of the Onion River Company, and to the Committees of Safety of the Atlantic Colonies, now forced into a shooting war.

By sunset, May 9, plans for Ethan Allen's attack across Lake Champlain had been made and were under way. Allen was at the rendezvous in the cove, welcoming the Green Mountain Boys as they came in, armed for war and thirsting for the drink promised them when they got to "Old Fort Ti." By moonrise (the moon was in the last quarter) Allen had two hundred men, ready and eager to go. Courage had been rising all through the night, as each new contingent arrived at the water's edge.

There had been a bad moment earlier in the night, when a red-coated officer and his servant rode in on tired horses. Red coats were suspect, and few of the mountain men had seen the muster of the Governor General's Foot Guard of Connecticut, or knew them for Whigs in spite of their British trappings.

Captain Benedict Arnold had arrived on Lake Champlain. He had an air of command, and written orders from the American Army besieging Boston, to take the command from Ethan Allen and to capture Fort Ticonderoga. For a moment the two men stood facing each other: Arnold in his red coat, squat and dark as a wolverine; Allen in his epaulets, hulking as a ten-ton catamount with a hundred or more cubs at her back. Arnold was a soldier, neither foolhardy nor a coward, so he bowed to the troop commander, and told of the need for the cannon at Ticonderoga by the growing colonial army, fighting to free Boston. Allen, a good politician with the votes all counted for him, welcomed Arnold's orders from yet another New England colony as authority that might prove useful to Allen himself. He invited Arnold to head up the attack by his side and gave Arnold his own blunderbuss to carry at the assault. While a sword made one very brave when it was brandished against any enemy, the blunderbuss was a practical firearm adapted to killing in close quarters, and Arnold accepted it in the spirit in which it was given. When once the job was done, the sword of command would come to the proper hand.

All was ready on the eastern shore. The sentry on the point reported all quiet at the fort. But there were no boats to take the Americans across the water!

Samuel Herrick had gone to Skenesborough with thirty men, with his object to take that place and its Tory family and to bring a boat with all haste to the rendezvous. No boat came. Meanwhile, Asa Douglas had gone north to Crown Point, where his brother lived on such friendly terms with the sergeant and his guard (the only soldiers stationed there), that there was no doubt but that Brother Douglas could hire one of the King's boats for the night. But that boat, too, failed to come up the lake to the cove.

With the passing minutes, the boat question was fast becoming a serious problem, when it was answered by two young boys, Jimmy Wilcox and Joey Tyler.

The two friends were at the edge of the curious crowd at Bridport, four miles back from the lake shore, when Asa Douglas stopped there long enough to alert the Green Mountain Boys to Allen's call and to tell of his going to Crown Point. In the resulting excitement, no one would listen to what Jimmy and Joey had to tell: that, even then, Skene's big scow was tied up in a cove south of Crown Point, where Negro Jack, one of the major's slaves and the barge's only attendant, was sleeping while he waited for a fair wind. Ignored at home, the boys took matters in their own hands. They raced to the cove and roused "Captain Jack," who was easily persuaded to let them help him row the scow up the lake, where they knew a big old wolf was penned up. So

Ethan Allen got his boat, delivered to the cove, and Jimmy Wilcox and Joey Tyler were heroes beyond their wildest dreams. But alas! When the men piled into the boat to cross Lake Champlain to the attack, the two young heroes, though they had produced the boat, were left behind.

Forty men made the first crossing, and against wind squalls from the north, the boat went back for a second loading. When it returned with another forty men, less the crew that had taken it back, it was accompanied by a small rowboat. This was the contribution of Asa Douglas. Allen now had eighty-three men around him in the bushes on the shore below the fort. Dawn was breaking, and the sharp prow of the northeast bastion cut clear into the sky above the waiting men.

The time was now.

Allen and Arnold led the eighty-three into the fort with a rush and a holler. The sentry was bowled over in the archway, and one other soldier got a crack on the head from the flat of Ethan Allen's sword. Arnold did not fire his blunderbuss.

Fort Ticonderoga had fallen to the Americans, and its great store of cannon was in the colonists' hands! It mattered not at all that the great fortress of the north had been held by only two officers, forty-one "other ranks," and twenty-five women and children. To the veterans of the Old French War and to their grown sons, Fort Ticonderoga was the place of Abercromby's and Amherst's thousands, and of Montcalm's defense. Now American colonists in arms had taken it with ease on a May morning before breakfast. Wiser heads who heard the news remembered the fleets of bateaux, the whaleboats, and the clumsy radeaux assembling on the shore of the peninsula on which stood the great stone fortress, the key to all Canada. All along the Atlantic seaboard where men were rising against tyranny, a roar of laughter went up at the confusion of George III, who had lost his fort to Ethan Allen and the Green Mountain Boys.

The "Boys" themselves gave little heed to the larger aspect of their morning's work. Ethan had lived up to his word, and had trundled out the ninety gallons of rum belonging to Captain Delaplace. Drinks were on the house. Looting came next on the agenda of victory, and in this Allen's men were joined by the neighbors, shifty of eye and light of finger, who wanted only a little souvenir.

Allen himself ignored the gaiety. He was busy writing a letter to go with the captured flag to the Continental Congress, sitting that very morning in Philadelphia. Arnold, who had been a ship's captain as well as a trained soldier, saw the need to restore order and attempted to do so. But there was no basic discipline on which he could call with authority. He *had* no authority, nor could the big man closeted with his cronies in the officers' quarters lend any authority to him. Ethan Allen's gifts to Benedict Arnold ended with the blunderbuss.

Arnold wandered out through the covered way, to look at the condition of the battery on the Amherst Wall. A shot from inside the fort whistled close by his head. The man must have been drunk to miss! Perhaps it was his red coat that drew the shot; perhaps not. Arnold hurried back to the Place d'Armes, where for companionship he joined the British officers, disconsolate but self-controlled, who were seated on a bench under guard.

Liberty Is a Schooner

Philip Skene's schooner sailed down the lake to Ticonderoga on Sunday, May 13. Captain Herrick had captured her at Skenesborough, together with the major's family, his property, and his late wife's legacy.

Arnold, still in a tenuous position at the fort, welcomed the schooner, for she brought three much-needed friends. Eleazar Oswald, a literate man who became Benedict Arnold's secretary and historian, had come with him from Massachusetts and had been sent to Skenesborough as part of Arnold's plan to capture Lake Champlain under his commission from that colony — the commission which Ethan Allen had brushed aside. Two captains of vessels, Brown and Sloan, were on deck with Oswald when the schooner dropped anchor below Fort Ticonderoga, and all three were happy to have Arnold come aboard. He had news for them, and plans.

Perhaps it was because he was the only qualified and experienced sailor in all this mountainous region, but also, no doubt, because Arnold's Massachusetts commission pricked Allen's political conscience, he gave Arnold command of the schooner.

Included in Arnold's plans was the seizure of the whole lake, entailing the defeat of a well-gunned, well-manned British sloop, the *George*. In his council, Allen visualized ten days as the minimum time required to ready Skene's

schooner for battle with the *George*. Arnold, who attended
the council, urged an immediate departure of the schooner,
to exploit the element of surprise which the Americans still
held. Temperamentally unfit for leadership in military council, where his roar and dash left scheming men unmoved,
Allen saw that by giving in to Arnold's impetuosity he might
quiet his conscience while ridding himself of his rival. The
loss of the schooner, which he could picture to himself
sinking under the well-served guns of the *George*, was good
riddance to a piece of heavy equipment which Allen, a
Ranger-type soldier, could not use. Ethan Allen planned to
capture the British sloop in a bateau expedition, with cutlass and tomahawk, and with boarders swarming over the
enemy's bulwarks.

In command of something at last, and with his friends
around him, Arnold burst into one of those surges of energy
which were to carry him, and the cause of the colonies,
into so many telling battles against the British.

From her quarter-deck, Benedict Arnold renamed Philip
Skene's topsail schooner the *Liberty*. That formality dis-
pensed with, he turned on his crew with all the fury of his
own energy, to get the vessel victualed and under way. He
urged on his men the necessity for surprise. Crown Point
had fallen to the Green Mountain Boys on May 11, but,
more important to Arnold's plans for the capture of the
George, Captain Remember Baker, coming south by boat
with the Winooski Valley Green Mountain Boys, had
captured the English boats which were carrying the news
of the fall of Fort Ticonderoga to the British at St. Jean.
They had not yet made contact with the British sloop, believed to be cruising in peace and ignorance on the wide
lake.

The *Liberty* got under way late in the day on May 13. She
made such poor headway that Arnold impatiently went

ahead in a small boat to Crown Point, leaving Captain Sloan to bring her up. On the evening of May 14, Sloan arrived at the Point, only to find that Arnold had gone ahead to scout the lake. The *Liberty*, having proved a poor sailor to windward, could not follow until the wind shifted to the south, which it finally did on May 16. With a good wind at her stern, she was able to overtake Arnold, merrily sailing north to St. Jean with a prize already in company.

Arnold had taken the British mail boat innocently enough, on her way to Fort Ticonderoga with letters and garrison gossip for Captain Delaplace's detachment. Arnold's red coat in the stern of a Crown Point bateau was a welcome sight to the crew of the mail boat. With the wind behind, she came smartly alongside the rowing boat in a courteous gesture from which there was no retreat. The surprise of the mail boat's crew was complete, and in their obvious astonishment at the turn of events at Ticonderoga lay hope of success for Arnold's expedition against the *George*. St. Jean was still unaware of the happenings up the lake, and the *George* was not on the lake but at St. Jean. She was ready to sail, however, and with this intelligence, Arnold pressed on. He raced for the narrow waters of the Richelieu, where, with surprise and his bateau crew, he could hope to board and take the sloop before she gained the lake itself.

North of Ile LaMotte, the wind dropped with the coming of evening, and the *Liberty* was becalmed. But Benedict Arnold would not be becalmed; with thirty-five staunch men, he took to the small boats and the oars. All night they rowed up the Richelieu River, a lookout in the bow straining his eyes for a blacker shadow against the black shores, or for a single slim spar, black against the deep night sky, that would be the hull and the single tall mast of the *George*.

They did not see her until they drove around the last gentle bend of the river, two miles below St. Jean. Bows

on into the current, she was at her berth in the river —
asleep, as was the fort and the town on the riverbank.

Arnold awakened the town by walking boldly into the
fort and sending Oswald with a party to take the sloop. No
one was expecting him, he learned from the startled sergeant who surrendered the fort and its garrison of twelve
men. But at St. Jean they did know that Fort Ticonderoga
had fallen to the Rebels, and on hearing the news the previous day, the captain of the sloop had set out at once for
Montreal, to get reinforcements with which to sail up the
lake and retake the forts. This accounted for the fact that
there was no officer at St. Jean.

With the sloop intact and the fort open to him, Arnold
did not press his luck, particularly as a good north wind had
come up with the sun. He set his men to staving in the British bateaux, lined up neatly on the shore, while he got the
thirteen soldier prisoners aboard the sloop to join the seven
disconsolate sailors, who were lying in the slung hammocks
in which they had been captured — asleep! An American
crew slipped the mooring and hauled up the jib and gaff.
The last that the gaping *habitants* saw of the British vessel
was the naval ensign, climbing the halyard to the peak of
the gaff; it was flying upside down.

Benedict Arnold had been in St. Jean for two hours and
had done his work. In that brief time, the Americans had
gained complete naval domination of Lake Champlain, at
least for the entire campaign season of 1775. The British
could not hope to build, in time, a fleet to match the sloop's
six 6-pounders, or the *Liberty*'s two 2-pounders and two
4-pounders, which armament would be increased in number of guns and weight of shot as soon as Arnold could pick
over the great store of cannon captured at the two forts.
The capture of St. Jean and of Chambly, on the St. Lawrence side of the Richelieu rapids, would have to await

a larger American force, under competent commanders. The wild Green Mountain Boys could never hold the post at St. Jean, with the British army at Montreal, little more than twenty miles away.

Arnold tried to explain this to Ethan Allen, whom he met a few miles up the river, heading an expedition of four bateaux on the way to take St. Jean. The two men sat in the cabin of the sloop, over a drink of navy rum. They met as equals, each with his own command; and they parted, each going his own way, Arnold in the right and Allen unconvinced.

On May 20, Arnold got back safely to Ticonderoga with his two proud ships: the *Liberty*, and the *Enterprise*, as he had renamed the *George*. Allen arrived two days later, having been driven off from St. Jean by two hundred British regulars with six field pieces. The two rival commanders immediately turned their separate energies to ways and means of invading Canada, while carefully keeping out of each other's way.

Arnold cruised the lake as commodore of his squadron. To Brown, who had come up from Skenesborough in her, he gave command of the *Liberty*. Sloan, who had been Arnold's second-in-command on the cruise to St. Jean, he took with him as captain of the *Enterprise*, when he found her the more agile of the two vessels and made her his flagship. Though he was gathering to himself loyal men, not in sympathy with the cabal surrounding Ethan Allen, Arnold found it necessary to write to the government sitting in Albany, urgently requesting that twenty sailors, two armorers, and two gunners be sent to him for the fleet. The local riflemen made good marines, but they were not sailors to satisfy a man who had captained his own vessel in the West Indian trade.

While, for the moment, the lake was secure to the Americans, the British were building a new boat at St. Jean. This town, with its shipyard, was to be a constant threat to Lake Champlain and its colonists. Benedict Arnold urged that he be given command of troops to take St. Jean; with two thousand men, he could take Canada itself!

Ethan Allen wished to have the same troops and the same command, but his approach was a different one. He connived with malcontent correspondents in Canada, and listened to their overly hopeful promises that the French Canadians would flock to join the rebellious colonists on the seaboard. He forgot the *habitants'* long years of distrust of the Puritans, and their deep Roman Catholicism, made secure to them by Britain under the Quebec Act. Allen felt sure that he could regain command in fact, over Arnold or anyone else sent up by a fickle Congress, if only his Green Mountain Boys could be enrolled as a regiment by the Continental Congress itself. The hero of Ticonderoga, he went to Philadelphia and succeeded in having his band regularized. But the backwoods giant, bragging in the messrooms of the forts he had captured, was no match for the city politicians. When the time came for the election of officers, the Green Mountain Boys were voted away from him, and it was only through the courtesy of the Congress-appointed New York State general, that Allen accompanied the expedition which eventually took St. Jean. He went as a volunteer; even his title of "Colonel" was complimentary!

A natural soldier, Benedict Arnold gave up the distasteful political struggle for command on the lakes, throwing it over with characteristic impetuosity. His wife had died while he was on the lake, and with his devoted sister caring for his three small children, he felt free to follow the dedicated soldier, George Washington, who became Commander in Chief of the Army on July 2, 1775. Nine days later, Arnold was on his way to join Washington at Cambridge, Massachusetts. As he rode back the way he had come to Lake Champlain, Arnold matured his new plan for the invasion of Canada by a surprise march overland to Quebec. His fleet and his forts were left to the New York general who, as Arnold shrewdly predicted, eventually would win command of the lakes. The *Enterprise* and the *Liberty* would keep for another day.

Lieutenant Jeremiah Halsey, of Preston, Connecticut, took over the fleet. But he was bewildered, and between his friends on shore and Arnold's friends who had been left on board, Halsey soon cried out to be relieved of his command. The sloop and the schooner were left to ride at anchor below Fort Ticonderoga, sails furled and guns secured, waiting in the summer heat.

The claims of the colonists in the New Hampshire grants, and the ambitions of their leader, Ethan Allen, were beneath contempt when the rich and populous colony of New York started negotiations with her neighbors regarding participation in the revolt of the thirteen Atlantic colonies. The Americans occupied New England around Boston; a Virginia soldier had been given over-all command there. Philadelphia was not threatened by the King's troops, and in that city, well-placed between the north and the south, delegates from all the colonies sat in Congress.

All these colonies were pressed to the seaboard by a long, rugged mountain chain, stretching from the mouth of the St. Lawrence to the back country of Georgia, and dwindling to rolling hills along the coast of the Gulf of Mexico. Here and there, mountain passes led through to the Indian country beyond, and to the rivers that flowed to the west and south, beyond the blue peaks in the distance. Still, as in the old wars against the French, the waterway of com-

merce and of army baggage trains reached northward up
the Hudson, from the great port of New York to Albany,
and the big Dutch settlement there. West of Albany lay
the valley of the Mohawk — Iroquois country loyal to the
Crown, and peopled by the descendants (both red and
white) of Sir William Johnson. Skirting the Mohawk country of the Iroquois, and just over the mild hump of the
watershed above the Hudson, was the second half of the
road through the Appalachian Range. This was a boat road,
which, with easy portages, carried down into the new English colony of Canada, which capped the Atlantic coast and
reached a long arm of waterways into the unknown and
undeveloped resources of the whole continent.

The geography had not changed a whit, nor had eighteenth-century man's ability to overcome it. New York remained in command of the lower half of the northern gateway and was thus the dominant government in dictating
policy as to any move down the other half of the road.
Regardless of who conceived of an expedition down the
lakes, be he Sir William Pepperel, Ethan Allen, or Benedict
Arnold with his Massachusetts commission, New York appointed the commander, as in the past she had appointed
Sir William Johnson. And it was New York's merchants
and builders, purveyors and innkeeprs, who would reap the
lion's share of spoils from a northbound army. When cohesion came, as it did with British armies in the French and
Indian Wars, and as it was to come in the Revolutionary
War, with the northern command under its own commander in chief, New York generals might give way to
men from other parts. But New York would always control
movement northward on the lake, vying only with Montreal, which under the French, and later under Carleton
and Burgoyne, controlled the lake road to the Hudson from
the north.

In the summer of 1775, New York made her deals with Boston in guns from the captured stock piles at Ticonderoga and Crown Point, and, with her own regiments and regiments sent by other colonies, undertook to force her way into Canada.

In New York City an enterprising merchant by the name of Peter Curtenius, who many years before had supplied William Johnson's expedition, got the contract for the green and red uniforms to outfit the newly legitimized regiment of Green Mountain Boys. Bateau-builders in Albany prepared for a rush of government orders by stocking up on green timber, while farmers goaded teams of young oxen up the paths toward the long portage from Fort Edward to Lake George, and boasted of their teams' hauling power in order to put up the prices.

To command the expedition, New York selected a patrician. General Philip Schuyler was the head of a family that for generations had supplied military and economic leaders to the Upper Hudson Valley. His loyalty stemmed from his wealth and responsibilities in it. While a parvenu such as Johnson must remain loyal to the Crown which had raised him up (and to Johnson's credit, he *did* remain loyal), a Schuyler owed loyalty to his tenants and to their economy, which a Schuyler always led. So it was that Philip Schuyler, forty-three years old, of the big house in Albany and the plantation up the river at Schuylerville, and with a commission from General Washington, his peer, easily assumed command of the expedition of 1775.

Richard Montgomery was commissioned brigadier general, and given the appointment as second-in-command. Though not himself of an aristocratic New York family, Montgomery had married the daughter of the Livingstons. As lords of the manor, the Livingstons were as grand, in an English way, as were the Dutch Schuylers, who accepted them as equals. In appearance and deportment, Montgomery was as gracious as his chief, and as a former British officer of eighteen years' service and experience, he knew how to give an order and to take one, and how to lead the way if his subordinates held back.

After completing his initial preparations at Albany, General Schuyler came to Ticonderoga on July 18 to make ready at the embarkation point the final stage of the invasion of Canada. He found the fort in a deplorable state. Colonel Benjamin Hinman, in command, had done nothing whatever, and was cowed by his disorderly and undisciplined troops, who were useless as soldiers. There were no bateaux, no workmen, no boards or other materials. The sawmill was so out of repair that it could not saw the boards to rebuild itself.

As much as he needed boats and stores and troops, Schuyler was in need of information. What could be expected from the English Canadians? What from the French Canadians? And which way would the Canadian Indians jump? Or could they be counted on to sit neutral over the buried hatchet? Major John Brown, who as a lawyer had been King's Attorney to the Caughnawaga Indians (as the Iroquois in Canada were called), was Schuyler's logical and willing secret agent. He was to be accompanied by Captain Robert Cochran.

To conduct the party down the lake and to act as guard, Sergeant Bayze Wells was found in the midden that Hinman's Connecticut regiment had become. A young soldier of conviction, principle, and ability, Wells found a bateau with a Canadian boatman, equipped it for the journey, and volunteered two reliable friends, John Legger and Peter Sherlon, as crew.

Wells himself logged the journey. The party left Crown Point at ten o'clock in the morning on July 24. They journeyed for sixteen hours that first day, sailing when they could, rowing into a north wind when they had to. Twice they were delayed, first at the entrance to the narrows and later at Split Rock, where Major Brown went aboard the watch ships *Enterprise* and *Liberty* to convince their captains that the bateau carried neither British spies nor American deserters.

Though beyond their own outposts, they were reasonably safe on the lake during the second day of travel. Again the south wind dropped about the middle of the afternoon, so they put in to a small island — little more than a dry rock — to cook and eat their dinner and to hope for a favorable wind. But the wind came up out of the north, forcing them to buck it at the oars until Brown called a halt at the north end of Cumberland Head. The bateau was now in waters where British patrol boats could be expected, and Indian canoes, too, if the Canadian Indians already had dug up the war hatchet. Caution, therefore, kept them concealed ashore through all the daylight hours of July 26. They set out after dark, with thole pins wrapped and the leather collars of their oars well greased, and rowed the fifteen miles to the end of Lake Champlain, where they arrived just as dawn was breaking.

They chose a landing place to the east of the marsh that made an island of the point at the mouth of the Richelieu River, where the old French windmill stood. There they concealed the bateau against their return, and changing into moccasins, they shouldered their packs and set off into the bush of the great plain, through which the Richelieu flows in its gentle drop into the St. Lawrence.

Their mission successfully accomplished, the men did not return to the bateau. Their presence in the vicinity of Chambly and St. Jean had become known, and when the enemy closed in, the party scattered like a covey of quail, and made for the alternative rendezvous: Simon Metcalf's house at Robertson's sawmill, far to the east around the full sweep of Missisquoi Bay.

The reunited party, now augmented by a Canadian agent returning to make his report, left the sawmill in a bark canoe they had borrowed from Mr. Metcalf for the return journey. They kept to the east shore of Lake Champlain, putting up at friendly cabins on the way. The lake proved too rough for their canoe, but they were able to borrow a bateau in which they completed their mission at Crown Point on August 9.

Sergeant Wells, however, had not yet finished with his detail. After a few days' rest, he headed another party down the lake to return the bateau to Mr. Parsons, and Mr. Metcalf's canoe to its owner. Then, too, Major Brown's bateau had been signed out in Wells's name, and unless he could report it discovered and captured by the enemy, the army might make him pay for it. Bayze Wells was a good, durable noncommissioned officer, with a fighting man's natural instinct for avoiding trouble with paper-workers. He located the bateau, and returned it to the boatmaster sergeant at Fort Ticonderoga.

To Quebec-and Back

For sixteen days, Major John Brown had been away from Ticonderoga on his intelligence mission. In that time, General Schuyler had taken over. Such fear of disgrace had been put into Colonel Hinman that Brown scarcely recognized his old post commander, nor Wells his ailing, sloppy, almost mutinous regiment.

Jeremiah Halsey, Commodore of all Armed Vessels on Lake Champlain and Lake George, had departed, trailing his long title behind him. A New Yorker named James Smith had been given command of the *Enterprise* and the over-all command afloat, with James Stewart as captain of the *Liberty*.

On the foreshore were bateaux in every stage of construction, and from the sawmill were coming carts laden with more boards for more bateaux. Major Elmore seemed to be in charge, for John Brown, on his way to Schuyler's headquarters, passed Elmore hard at work, signing orders for oars and paddles. Before they finished the job, David Ives and his thirteen oar-makers would have worked a total of 330 days, making 332 sixteen-foot oars from 5317 feet of lumber, as well as 285 paddles, each cut from an eight-foot plank. The shavings swept from the oar-makers' shop were salvaged by the encamped soldiers and used in their cooking-fires.

Brown's report implored the general to strike at once. In all Canada, General Carleton had only seven hundred men from three weak regiments, the 7th, 8th and 26th. Less than three hundred of the men, with a few artillerymen, garrisoned the two new forts, still under construction at St. Jean. According to Brown, Schuyler could count on the English Canadians, who were Whigs, while the French Canadians would not fight, either for the Crown or against "les Bostonais," a category in which they lumped all heretical Americans. Of the Indians, Brown was not so sure. The old men of the Caughnawagas talked peace, but Louis St. Luc de la Corne, the fiend incarnate of the French Indians in the old wars, had come out for George III. In the hunting camps, the wily *coureur de bois* was stirring up the young bucks of the tribe with brandy, and with brass-trimmed fowling pieces made in England to the Indians' gaudy taste. These were sent out with other gifts, to be distributed by Carleton as an inducement to fight with the white King-Father in London. Schuyler must strike quickly, while Canada was weak in defense and open to friendship, and before the two vessels that Brown had seen building at St. Jean could get onto the open lake.

While Major Brown was still at headquarters, word was received that Colonel David Waterbury's 5th Connecticut Regiment was arriving at Skenesborough and would come up to Ticonderoga that same night in the boats that Schuyler had provided. The troops arrived on August 11, but their tents and baggage, which came by way of Lake George, did not catch up with them for two days. Meanwhile, they bivouacked on the flat ground below the escarpment, crowned by the walls of the old stone fort.

Even with these fresh troops, Schuyler did not move. Command, personnel and matériel had not yet coalesced into an army, though around Ticonderoga the Connecticut men were sufficiently united to murmur in concert against the inaction of the Yorker general.

At the end of August, Schuyler went to Albany for an Indian conference, leaving his second-in-command in charge on Lake Champlain. It was as commander in chief of a theater of war that Schuyler's attention was claimed by the Indian conference. Every effort must be made to win over to the Americans the powerful Iroquois Confederacy. From its position on the Mohawk River, the Confederacy was a threat to Albany, at the crossroads of the Hudson-Mohawk-Champlain line, and a menace on the flank of communications for the army, soon to move north from Ticonderoga.

Thus it was that Schuyler was absent when, on August 28, Brigadier General Richard Montgomery moved the army out of Ticonderoga on the first leg of its journey to Montreal. It was a bold move to be made by a second-in-command, and it reflected the mutual understanding that existed between the two men. The naval situation had forced Montgomery into positive action — a responsibility which it was characteristic of him to assume. While the Americans, by the inaction of Colonel Hinman and "Commodore" Halsey early in the summer, had been committed to a naval policy of controlling the lake by commanding the inlet to the Richelieu River, the British had carried out a shipbuilding program at St. Jean. By the end of August the British vessels were so near to completion that, ready or not, the American army had to move into its selected position on Ile aux Noix or lose the whole Lake Champlain waterway as far south as Crown Point to the newly built British flotilla, for which the *Enterprise* and the *Liberty* were no match.

Montgomery embarked about twelve hundred effective soldiers; a week later, he disembarked between nine hundred and a thousand men at the northern end of Lake Champlain. The difference in force was made up of sick soldiers of the 5th Connecticut Regiment, which with two hundred to two hundred and fifty healthy men of the 1st New York Battalion, comprised the force.

General Schuyler himself, bilious and wracked by rheumatism, had caught up with the army waiting for him beyond Ile LaMotte, its bateaux drawn up on a fine sandy beach. The schooner and the sloop, with two rowboats each mounting a 12-pounder, made a show off the entrance to the Richelieu. Schuyler brought reinforcements from Hinman's and Colonel Goose Van Schaick's regiments.

He immediately ordered the army to Ile aux Noix, where work was begun and batteries erected to command the traffic on the river. The Americans had arrived just in time. The British had launched a schooner, now being fitted out with fourteen guns (6-pounders and 4-pounders) and as many swivels. The Americans heard that she was named the *Brave Savage*, or maybe the *Royal Savage*.

Having established his advanced base on Ile aux Noix, Schuyler waited for two days for the Whig Canadians to rally to him. When they did not come, he advanced his still high-spirited troops to the attack of St. Jean, building two entrenchments on the west bank of the river. One of these was within range of the British guns, the other beyond the reach of the cannon; prudently, the army occupied the latter.

Schuyler had been worried by the failure of the Canadians to rise up, so when a spy came to his headquarters behind the second entrenchment on the night of September 6, he was prepared for the worst. The fort at St. Jean, it appeared, was strong; the *Savage*, her sixteen guns (not the fourteen of earlier intelligence reports) blazing, was almost ready to make a dash down the river and into the open lake. The only American hope was to return to Ile aux Noix and go into defensive position there, while the Canadian

Committee of Correspondence stirred up support behind the British lines.

On September 7 the army fell back on Ile aux Noix and the boom which had been made was towed across the river, secured to the west shore, and a guard set over it.

One look at General Schuyler, lying on his camp bed on the island, was enough to convince his staff that no longer could he take command of the army in the field. He shook with the ague, and fever burned in his eyes. There were moments when he was completely rational; then the rheumatic pain surged up to cloud his reasoning. At last he was persuaded to bow to the inevitable. On a bed hastily made up in a covered boat, he returned up the lake to Ticonderoga, leaving Richard Montgomery in command of an army bent on the capture of Montreal. Before this could be attempted, however, Montgomery had to master a troublesome element in his army: the Connecticut men. Also, he had to capture St. Jean. He accomplished the latter, in spite of the former.

Connecticut men made up three-quarters of the army. If an order or a plan did not originate under a Connecticut hat, the officers were quick to transmit their pique to their men. Even the "padre," so "Connecticut" that his name was Trumbull, entered into the debates, spread gossip, and clicked his tongue. Occasionally, without the demarcation line of the pulpit between them, he went so far as to hint to the boys in the trenches that they were being put upon. When Montgomery called on the army for some three hundred volunteers for a particularly dangerous mission, he was excoriated by the Reverend Benjamin Trumbull in as fine a bit of double-thinking as ever rationalized a political argument. To call for volunteers, he argued, when all the men considered themselves as volunteers, having joined the army voluntarily in the first place, showed that Montgomery was a defeatist. He reasoned that Montgomery, no doubt, had not *expected* any response and had called for volunteers only so that, by their refusal, he would have in his men and junior officers a scapegoat for any blame arising from his own unwillingness to advance the army.

Undaunted, Montgomery again tried to set up siege lines around St. Jean. He hoped to put five hundred soldiers into position north of the town to cut the supply road, while re-occupying the American trenches dug on the unsuccessful first attempt. The flanking party got lost in the woods. The main party was successful in driving the British picket from their upper works, killing two men but themselves coming under fire from British gunboats on the river. When Commodore Douglas arrived in one of the American gondolas and drove away the British boats, a cheer arose from the men. When the *Royal Savage* was brought up, Douglas thought it prudent to withdraw his navy; the army also withdrew.

In common with all the American fleet commanders on Lake Champlain, Commodore Douglas came out of the commissioned ranks of the army, his qualification to a ship command being based on earlier service in the West Indian trade. His bravery was never questioned — perhaps it was the bravery of a man soon to die from tuberculosis — and he handled his ships with boldness and wisdom throughout the campaign of 1775. The weakness of this tall, slender, erect, and strong-featured "Commodore of the Lakes" stemmed from the fact that he was born in Connecticut, had married a Connecticut girl, was a major in a Connecticut regiment, and was partial to Connecticut.

Douglas urged that, as part of the Americans' third attempt to set up a siege, a try be made to board the *Royal Savage*. Montgomery called for three hundred and twenty volunteers to go on the expedition with Douglas, and Connecticut men rose in indignation. Though eventually the boarding party was raised by the commodore, with the help of Colonel Waterbury (also of Connecticut), both of them eager to make the attempt, the whole plan sputtered out in internecine debate.

On September 18, Montgomery succeeded in circumventing the British, and established a post of five hundred men astride the St. Jean–Chambly–Montreal road. He did this adroitly, relegating the old, grumbling Connecticut regiments to man the southern works, while he himself led Colonel Timothy Bedel's New Hampshire regiment west of the town, and into the position prepared by Major Brown's advance scout. Montgomery had to fight for his position, which the British had taken from Brown in a desperate sortie, to prevent encirclement. It was a bloody little skirmish, and after it was over, Captain Watson, the lieutenant of marines of Captain Sloan's *Enterprise*, was found among the British wounded. He had sustained a desperate wound in the abdomen, but he survived, and the post, known as "Bedel's Encampment," was firmly held in American hands.

In addition to the New Hampshire regiment, Colonel Seth Warner's Green Mountain Boys, newly uniformed in green and red, joined Montgomery and were sent north of St. Jean. There, with Major Brown's detachment, they raided Montreal and beat up the countryside in general. Ever wild, as rangers should be — sometimes they were referred to as the "Green Mountain Rangers" — they caroused on captured wine, lived high on pork and butter, and with difficulty were restrained from casting aside their new green coats and dressing up in British ones which they discovered, baled, in a commissary wagon. They sobered to the seriousness of war after their old leader, Ethan Allen, now without rank, disappeared into Montreal, a prisoner, after a fool-hardy and almost single-handed attack on the city.

With pick and shovel, Montgomery's main army was erecting batteries and building roads north of St. Jean. By September 25, the first American battery was completed. It had two cannon firing from embrasures, and, set back a little, a mortar squatted on its bed. At three o'clock that afternoon fire was opened on the British forts. This was a mistake, for, from the same number of guns, the enemy returned the fire at the rate of seven shots for one! General Montgomery's gunners were no match for their English opposite numbers; they simply did not understand their pieces. Later, a second mortar was sent up, with a powder chamber too small to loft the 8-inch shell to its target. No sooner had the master gunner enlarged its capacity by reaming out the chamber in the base of the bowl than a trunnion broke, wedging the squat bronze gun into its mount. Nothing daunted, the gunners mounted a tripod over the piece; she was hoisted up and hung suspended like a butchered pig, until, in a burst of Yankee ingenuity, an emergency bed was contrived. The men might have saved their energy, because, while the mortar crew was working (aided by the best of advice), all the powder was being used up by the guns and the other mortar. However, everyone felt sure that things would improve when the "Old Sow" arrived; she would throw her 13-inch shell right into the cabin of the *Royal Savage*'s captain!

Discomfort came to add to embarrassment. A cold rain set in, lasting for eight days and making deep mud of the new-turned earth. The main camp was found to have been set on miry ground, and in the biting October cold, men sat hunched in their wet blankets and coughed until they were sent back to the base camp on Ile aux Noix. There, the hospital tents provided little more comfort than those up front in the lines.

In a thin picket line across the Richelieu River from the upper works to the eastern shore, the six vessels of the American Navy on Lake Champlain rode through the rain and the squalls. Commodore Douglas had anchored the *Enterprise* and the *Liberty* from the bow and stern, so that they lay across the current, and had rearranged the downriver broadside to give maximum fire power toward the enemy. The waters of Lake Champlain and Lake George, fed by hundreds of brooks and mountain streams, rose as the rains continued and flooded into the great spillway of the Richelieu. Douglas had reason to be anxious for the girt cables of his two capital ships, lying crosswise in the swift-running water. Being a seaman, he arranged a slip to the stern anchor on each vessel.

In line with their big sisters, but anchored stern to the flow, were the two gondolas, the *Schuyler* and the *Hancock*, their sails rigged over their racks built up from the gunwales. A heavy 12-pounder poked its capped muzzle out over each bow, pointing down the empty river. The twelve swivels on each gondola lay in the waist, ready for loading (if any dry powder remained on board) before being mounted in their sockets.

Douglas had added to his fleet two large bateaux, armed with swivels. These he used as shore protection to the east of his line. Now they lay at anchor, their crews of oarsmen and swivelmen cramped and crowded among the benches, their masts forming ridgepoles for the soaked canvas sail, stretched tentlike athwart ship.

The sailors aboard the armed bateaux and gondolas merited no envy from the soldiers on shore. Even on the flagship and her consort there was little comfort to be found, as three hundred and twenty men were crammed into the six vessels, and little warmth could be coaxed from the smoking fires in the brick fire beds that were the cooks' galleys.

Between October 4 and October 8, the weather improved somewhat, but a storm still raged around Montgomery's head. Commodore Douglas, fussing over his fleet, petitioned the general for a riverside battery on the American right — a battery that could reach and pound the *Royal Savage*, should she come against him. Short of cannon (despite the arrival of the "Old Sow"), Montgomery vetoed this idea, and continued with his plans for a battery to play on the southwest bastion of the English fort, the point he had chosen for an assault. Hearing this, Douglas marched into a Connecticut regiment and by bribery brought together his own work party from among off-duty men and began to build his battery. When it came time to give the men their promised treat, the commissary refused to issue the rum, but Douglas was less disgruntled at this than were the soldiers from his own colony.

As a quartermaster had embarrassed Commodore Douglas, so did a Council of War humble General Montgomery into giving over work on a west battery in favor of a field work on the east shore of the Richelieu. In a Council of War, the most junior officer present is the first to state his views, followed by the others in ascending order of rank. As each officer spoke, on this occasion, the crescendo rose against the general. Montgomery's hopes for a quick end to this campaign fell, and when it came his turn to speak, he bowed to the wishes of the Council. It was his right to go against them, but he sensed mutiny in the oratory of the Connecticut officers, and with the possibility that, should the Connecticut regiment go home, the troops below the town would be abandoned to their fate, he gave orders to build the battery on the east shore, close up to the British forts.

The Reverend Benjamin Trumbull gloated at this; two days later, when the new battery on the east shore sank the *Royal Savage* at her moorings, he became magnanimous, as befitted his cloth.

Patience achieves purpose. Montgomery forwarded his purpose by biding his time and by taking advantage of opportunities as they presented themselves. A Canadian Whig, with the complimentary title of "Captain," undertook to run the river past St. Jean during the night and deliver a 9-pounder with which to lay siege to Chambly, twelve miles below St. Jean. The venture was successful, and by the time Major Brown came up from Bedel's Encampment to take command, the gun was in action, served by seven old French gunners who were tearfully happy again to be at their trade. With reports from Chambly that the French Canadians were rallying at last, Montgomery sent three more cannon down the rapids, and on October 18, the commander at Chambly, Major the Honorable Joseph Stopford, son of an Irish earl, surrendered his fort, his troops, his stores, and his honorable self.

This first tangible result of the campaign was fully exploited by the Americans. The one hundred and eighty-four captives, of whom a hundred were women, were paraded under a white flag past the garrison at St. Jean. Then the siege of that place was reopened in ernest.

The cannon pounded the parapets, and mortar bombs crashed in among the barracks and storerooms. There was little opportunity for the British fort to fight back, as the artillery stores were running low and had to be conserved. There was equally little hope of the Americans running out of powder and shot, with the supplies from Chambly in their hands. At last, when its special bombs ran out, the big American mortar was still, and once again there was safe shelter for the women in the great white house around which the fort had been built. Before she went quiet, however, the "Old Sow" had completely demolished the wine and liquor cellar with its precious stores.

Time was running out for Major Charles Preston and his five hundred and twenty-nine combatants, cooped up in their fort at St. Jean. Time was what General Guy Carleton had sent Preston to buy there. The major had presented his general with a lavish two months, bought at little cost, much of it given away by the Americans in cautious committee. But now, at the end of October, the confines of the British fort were close and heavy about Preston's shoulders. General Wooster, a bibulous old veteran of the British army, had arrived with additional American troops, raising the size of the investing force to some twenty-six hundred men. Control of the river had passed over to the Americans when the *Royal Savage* was sunk, and now her crew of twelve seamen, under a midshipman — all out of H.M.S. *Gaspé* — were serving on the ramparts. Allgee, the Royal Navy officer, had been caught in Chambly Fort with naval stores; Preston had recognized him among the prisoners from there. Now, on the night of October 27, Major Preston had been called hurriedly to the southeast corner of his fort to watch the dark shadows of American boats go by. He forbade firing on these will-o'-the-wisp shadows, and from their number and shapes he estimated that a general movement was under way to pass the whole American army to the north of him. There, it could block any relieving force that Carleton might send in an attempt to extricate him. Preston could only wait, perhaps squeezing out another day with a sortie by his still eager garrison.

On the American side, David Wooster's arrival had brought to fruition Montgomery's taut patience. Though a Connecticut man, Wooster had learned soldiering in the same school as Montgomery, where a second-in-command supported his commanding officer. So, though people like the Reverend Mr. Trumbull still counted Connecticut men as comprising over half of the American force, the new general did not call for democratic support on a political basis but insisted only on obedience to military orders.

At last Montgomery was able to move, and finally he could build his battery on the landward side of the British fort. He put up a battery of five big guns and five small mortars to play on the British northwest bastion, and the work was completed so quickly that Major Preston's last sortie was easily repulsed. As Montgomery had anticipated when, with Wooster leading the recalcitrant Connecticut troops, he had interposed the main army between St. Jean and Montreal, General Carleton tried to relieve the fort from the latter city. Montgomery's men turned back Carleton's eight hundred, after which he was ready to tackle St. Jean in earnest. At nine o'clock on the morning of November 1, the American batteries opened the bombardment and the British answered, killing two American gunners from New York. All day the American guns hurled shells at the British fort, and all day mortar bombs fell inside. Toward evening a truce was called, and to bring despair to the defenders, Montgomery sent in a soldier captured from Carleton's relieving force. Preston surrendered.

Preston marched his troops out in a ceremony that gave full honors to his men, whose perseverance and fortitude were fully recognized. After the parade, the officers mingled together, and when their talk touched briefly on politics, all concurred in the unhappiness of the current disputes and differences. A tall lieutenant of the British 7th Foot, fair and delicate of feature, caught the eyes of the rough officers from the farms of the Connecticut shore. They began to mimic his extravagant gestures and almost feminine grace of movement. Sensing danger, while recognizing the type and being undeceived, General Montgomery, with Wooster at his side, asked Major Preston to present the young lieutenant. The introduction was made, and the two brave men exchanged compliments and stood talking for all to see. Lieutenant John André, that morning of his first capture by the Americans, was wearing a stock of fine cambric around his graceful neck.

While the British officers had months of time on their hands, Montgomery did not. Snow was due to fall, and he wanted Montreal before then. Leaving his siege equipment and taking only his light artillery (Colonel Lamb's uniformed battery from New York), he raced for the St. Lawrence and crossed the river with New York troops and Wooster's Connecticut regiment. Indefensible, as it had been in 1760, Montreal fell to the Americans on November 12, 1775.

General Carleton escaped down the river to Quebec. Montgomery tried to stop him at Sorel, where the Richelieu flows into the St. Lawrence, but Carleton slipped through in the night, his boat crew paddling with their hands, silently, past the American watch boats on the cold, cold river. Montgomery did not much care. He himself was on his way to Quebec, as soon as he could regroup his army. The troublesome Connecticut troops, with their smug chaplain, were going home — and good riddance. Arnold should now be at Quebec, to intercept the governor general; he might even have the city and the citadel in his hands, for Carleton, with all the time Preston had given him at St. Jean, had used it not only to win over the nonbelligerent French Canadians but to bring troops from Quebec. Carleton did not know, of course, that General Arnold had taken the long way 'round from Ticonderoga and was marching overland to the old capital of Canada.

On November 12 the same day that Montgomery took

Montreal, Benedict Arnold established a position outside the gates of Quebec. Except for that bit of land encompassed by the walls of Quebec City, all Canada was now in American hands.

~~~~~~~~~~

When their enlistment time expired, the Connecticut men quit the army at Montreal and set out for St. Jean, where they expected Commodore Douglas to have boats ready and waiting to convey them up the lake on their way home. To them, nothing was more important than their homecoming.

But Douglas was not ready; the Commodore of the Lakes sat in his office in the battered fort, with lists of naval stores before him and piles of supplies on the foreshore. Resting uneasily on the river bottom sat the *Royal Savage*, waiting to be patched and raised before the crushing ice came to crack her hull as though it were a big black nut. Douglas had salvaged and repaired the big row galley, a cumbersome craft with a bow gun of 24 pounds and two smaller waist guns, which he had been persuaded to name the *Douglas*. Among the captured shipping there were also ten or twelve bateaux which could be made serviceable and eleven birch-bark canoes.

Douglas was experiencing the frustration of responsibility without the men and means to carry out his orders. The homeward-bound Connecticut men clamored to be sent back. The old fleet was anchored in the roads, but after the hard campaign the vessels needed repairs to rigging and hull. His fleet of bateaux was either on the rear link with Fort Ticonderoga or was being hauled laboriously up the rapids from Chambly, where it had gone at the end of October when the army passed the British forts. The better of the two gondolas was lost to him. Under command of Captain Lockwood, of Waterbury's regiment, she was cruising in the St. Lawrence at the mouth of the Sorel River, as the part of the Richelieu below the rapids was known.

In his office, Douglas was besieged, wheedled, and bribed to give boats to the southbound soldiers. In desperation, he told them to go and rig their own boats. They did so, wrangling and debating among themselves even as they shoved off from the beach, and giving no heed to the snowflakes blowing in on a small northwest breeze, which — as any seaman would have known — was veering around into a northeast blow. When the *Enterprise* returned from Crown Point, where Douglas had sent her as a shepherd, her captain reported the severity of the storm they had encountered. He told how they had been lost on the lake, and how, under a small sail, they had been driven up the lake for a distance of eighty miles. On the exposed decks, the soldiers had huddled in what lee they could find, and there were many frozen noses, fingers, and limbs. In his own cabin, Captain Smith reported, the Connecticut officers had crowded, protected from the force of the wind but exposed to the resounding blasts of prayer delivered by the fervent Reverend Mr. Trumbull. None had actually died on this terrible passage on Lake Champlain, but at Crown Point all the men had elected to walk the rest of the way to Connecticut, leaving their officers, encumbered by baggage, to continue the voyage on Lake George.

The time of year was at hand when the Commodore of the Lakes had to secure his fleet for the winter. Until spring, Montgomery's army in Montreal and the small neighboring towns must live on the inhabitants — in spite of the Americans' stated abhorrence of being themselves billeted upon! Outside the walls of Quebec, Benedict Arnold would have to fare as best he could; the lake route could not support two armies through the winter.

Douglas got up the *Royal Savage* and renamed her the *Yankee*. She was a good addition to the American fleet, all of which had been acquired by capture.

There was another vessel on the ways, only partially built, but with her timbers and planks all neatly stacked. She was to be a small sloop, if the quantity of sails and rigging which had been found in the fort at Chambly was properly sorted and listed. Douglas left this vessel on her cradle. She could be completed in the spring, if enough ship's carpenters could be found among the soldiers of the next campaign.

In the first hours of the New Year, 1776, Montgomery died, shot through the head while storming a barricade in the Lower Town at Quebec. In another part of the Lower Town, Benedict Arnold was down, too, a leg wound bleeding onto the snow in a crooked, ancient street.

Deprived of their two leaders, the Americans saw their hope for the conquest of Canada dashed to the ground. The army slipped into a desperate routine of trying to subsist in the harsh northern winter, and old General Wooster, who came up from Montreal to take charge of the suburban occupation that comprised the winter siege of Quebec, was a worn-out flint of a man, unable to strike fire from his troops. Arnold, up at last after his leg wound, took to horse too soon, with the result that he was unable to save himself from a bad fall when his beast slipped on a patch of ice, and they crashed down together. He was sent to Montreal. By that time it was April. Nothing had been done by May, when General John Thomas came up through the lakes, and command of the siege was turned over again. An able general, Thomas could accomplish nothing with the thousand healthy men that were left for him to work with.

The British fleet arrived off Quebec on May 7, the fifty-gun *Isis* leading through the ice floes: fifteen ships in all, with eight regiments of British and two thousand German mercenaries aboard.

General Thomas could not wait for his Jersey and Pennsylvania regiments to come up, and though Washington poured troops through the funnel of Lake Champlain, they all turned back on the Richelieu River, driven before Carleton and the new British general, Sir John Burgoyne, and the gun-studded wooden walls of British ships of the line.

Where the Americans might have rallied, with their back to their fleet, they were struck by an impartial ally now favoring the British: smallpox. Those it did not strike went down under the induced fever of inoculation, while the immune and the convalescent had only energy enough to care for the sick. With all his promise, General Thomas himself died in obscurity of the smallpox.

The Americans, however, were rich in generals. As one died on the St. Lawrence, another stepped off the boat at St. Jean. The quality of the American generals was improving, too, as General Washington molded a Continental Army from the clay of minutemen and militia. Pugnacious and punitive, Brigadier General John Sullivan swept through the sick and exhausted men of his predecessor's army, and with his fresh troops — thirty-three hundred New Yorkers and over a thousand Pennsylvanians — made a counterattack. He deserved better luck than was his. Brigadier General William Thompson, yet another American general, and Sullivan's deputy, carried the Pennsylvania brigade head-on into the British army and fleet, just arrived at Three Rivers. The troops recoiled into a swamp and forest filled with mosquitoes and black flies, where the terror of a vast land of deep, close woods, pressing in on them from incomprehensible distances, completed the degeneration of the young soldiers. They fell back on the smallpox camps along the Richelieu, dispirited, dejected, and with malaria germs incubating in their worn-out bodies.

Sullivan wanted to hold at Sorel, but casting about through his returns of regiments, he could count only twenty-five hundred fighting men at Sorel, with possibly a thousand more at other posts along the Richelieu and the St. Lawrence. He knew that he was fooling himself with this count; the will to resist the enemy had gone out of the troops. Sullivan ordered the army to fall back on its stores at St. Jean, near to where its sick lay in the low, marshy ground of Ile aux Noix. They had been gathered there to die or to recover — a loathsome, rotting concert of wretchedness, orchestrated with moans underlying fits of hacking coughs and spitting, that swelled and subsided up and down the mile-long island.

Burdened with these sick and dying, and with malaria fever beginning to pop up like mushrooms among the regiments, Sullivan had no choice but to fall back behind the fleet on Lake Champlain.

The island was evacuated, the less sick struggling at the oars of the cumbersome bateaux which had been sent up from Crown Point and Ticonderoga. Sullivan himself withdrew and left the rear guard to Benedict Arnold, since the winter a very junior brigadier general with a certainty of purpose that angered his equals and overburdened his superiors.

Arnold long since had despaired of wresting Canada from the British, and as he had done the previous year, he had given over the job in hand for a new scheme. He had evacuated Montreal, where he was in command, and was now back at St. Jean with the last American troops. He had come the full cycle to that place where he had been the first American soldier.

The British were downriver and coming fast. Arnold increased his characteristic hurry. The mounds of American stores he scattered; some supplies he salvaged; what he could, he destroyed; much he gave away into the keeping of the *habitants*.

As he stood looking at the shipyard and regretting its loss to the Americans, his attention was drawn to a boat that was building on the ways. Since Commodore Douglas had found it there seven months before, no one had thought it important to complete its construction. Arnold's ship-wise eye noted an unusual proportion of length to beam, while the curve of the few ribs already assembled excited his imagination. Here, in the shipyard at St. Jean, was an idea to be used in the scheme that he was hatching. He called up a work party and set it to dismantling the assembled pieces of the boat. This done, he set off for the shipyard shed and office, where, in the dark interior, he discovered a large bundle of sails belonging to the vessel outside. There were boxes, too, bearing the broad arrow mark indicating Crown Property. On hefting some of them, he guessed that they contained bronze and iron fittings. Further search of the deserted premises uncovered a draft of the vessel on the ways, which Arnold folded carefully and put in the inside pocket of his blue uniform coat. Back in the sunlight, he quickly gave the order that loaded all the separate members of the new vessel on the special bateaux which were to take them to safety up the lake, for assembly behind the American defense lines.

Benedict Arnold left St. Jean in the last boat. Burgoyne's light infantry, easily identified by their little round leather hats, were moving in short, hurried rushes across the open spaces among the last remaining buildings of the old encampment when Arnold gave the order to shove off.

Benedict Arnold's Plan

Five American generals met in grave council in a dilapidated building in the old English fort at Crown Point. The date was July 5, 1776. Philip Schuyler was in the Chair, by virtue of his over-all command of the northern frontier. He had been the first general officer casualty of the Canadian campaign, which had begun ten months before and was now ended where it began, its regiments lying shattered, beaten, and diseased on the wide camp ground outside the walls of Fort Amherst. John Sullivan sat at the long table: a bewildered man, shocked by the catastrophe that had overtaken his command, and haunted by the image of the pestilence that had wilted the flower of the army — *his* army. In time, his native resilience would rationalize his personal defeat, and he would yet be useful to the new nation he served, though on a field far removed from this deceptively beautiful lake of malign leprechauns.

Horatio Gates was there, ranking with Schuyler, yet, by their mutual agreement on the seriousness of the situation, serving under Schuyler in command of troops — the sick and the well, if, indeed, there were any of the latter — to supersede John Sullivan. Gates had come to the lakes with dictatorial powers over the northern army, powers given to him by George Washington, whose adjutant general he had been and whose confidence he held. Gates hid his military ability beneath an unsoldierly appearance. Artists, when he posed for them, had to square his round shoulders, restore youth and vigor to his old man's face, and insist that he lay aside his spectacles, lest he look like a dilettante philosopher. Gates's soldiers referred to him as "Granny," because they could not see the painstaking labor that brought them up to a battle, where a dashing general on a splendid chestnut stallion rushed them forward against the enemy — an enemy often already plucked and parboiled by Gates's strategy.

At the time of the outbreak of the American Revolution, the young British officer of Louisbourg, the Monongahela, Oswego, and Martinique (in the West Indies, where men age quickly) had become, at age forty-eight, the retired Squire Gates of Virginia, an ardent Whig. As Washington was not misled by Gates's mild appearance, neither was Benedict Arnold, the fourth and junior member of the council. He, too, knew Gates, who, as adjutant general, had found the troops for Arnold's overland march to Quebec. From that Quebec expedition, Gates knew Arnold, too; knew him as a firebrand apt to inflame the angry and not altogether unjustified passions of his associates, but a firebrand whom Gates thought he could wield to advantage, as long as he could keep it brandished toward the enemy to the north.

Furthermore, Benedict Arnold had a plan.

The fifth member of the council interrupted, and the four Americans listened politely as he expounded his views on an irrelevant detail of his service in the field under "Old Fritz," the King of Prussia. The speaker was Baron de Woedtke, who wore the pink ribbon of an American general and was one of those foot-loose, titled European Swords, so impressive to the Continental Congress, but whose stability was so shrewdly assessed by the American generals on whom they were foisted. At last the Baron subsided, and at a nod from General Schuyler, Arnold continued with the explanation of his scheme.

The sloop *Enterprise* and the schooners *Liberty* and *Royal Savage* (her original English name persisted) were all that kept Carleton from driving up the lake in small boats, borrowed from the British fleet in the St. Lawrence, or found in obscure bays and inlets which had been overlooked by the rear guard of the retreating Americans. Of the gondolas, the *Hancock*, *Schuyler*, and *Douglas*, one had been taken into the St. Lawrence and the other two were now unfit for service as gunboats. Green timber and hard use had shortened their military lives.

Arnold, however, had drawn up rough specifications for a new type of gondola particularly suited to the requirements he had in mind and which took into consideration the building limitations imposed upon him. From his attaché case, Arnold drew a paper which he passed to General Schuyler for circulation. The sheet bore a rough outline (which Woedtke thought to resemble a North Sea sole) on which specifications were indicated. Down the right-hand side of the paper there was a long list: "deadrisings 4 inches; wale knees 16 feet asunder," etc. — details, in Gates's opinion, best left to the shipwrights.

For the present, according to Arnold, the Americans were safe behind their fleet, now at anchor off Crown Point. But Carleton could draw upon the brains and the hands of the British navy, and there was little doubt but that in the shipyard at St. Jean (by no means irretrievably destroyed) he would built a fleet capable of sinking the three American vessels. Already — and Arnold himself had seen it — a British frigate was building at Quebec City. Though this big ship would scarcely climb the road around the rapids between Chambly and St. Jean, there was also a tubby-looking little vessel, ketch-rigged, with high sides, which Arnold himself had built and sailed on the St. Lawrence. This could be hauled overland by a competent sailor, using blocks and tackles and rollers. Arnold referred to her as the *American*, but whether that was her christened name or a sobriquet he did not say.

In exchange for the *American*, now in British hands, Arnold had taken the timbers, planks, and fittings of the vessel on the ways at St. Jean and had found there the plans to complete her on her intended lines. On these plans Arnold wished to lay the whole American naval policy for Lake Champlain.

The drawing which Arnold had now introduced to the meeting was that of a small, narrow vessel of light construction which would be fast under sail and, more important on the narrow lake, would be fast and agile under oars. With vessels of this same construction, but larger, he would have a force that could maneuver against the British ships, which he did not doubt would be slow-sailing, strong ships, full at the ends and of deep draught, suitable for the traditional tactics of the Royal Navy: to "sail in and engage."

Schuyler and Gates listened to the exposition of naval tactics and construction for Lake Champlain, detailed by the dark young brigadier who spoke with such surety and conviction. On their shoulders would rest the responsibility for implementing Arnold's ideas. From his headquarters in Albany, Schuyler would have to find the raw material for the new American fleet. Gates had a man-sized job to do in rebuilding the northern army and making defensible the fort at Ticonderoga. It had been decided to evacuate Crown Point. In Benedict Arnold, Gates had a deputy commander qualified to take complete charge of building the fleet, and one who seemed eager to fight that fleet when built. Gates was ready to back Arnold, as chief of naval construction and as commodore, in any altercation in which his impetuous nature might embroil him.

The new fleet was pioneered that very afternoon. The Council of General Officers scarcely had time to rise before Arnold was on the foreshore, giving instructions to a Captain Winslow, who, with a few carpenters, was bound for Skenesborough. They were to repair the sawmill there and prepare the ways on which to build the hulls of the gondolas and row galleys.

Skenesborough had been chosen as the site of the shipyard because of its sawmill, and because of a second sawmill only seven miles distant, which was owned and operated by a former tenant of Major Skene. Convenient to the mills, there was a plentiful supply of oak and pine, and Wood Creek (which turned both wheels) was a good road from the upper mill to the shipyard. The launching-site, the arm of Lake Champlain curving to the east and south out of South Bay, was protected by barrier hills. The south shore, below the last falls of Wood Creek, was flat enough for the ways and dropped off into water sufficiently deep to receive the new hulls. Also, removed as it was from Ticonderoga, the shipyard at Skenesborough would keep separate the ordinary soldier and the high-priced shipwrights and ships' carpenters that Schuyler would hire down-country.

From his Albany headquarters, Philip Schuyler beat the coast in an attempt to supply the men, tools, and materials to fashion the fleet. On it, his whole Northern Department of the Continental Army must depend for its continued existence that year of 1776. Somehow, he managed to make good, and sometimes to exceed, his promises to Gates. The latter bore the triple responsibility of restoring to usefulness a shattered army, rebuilding the defenses at Ticonderoga and erecting new ones across the lake, and creating a fleet of warships — all this in the space of two summer months.

In the hot little rooms of Fort Ticonderoga, windows and doors were opened wide to catch the smallest breeze. The staff worked long and late. Stockless and coatless at his littered work-table, the plump old general watched over the work of jealous clerks and self-important staff officers, and he made sure that no urgent demand was ignored or purposely mislaid. Patiently, he sweated through the priorities, again and again turning aside a brigade commander, mildly but emphatically, in order to expedite something requested by Arnold for his fleet.

The energetic, impatient brigadier wanted so much! So many sinews and so much muscle must go into the vibrant body of a fighting ship under way: big anchors weighing from 200 to 250 pounds were offset in size by needles and sailmakers' palms. Arnold needed 6-inch hemp rope and spun yarn of only two or three strands. Three hundred single blocks and two hundred double ones had to come up the supply line from Albany, in addition to all the artillery required to give the vessels their voice and their authority in the battle to come.

One day, Arnold limped into Gates's office with the observation that he had noticed the darkness of the nights after the moon went down. He had ordered three dozen lanterns of horn or tin, in addition to two dozen dark lanterns; now he wanted 800 pounds of chalk, to whiten the stern rails so that a following ship could guide herself in convoy through the blackest night. Gates forwarded that request, too, and the order was filled.

On July 22, General Arnold, whose "headquarters" was his field desk and whose "office" was his saddle, his boots, or the stern sheets of his boat, arrived at the dockside in Skenesborough as the first big drops of a summer thundershower were falling. As he seemed to bring the thunder and lightning to the shipyard, he left it cooled and refreshed and encouraged, drenched by his own eager certainty and determination.

During the course of his two days' inspection, Arnold had seen everything. Accompanied by General Waterbury, whom he had placed in over-all command of the shipyard, he had gone everywhere: down the forest roads where the lumberjacks were felling the great trees, and where the skid-horses stood, steaming, while the lame brigadier talked to their drivers of linament or harness, or of other great hauling-horses. From the platform around the big water-wheel, the two generals had looked down to view the results of twenty days' work. Already, Arnold had been aboard the two gondolas being finished at moorings in the basin. Now three more gondolas sat on the stocks, looking like broody ducks, each on its nest of yellow chips and shavings. Waterbury pointed to where groups of carpenters were shaping long keelsons and carelines and whale knees for yet another three gondolas, readying for a launching and a free stock. Beyond, a row galley was beginning to take shape. Thirteen carpenters had begun work on her on July 18, the memorable day on which Waterbury had read to the assembled camp the fiery and daring words of the Declaration of Independence, dedicating them and committing them to a new Nation.

The real work of the inspection trip was in the decisions met and made by Benedict Arnold, with the advice of his second-in-command. David Waterbury, like Arnold, was a Connecticut man, a veteran of six campaigns in the French and Indian War, a dedicated — almost rabid — Whig, and, at fifty-six, a man who knew ships. On careful observation, the two officers decided to complete the eight gondolas and to rush construction on three additional row galleys yet to be set up. At Arnold's insistence, Waterbury rearranged his yard schedule to allow for the assembly of the ships' timbers sent down from St. Jean.

With the sloop and the two schooners at Crown Point, this would constitute the fleet which Arnold could count upon to go forth and fight. He had hoped for four more row galleys, but with the means at hand there was no time to build them.

One other vessel was built that summer, but, though she joined the fleet, Arnold appears to have ignored her. This was the *Revenge,* built at Ticonderoga by Colonel Jeduthan Baldwin, chief engineer of the northern army, and a very harassed man. As the slim, fast, hard-hitting row galley was Benedict Arnold's brain child, so the rotund, shallow, lightly gunned schooner *Revenge* was built to specifications seeming to resemble those of Jacobus Wynkoop, Captain of the Lake. In May 1776, when Douglas declined that command, Schuyler had given it to Wynkoop, colonel of a regiment of stolid New York Dutch troops. In the interim, no one had thought to spell out to him the fact that he had been superseded. Three weeks' work went into the *Revenge,* but Wynkoop never used her. The head-on collision between the Captain of the Lake and Arnold, Brigadier General and Commodore in Chief on Lake Champlain, was ended by the adroit intervention of Gates, who sent the baffled old Dutchman home, the better to "recover his health."

The Wynkoop affair was the least of Arnold's personal problems. Though he had the finest and fastest, the best armed and most completely found ships that he could design and build, Arnold could not fight them without men on the decks and in the rigging, behind the guns and at the wheels or the tillers. He started the recruiting of his soldier-sailors in that busy July, when Colonel Baldwin wrote, truthfully and in disgust, "I am heartily sick of this retreating, ragged, starved, thievish, pock-marked army in this unhealthy country."

A call for volunteers was published, quotas were established for each brigade, and, as inducement, Gates offered eight shillings a month extra pay for "service aboard the armed vessels." The men stepped forward: some, ignoring the soldier's Creed — "Never volunteer for anything" — in the hope that pulling an oar would be less arduous than digging with a spade; others were pushed out of the ranks of their own regiments by exasperated adjutants glad to see the last of them. Some who were good men managed to escape from their colonels and so offer their experience, trade, or talent to the fleet's mustermaster. It was this officer who sorted out the three hundred and forty-eight land lubbers, naming them seamen, gunners, and marines. The bulk of the new sailors went down to Skenesborough, receiving their first lesson in boatmanship on the twenty-mile row through the reed-lined channel of the Champlain marshes. Twenty-five good men from Wayne's Pennsylvanians marched north to be the marine detachment of the *Royal Savage* under Mr. Hops. It was felt that an after-guard of loyal marines might well be needed!

In the dredge-net for crews to man the Lake Champlain fleet, General Schuyler's agents scooped up three hundred men along the Atlantic coast, from Portsmouth to the Virginia Capes. They did well on the head count, though with thirty thousand American seamen off with the privateers, showing rich profits for their patriotism, the three hundred who took the bounty money were mainly the flotsam of the waterfront and the jetsam from the taverns. Arnold's captains took the volunteers as they came, straightened them out as best they could, and bent them to the heavy work aboard the ships. In the final tally, those ships would be two hundred men short of the nine hundred called for in the tables of organization.

As the captains had to make up their crews from the material they received, the commodore was forced to fill up the fleet from the ships' captains he could find. In an attempt to get his own men, General Arnold had written to five skippers of his acquaintance, inviting each of them to accept a command in the Lake Champlain navy. He promised them a good deck to stand on, and some fine action, but he urged each man to bring with him his own crew of forty sailors. Of the five, only one man, Captain Warner, received and answered Arnold's call.

Captain Warner rode out of the woods in an ox-cart, seated on his sea chest, his sextant in its wooden box on his knee. He made a strange figure of the sea in the wide clearing where the shipyard lay, the only visible water being the narrow stream on which floated two gondolas receiving their finishing licks. While she was still building, Warner took command of the *Trumbull*, a galley named for the Connecticut governor. He finished her to his own inclination, saw her launched, and stepped onto her deck, once more a seaman with a crew to train. His was the first row galley to join Arnold's fleet.

John Thatcher came up to Ticonderoga with Colonel Swift's Connecticut levies and immediately sought out General Arnold to beg command of a galley. He was given the *Washington* on whose quarter-deck he was to receive his death wound. Of the two remaining galleys, Arnold reserved to himself command of the *Congress* while the *Gates* was commanded by a New Hampshire man, Frederick Chappelle, recruited by Governor Trumbull in response to Schuyler's urgent request for sailors. Captain Chappelle brought a company of seamen with him to Lake Champlain.

The captains of the gondolas came from wherever Arnold

could find them in the army, or where Schuyler was able to recruit them along the seacoast. Some came alone; others, like Captain Rice of the *Philadelphia*, brought sixteen skirted sailors, the nucleus of his own crew. Sumner of the *Boston* was a Bostonian, in accordance with the policy Arnold tried to carry out, where and as he could: to identify a crew with its vessel by a home state or city name. Simonds, Grant, Reed, Mansfield, and Grimes — all were captains of Arnold's new-built gondolas, and each was proud of his command. Even Ulmer, captain of the gondola *Spitfire*, the smallest vessel of the fleet, was the envy of those captains who waited, impatiently and seemingly in vain, for more ships to be built.

One would-be captain was bitterly disappointed. Master Carpenter Titcomb, working on a galley at Skenesborough, conceived the idea that he would command her. He made the request, and the command was promised to him. But in spite of his good physique, Titcomb was a sick man, whom Arnold had to leave on the beach when the vessel he had built sailed proudly north to the rally, another captain on the quarter-deck. Captain Lee, of the *New York*, also was unable to sail with the fleet, and had to give over his command to Captain Reed.

Volunteers for junior officers were easily found among the high-spirited young officers of the army, who spoiled for a fight ashore or afloat. In battle, blind courage is a liability, mistrusted by a captain who recognizes the true hero in the trained man. Arnold and his captains screened the volunteers, rejecting the firebrand in favor of the man who, in the short time left to teach him, could master his new trade of officer on board a man-o'-war. Duties aloft, setting sail, giving a beat to the long sweeps that were counted on to give the American fleet the advantage of maneuverability; learning how to deploy marines on a deck crowded with guns

and their crews, or in the tops so as not to hinder the top-
men; the laying of a cannon to hit a moving target from an
unstable deck, while under fire oneself — all these things
were in the curriculum of a young officer in Benedict Arnold's fleet.

Ready or not, in mid-August the time came when General
Arnold was forced to turn over his brigade to his second-in-
command, and as Commander in Chief on Lake Champlain,
hoist his broad pennant on the *Royal Savage*. As the bunting
broke out on the mainmast, the other vessels greeted it with
a gun salute and three cheers, which Arnold, scorning naval
rank of commodore or admiral, acknowledged as brigadier
general.

All the vessels in the bay were familiar to him. The little
Liberty, commanded now by Captain Primmer, had been
Arnold's first command on the lake. When he had captured
the tall-masted sloop *Enterprise*, now lying a little further
out where in an emergency her speed would get her down
the lake first, he had named her flagship of the then two-
vessel navy. Now Dickenson commanded her, and Arnold
was confident of both captain and ship. Captain Seaman's
capabilities merited a better craft and a better gun platform
than the schooner *Revenge*, but there was a compensation
to the senior captain, for the after cabin was as large as
Arnold's own aboard the *Savage*.

Four of the new gondolas — the *Providence*, *New Haven*,
Boston, and *Spitfire* — were anchored in a neat row inshore
from the *Royal Savage*. As Arnold crossed the quarter-deck,
better to view these first fruits of his imagination and perseverance, he noted approvingly that the deck officers had
learned enough ship's manners to keep opposite station to
him. The vessels were in disorder, as they were still coming
in, but already the *Providence* had painted her masthead
white, and it was bold and clear, as it should be on a man-o'-

war. On the *Boston*, too, Captain Sumner was painting, to judge from the deckhand on the cross-tree, a bucket dangling from his wrist, and the spars athwart the gunwale.

The tactical concept which Arnold had envisaged for his gondola fleet was that of fire and movement. Working together in flotillas of four, with all their heavy guns loaded, the boats would move out under oars into range of the enemy; they would fire all four cannon broadside on the enemy's quarter; then, turning inward, they would bring to bear the four bow guns and the four guns of the other beam in two more quick broadsides before retiring out of range to reload. Such a maneuver would require much teamwork, practice, and time.

The Americans Make Ready

No British ships had yet been launched when Benedict Arnold took active command of his fleet (as she then was) in mid-August of 1776, but Arnold was not a man content to sit idly in the shade of an awning contemplating his navy at anchor.

At seven o'clock on the morning of August 24, the gondola *Connecticut* joined the fleet off Crown Point, and her Captain Grant reported on board the flagship. If Grant expected time to shake down his crew, fire his guns, and dress up his ship (so new that pitch oozed from the pine planking), he was disappointed. Arnold welcomed him heartily, gave him his signals for "Send a boat," and "Captains called," assigned his station in the line, and ordered him to be ready to sail that same afternoon. There was little rest, that day, for anyone aboard the *Connecticut!*

The fleet sailed at sunset in two columns: the *Royal Savage, New Haven, Providence,* and *Philadelphia* to port; the *Enterprise, Boston, Spitfire, Connecticut,* and *Liberty* to starboard. Arnold chose with great care the time of his departure. For the advance guard of the army at Crown Point, the day's work was done. It was the hour after supper, when men would be smoking their pipes in the soft coolness of the summer evening, relaxed in mind and body. All eyes, then, were on the American fleet, white sails spread, lines as true as any drill sergeant could wish, as it sped into the darkening north, a protecting sword and shield in the months to come. When the red glow had died out in the clay bowls, the hot ash been beaten out on the rough, work-hardened palms, and the fragile pipes wrapped carefully in handkerchiefs before being thrust deep into inner pockets, the boats had disappeared. But the sight of ten American sails going out to fight was a memory burned deep in the minds of the men of the advance guard, and the telling did not want for additions of proud identity with Benedict Arnold's fleet.

Four miles down the lake, the fleet hove to in line of battle, and out of his speaking trumpet Arnold's voice boomed over the darkening waters, encouraging and instructing the captains as they carried out their first maneuver together.

They were off and away under a red sky at sunrise, driving fast to the narrows. All day Arnold worked slowly north, testing the water's depth in sheltered bays, at the mouth of the Otter River and in Gilliland's Creek, or under the high walls of Split Rock Mountain and close in around its northernmost point — insatiable in his inquisitive search for knowledge of Lake Champlain.

On August 26, a storm struck from the north.

Caught in the open lake, Arnold ordered the fleet back up through the narrows. It was a ragged race before the wind, which came in swirling gusts off the high mountains at the narrows and called for seamanship of a high order. Captain Grant's *Connecticut* was the first casualty — a casualty which resulted more from the crew's lack of training than from the wind. The vessel's mast snapped, and, opposite Highlander's Bonnet, the *Revenge* came up to take her in tow. Captain Ulmer, who had had more time for training his crew, fared better. When a squall carried him on shore, his sailors jumped to it and got the sails furled and an anchor out, before the *Spitfire* got herself fast aground. Two days later, Captain Ulmer rejoined the fleet at the appointed rendezvous. The *Enterprise*, too, had her troubles. As she was luffing, a trick of the wind grounded her on a point of land, but she got herself away and joined the fleet, to wait out the storm at anchorage in a sheltered bay.

For three days, the wind blew out of the north and the rain soaked officers and men alike, as they huddled in their crowded boats or ashore in leaking temporary shelters. On the fourth day the sun came out, and the men emerged from under their wet canvas to stand about, hands in their pockets, sniffling and listless. The officers were little better off, and the captains of the *Connecticut*, *Spitfire*, and *Enterprise* were shamefacedly truculent over their accidents during the storm.

Arnold saw that morale must be restored, and so he began with the captains and lieutenants, all of whom were invited ashore for a pig roast. With punch and wine, the games and songs lasted far into the night.

On September 4, Arnold placed his fleet in a watch line across the lake above Ile LaMotte: the *Revenge* nearest the west shore, the *Liberty* on the east, the *Enterprise* and *Royal Savage* in the center of the lake, and the gondolas filling the gaps on either side.

Two days later the *Lee* came up, escorting the gondola *Jersey*. The little forty-three foot *Lee* was a pretty sight, her big sails bellying before the wind, so that she seemed to skip along the water after her long running bowsprit, in striking contrast to her plodding escort. Arnold welcomed the new arrivals with a salute of cannon, begun by the *Liberty* and taken up by the *Revenge*, then alternating right and left until all had fired. Captain Davis replied with a shot to the English shore from the *Lee*'s 12-pounder.

Earlier that day the fleet had suffered its first casualties through enemy action. A boat party was sent ashore from the *Boston* to cut fascines, with which the gondolas lined their rails as a screen. The party was ambushed by British Indians under a white officer, and four of the Americans were killed; four others were seriously wounded. After this episode, no further work parties were sent ashore, though the American fleet held to that station through most of September.

A supply line from Ticonderoga kept the ships provisioned with food and news. When Colonel Edward Wigglesworth came up to take command of the *Royal Savage* as captain, he told of a big battle being fought between Washington and Howe. It would be several days, however, before the fleet would have word of the outcome of the Battle of Brooklyn and the American retreat to the Hudson Highlands. News came out of Canada, too. Benjamin Whitcomb, the American scout, stopped at the flagship for a word with Arnold, and to display the red coats of his two prisoners, taken from behind the British lines. Word also came that the British had launched their schooner, the *Carleton*, on September 4, and that the *Lady Maria* was soon to follow.

Still waiting for his fighting ships — the row galleys — on September 24, Benedict Arnold ordered his fleet back up the lake to a position already determined upon: St. Anthony's Bay, on the west coast of Valcour Island. The galleys would have to find him there.

———————

Meanwhile, as August gave place to September, General Waterbury was still at Skenesborough, pressing forward work on the four row galleys, none of which had yet been launched.

Skenesborough itself had changed in appearance. Already, it had the look of an old Fair Ground — the races over, the

cattle gone home, only the midway still busy, packing up
to move on. Four gondolas of the type used on the Schuylkill River in the vicinity of Philadelphia stood in their cradles, unattended and forgotten. They required more oak
than was to be found in either sawmill, and all work on
them had been stopped. Every effort was now concentrated on the four big row galleys. One of these was ready
for launching, two others were almost completed, and the
fourth still without a transom, her deck beams casting
barred shadows into the narrow hold as the sun swung
high on its now southward arc. Pine deck planks for the
Gates, as the fourth galley was to be called, lay neatly
stacked beside her scaffolding, awaiting only the deck nails
which had not yet come up from Albany.

But the desolate look that had spread over the shipyard,
giving a distant, unreal clatter to the turning wheel and nodding saw of Skene's mill, came from the hush in the dark
barracks and from the listless pale men sprawled in the sun
at the wide doorways. Skenesborough had become a fever
hole and a pestilence camp in the mountains. Hands shook
when they tried to hold a chisel, and a tiredness staggered
the team of sawyers trimming a rudderpost. The men
stopped, bewildered and frightened at their sudden weakness.

Waterbury, who heard from Arnold the urgent calls for
his galleys, cajoled and drove the remaining healthy carpenters, and on September 5 the *Trumbull* kissed the waters
of Wood Creek. As she was launched on a Sunday, the men
felt sure she would be a lucky ship. Unfinished as she was,
Waterbury sent her out under oars, her two masts and long
spars lying on a deck which still gathered chips, as carpenters worked on rail stanchions and hammers sounded
below, where baffle doors were being fitted to the powder
magazine.

Before the week was out, the *Washington* and the *Congress* were tied to their fitting docks at Ticonderoga alongside the *Trumbull*.

General Waterbury himself had not waited in the pest-ridden camp at Skenesborough. Captain Chappelle could finish his own galley, the *Gates*, with the entire shipyard at his disposal for this last effort. Waterbury had done his best. Eight fifty-six-foot gondolas had been launched, and three row galleys, each over seventy feet long; a fourth galley, a seventy-two-footer, was on the ways. Though General Schuyler and General Gates had tried to move "Heaven, Earth, and the Continental Congress," the latter had shown a "strange economy and infatuation" which prevented further work on the Schuylkill gondolas and the laying-down of four additional row galleys, wanted by Arnold as possible replacements after the impending battle. General Washington was occupied with the battles around New York, and could give no further help to his northern generals, whose own resources, splendid as they had been, were now drying up.

Having exerted all the impatience of a veteran sea captain, Warner brought the half-finished *Trumbull* up to the wharf at Ticonderoga with tidy decks and a chastened crew of New York men. Though the day was spent, ten minutes after her arrival Captain Warner's vessel was again a shambles. Bateaux, filled with ballast from the Rattlesnake Hill shore, were bringing the gritty rocks in over the lake rail, while the rigging crew, stomping in muddy boots, were angling on board the long sheers needed to step the masts. Tactfully, Colonel Baldwin led the captain away to the engineer's own office, where Warner could select from stock a spyglass and a new lantern for the great cabin.

When Waterbury arrived at Ticonderoga in the galley *Washington* on September 9, with the *Congress* a day behind, the *Trumbull* was in ballast and set into the water nicely, showing her long lines with their promise of speed. Only the short stumpy mast looked out of place on the big North American inland lake.

Work was intensified with the arrival of each new rumor purporting to come from St. Jean, or the urgent calls that came back with the provision bateau from Arnold in St. Anthony's Bay. While the galleys were fitting, the *Liberty* had come down to get her new set of sail, which had been found in Albany. The sails had been bundled and carefully labeled "For Major Philip Skene," but had not been delivered to that gentleman. Then the *Lee* came busily into Ticonderoga to establish, with the *Liberty*, an alternate-voyage messenger and supply service for the fleet.

Behind Valcour Island and hidden from the lake by the high, pine-covered bluffs, Arnold's fleet rode at anchor across the mouth of St. Anthony's Bay. Except for the watch, the men were ashore in barracks. Daily exercises were held aboard the vessels, at the guns and at the oars. At night campfires twinkled, sharp in the crisp September air, and the wonder of the aurora borealis lighted the northern sky. One night it snowed.

There was a second officers' picnic, but it was a more serious affair than the first had been. The captains sprawled on the pine needles, red firelight picking out the seams and shadows of their grim faces. Arnold sat on the trunk of a fallen tree, dominating the group as always and guiding the drift of the conversation. Finally, when the last captain had said his say about the scurvy lot of dollards that was his crew, and when Arnold had noted the careful attention given by one of the lieutenants to a louse discovered in the kneeband of his patched breeches, the general quickly emptied his mug and swung around, squarely facing his officers.

Benedict Arnold spoke plainly to his captains that night,

agreeing with their low opinion of their patriot crews, then turning that weakness into a plan of battle. Unable to sail because of unreliable seamen, the American fleet would fight like an army, each vessel a redoubt set in line between the islands and the shore. When they arrived, the galleys — with the *Enterprise* and the *Royal Savage* — would be a rallying force with which to attack the British vessels, as one by one the Americans pressed into the bay from the south. The enemy would come around the point, yonder: Arnold's big hand shot out from his buff-colored cuff as he pointed to the southern tip of Valcour Island, where pine trees made steepled tents against a star-pricked blue velvet sky. They would come that way because the Britons are predictable and their sea traditions never alter. Ten years before, the British had shot one of their best admirals on his own quarter-deck, because he had failed to engage the enemy. In 1776, there was not an officer in the British navy who would not attack, and attack with eagerness. "Eagerness!" That was the word; the season was late, and the English must have their victory soon. They would sweep up the lake in line of battle, eager to engage the Americans. With a following wind, which they had to have for their ark and their gunboats, they would sweep right past the American fleet behind Valcour Island. It was when the British had to turn and beat upwind to get into the bay that the Americans would attack, and Arnold had little doubt that, poor specimens though they were, his own sailors would fight, once the enemy trapped them in the bay.

The *Trumbull* joined the fleet on the last day of September. Arnold was aboard her before the last gun from the *Savage* had finished answering her salute. He was disappointed: they had sent him a half-rigged vessel, too lightly gunned. But Captain Warner would take care of the rigging, and Arnold himself would see that two 4-pounders and three swivels were sent over from the *Liberty* before the vessel sailed for Ticonderoga.

On October 6, the *Washington*, with Arnold's own *Congress*, came down the lake and into St. Anthony's Bay. That night, Arnold slept in the after cabin of the *Congress*, his new flagship.

Now he lacked only the *Gates*, the galley which General Waterbury had assured him would sail from Ticonderoga, weather permitting, on October 10. That would be too late; Arnold had his full fleet already mustered for the battle.

There was not long to wait.

The British Make Ready

Hard on the heels of the British light infantry infiltrating the town and the military installations at St. Jean, on the afternoon of June 18, 1776, had come Lieutenant John Schank of the Royal Navy. He was the new superintendent of the dockyards, and he had come to see what was left of them. With him was Lieutenant William Twiss, the engineer officer whose duty it was to rebuild the yards and maintain the workshops.

On these two men rested General Carleton's hopes of beating the Americans in the shipbuilding race which England must win, if British armies were to force the Lake Champlain gate during the campaign season of 1776. Each of the men was an inventor, with a new idea which complemented that of the other. Twiss had invented a square-bowed landing craft for infantry: a shield in front, pierced with loopholes, could be dropped like the drawbridge of a castle, making a ramp to shore on which troops, dry shod and with powder dry, could land in ranks to the assault. Schank called his own invention "the drop-keel." This was a board that could be raised or lowered in a slot-shaped well set into the inside of a boat along the center line, to act as a keel when down, or, when raised, to permit the boat to enter shoal waters. For the British cause, it was regrettable that neither of these inventions, practical though radical, was sanctioned by General Carleton, or by Captain Douglas, the British naval commander.

On a staff and plans level, General Carleton was committed to a naval policy for the Lake Champlain expedition of 1776, long before the two bright young engineers were seconded for service in that expedition. Even in June 1776, when the naval plans for Lake Champlain became operative, Carleton had no reason to exercise his right to change them, since he was promised a fleet on the lake by mid-August.

When St. Jean fell, Carleton had such a fleet, but it was on the decks and in the holds, or floating in the St. Lawrence with Captain Douglas's warships and the transport fleet that had landed Burgoyne's soldiers.

Fourteen gunboats made in England were sent out as deck cargo. They were of a class thirty-six feet long and sixteen feet wide, with a bluff bow over which stuck the muzzle of a 12-pounder cannon. Each of the gunboats carried eighteen artillerymen, and enough sailors to man the oars from benches, built in on either side of a central passage where the soldiers sat. Each boat was commanded by an artillery officer, with a junior naval officer in command of the sailors.

In the holds of the vessels at anchor off the mouth of the Sorel River, there was a wealth of naval stores, including key members for a schooner. With the fleet there was another schooner, destined by the Lords of Admiralty for Lake Champlain. She was to be taken overland and launched again at St. Jean, where she was to be christened the *Lady Maria*. In compliment to General Carleton's wife, a daughter of the important Earl of Effingham; the figurehead represented that young lady, but did scant justice to her vivacious beauty.

The previous June, when the Americans had left the St. Lawrence in precipitate retreat, the gondola *American*

Convert had been abandoned to the British. Royal Navy experts looked her over and liked her flat bottom, pointed ends, rounded sides, and long quarter-deck. They approved of her armament capabilities of six to eight 9-pound guns, but they thought she was poorly rigged, and they gagged at her name. She was taken into the Lake Champlain fleet as the *Loyal Convert*, and her rigging was converted into that of a bomb ketch.

In planning the third capital ship of Carleton's fleet, the Admiralty had in mind a siege operation against a land fort. She was a radeau, of large dimensions and heavily gunned, and if the tactical situation so indicated, she, too, could be gunned as a bomb ketch. She was aptly named the *Thunderer*. Six 24-pounders and eighteen 12's was her maximum armament, after bow ports had been added to her original plans; but the *Thunderer* went into action on Lake Champlain with only six 12-pound guns, two high-angle howitzers supplanting the other twelve cannon. She was in the tradition of Amherst's *Ligonier,* and of Johnson's first radeau of the lakes, but the *Thunderer* differed in that, though generally square, she was shaped like a scow and had a scow bow and stern, which gave a certain grace to her lines. With all sails set on her high mainmast, she had an eager, forward-leaning appearance. The *Thunderer* turned out to be a good sailor, once logging ninety miles in nine hours; against the wind, however, she made little headway with her sweep oars. Lieutenant Schank had sought permission to install a drop-keel, but this was refused.

⁓⁓⁓⁓⁓⁓

Such was the composition of the fleet with which General Carleton expected to take Lake Champlain from the rebellious colonists. Two of his vessels floated in the pool below Chambly Falls; a third, the *Thunderer,* was only on plans, while the schooner to be launched as the *Carleton* was still in pieces in the hold of a transport. Fourteen artillery boats were on the Chambly shore, awaiting transport to St. Jean.

Labor, both skilled and unskilled, was readily available. Craftsmen and sailors from the fleet and from the army were Carleton's for the asking, and the *Corvée*, an old French law under which the *habitants* could be called up to public labor, had been retained under the Quebec Act. By use of the *Corvée*, the governor general conscripted some twelve hundred *habitants*, sending some of them into the woods as loggers, but using the main body to rebuild the road between Chambly and St. Jean.

While the boats and stores were accumulating at Chambly, Lieutenant Schank was busily preparing bases for the capstans and setting the rollers over which the *Lady Maria* and the *Convert* would make the long ten-mile haul to clear water at St. Jean. At the dockyard, Engineer Officer Twiss was busy, too, preparing stocks for the *Thunderer* and the *Carleton*, and launching-slips for the two vessels coming up overland. His work load was greatly reduced when it was decided to build elsewhere the five hundred and sixty bateaux needed to carry the army up the lake. Twiss, however, was to build twelve single-gun artillery boats at St. Jean.

General Carleton's plans were well laid; his army was strong and well equipped, poised ready to move; his naval plans progressed on schedule. His estimate of the American shipping, viewed in the light of the time he would give them, caused him no alarm. Their seacoast source of supply for sailors and stores was a long two hundred and fifty miles away, while his own was ten miles distant, and was concentrated in Captain Douglas's fleet. The ships included in Carleton's plans would descend on the existing

American vessels before they could possibly build more and stronger ones which could tip the balance in their favor.

The only fault lay in the Englishman's estimate of his time schedule. It took a week to get the *Maria* and the *Convert* out of the water and up on top of the rise out of the Chambly Basin. They had progressed little further before the rains came, and there they stayed, patient as a logging team at the noon hour, rain streaming down their barrel sides. Heavy timbers propped up the *Maria* on her port side, as the rain-soaked earth gave way and the rollers, with their tracks, settled into the mud. Still it rained — the same rain that stranded fifty badly needed Philadelphia carpenters on the road to Skenesborough, far away at the other end of Lake Champlain.

As rainwater and weeks of time trickled down the ruts in the Chambly–St. Jean roadbed, General Carleton's patience ran out. The *Lady Maria* and the *Carleton* must be cleared out of the supply route which their hulks successfully blocked. Lieutenant Schank gave the order to take the two vessels apart and to have them carried piecemeal for reassembly at St. Jean. The attempt to move them overland had been a costly failure. The advantage lost on the road could be regained only by increasing the size of the British fleet, so that it could meet the threat of the row galleys which Carleton knew could now be built in time to come against him.

Casting about for a ship, Carleton remembered the frigate that was building in the dockyard at Quebec City. When completed, she would be more than 90 feet on deck and of 300-ton burden. If she could be brought to Lake Champlain, her size and her three tall masts under a mountainous cloud of white canvas, backed up by eighteen big 12-pounders, would make a show to cow the rebels. The general's naval advisers told him this was possible, and he issued orders for the *Inflexible* to be dismantled (the ribs and planking already had been joined) and for the numbered pieces to be brought with all possible haste to the shipyard at St. Jean.

~~~~~~~~

William Digby's fever had subsided, and after three days of delirium, he regained consciousness on September 30, 1776, only to find that he had been left behind by his company of British grenadiers. He had come off advance guard on September 27, soaked to the skin and cold to the marrow. He had seen to his men and, before seeking out his own bed and blanket, had gone down to the shore to watch the two schooners *Maria* and *Carleton*, just up from St. Jean, drop anchor in the east channel. The two vessels were all ready to fight. Watching from the shores of Ile aux Noix, General Simon Fraser's advance corps — the grenadier and light infantry companies of ten fine British regiments, plus the whole of the 24th Foot — felt the excitement of approaching battle.

The advance corps had passed the last month of summer on Ile aux Noix, in danger of flooding when it rained, killing snakes under the tent flaps, and plagued by enormous yellow mosquitoes. Their duties had been to rebuild the old French fortifications and to build new ones, and to keep watch posts and guards up the river and on the big lake. Lucky officers seconded to the Indians scouted forward in offensive or defensive patrols, sometimes returning with a prisoner, or with a tale of a brush with the enemy. Now, with the big ships gathering, Fraser's corps again would be on the move.

When Lieutenant Digby awoke, weak and exhausted, he was in an unfamiliar tent; his brother-in-law, a captain of the 31st Foot, was with him; and Ile aux Noix was occupied by General William Nesbit's 1st Brigade. The advance guard had gone to Riviere Lacolle, six miles up the river, opposite Ash Island. During the days of his convalescence and mounting restlessness, Digby was made welcome by his brother-in-law's regiment. But it was not *home*, and his singularity was accentuated by his hat: it was the only grenadier's tall fur cap remaining on Ile aux Noix!

Impatient at his weakness, without army duties, and surrounded by acquaintances instead of friends, Lieutenant Digby roamed over the island, gaining back his strength through exercise, and seeking an outlet for his increasing energies. It was during one of these walks on the crowded island that he came upon the grave of four scalped Pennsylvania men. "Not hirelings but patriots," the marker said. He had to pull aside the tall grass to read the verse, carved into the wide board that marked the grave:

> Sons of America, rest in quiet here,
> Britannia blush, Burgoyne let fall a tear,
> And tremble, Europe's Sons with savage race,
> Death and Revenge await you with disgrace.

A British officer serving in North America had much to condone, with his government in London using Indians and employing Hessians, the "hirelings" of the grave marker, against the erstwhile colonials. Though the savages could be rationalized as indigenous, in this rather embarrassing family affair the presence of mercenary troops from over the Rhine was a source of constant intra-army irritation.

There were three thousand Germans in Carleton's army — the soldiers doltish, the officers and noncommissioned officers competent, efficient, and brave men. They were completely professional, without humor or conviction, bent only on giving satisfaction to their employer. A good job done in this campaign meant a higher asking price in the next, for themselves and for the princeling who hired them out. Carleton kept his Germans to themselves in a wing of the army. Only in the case of Captain George Pausche's Hesse-Hannau Artillery Company did he mix the nationalities, and he did it on the crowded deck of the radeau *Thunderer*.

If General Carleton's purpose was to foster a better relationship between British and Hessians by using the common bond among artillerists, the humorless Pausche was not the man, nor the swarming deck of the radeau the place, to try the experiment. Three hundred men were so crowded aboard the big vessel that their baggage had to trail along behind in twelve bateaux. Captain Pausche considered his assignment to the fore and aft batteries as a post of honor, which not only acknowledged the superiority of his men as gunners, but gave them privileges as to quarters. A downpour of rain their first night on board brought this matter of quarters to a head, but the rain also served to dampen a serious outbreak between the two nationalities. Tempers simmered during the two days' kedge up the Richelieu to Ile aux Noix. There the Hessians were put ashore, to await the arrival of the gunboats to which Major Griffith Williams, Royal Artillery, commander of troops on the *Thunderer*, had effected their reassignment. The uncomprehending Pausche merely considered Englishmen "unpleasant companions." Captain Scott moved his radeau upriver, and when the British and the Germans next saw each other it was October 10, the day before the battle at Valcour Bay, and plenty of blue water lay between them.

From Ile aux Noix, the *Maria, Carleton, Thunderer*, and *Loyal Convert* sailed for Riviere Lacolle. On board the *Convert* as a guest of her captain, Edward Longcroft, went Lieutenant Digby. He was bundled in his new winter clothes: warm undervest, mittens, and Canadian blanket-coat. He was still pale, the flush of fever drained from his face, but he was exhilarated by the chill wind that was taking him back to his fellow grenadiers.

~~~~~~~

Handsome General Sir John Burgoyne, who, even on a quarter-deck, looked every inch a dashing commander of light cavalry, stood at the taffrail of the *Lady Maria* with his staff around him, hailing the glory of the Canadian autumn which was touching the hardwood trees along the river bank with pale gold and making the swamp maple a splashed crimson. As the vessel passed, a small flock of pink and gray pigeons rose out of a big oak tree and darted off, flying inland over the gently billowing tree tops. One of Burgoyne's aides, a Canadian, pointed them out as harbingers of the myriads soon to come, in such numbers that they could feed the army — both armies — during the days it took the birds to fly overhead. High over the ensign at the masthead flew a ragged, changing "V" of geese, each one a small, dark cross against a lead-gray sky. The general and his group fell silent, as they listened to the faint, mystical call of the leader. It was a morning such as men remember.

When the *Maria* hesitated momentarily and then lurched ahead, as a soft mud bank stroked her bottom from bow to rudder, Burgoyne turned a courteous joke with the nervous captain standing beside the helmsman, forestalling any comment from Captain Pringle, whose flag, as squadron commander, was hoisted on the *Maria*.

The inexorable movement of a great British host had begun, and here on the placid Richelieu River was the advance guard of a mighty navy, about to debouch onto the lake; while, crowding the river bank, was the cheering advance guard of a stout-hearted army. Behind the elite were coming the solid regiments of four brigades, and following the fleet, soon to overtake it, was Britain's leviathan of the lakes, His Majesty's Ship *Inflexible*.

In twenty-eight days, Lieutenant Schank, with sixteen shipwrights, had built the *Inflexible* in the dockyard at St. Jean. The dismembered ribs and sides had come up from Quebec on September 2, and in one day, had been put together again. On September 30, she was afloat. The riggers went aboard, and were still at work as the vessel was towed up the river by teams of whaleboats, tugging at her rounded bows. Accompanying the *Inflexible* was a swarm of heavily laden boats, piled high with stores of every kind to be put on board the big ship, together with her guns and ballast, when she reached water deep enough for her in-ballast draught. Never had the inland lake received to her bosom such a noble vessel. Nine 18-pounders poked black muzzles out of her orange-painted sides, almost a hundred feet from her bow to the windows in her transom. Above deck, her square sails towered in diminishing perspective to the tip of her tapering pine masts, where her jack and pennants billowed out as though in a wind from the clouds themselves. There had been no time to carve a figurehead, or to ornament her rails or transom with fine-carved scrolls and emblems. Only a large blue ensign flew at her stern, signifying that the *Inflexible*, with the other vessels of the Lake Champlain fleet, was now an inland part of the Blue Squadron of the Royal Navy. There were three rousing cheers for the Red, White, and Blue, as the ship *Inflexible* joined the fleet at Windmill Point, the long corridor of the lake lying before it.

In Harm's Way

At five o'clock on the morning of October 11, the signal flags of the *Lady Maria* drew the other vessels of the British fleet in line of battle behind her. General Guy Carleton was on deck as the austere but graceful *Carleton* swung in astern, followed by the *Inflexible*, yawing a trifle as her captain sent his sailors aloft to trim sail for a good north-northwest wind. That wind would give the *Thunderer* trouble, as the course was a point west of south, and on a course that was slightly across winds, the heavy radeau was not able to keep up with the squadron.

Four sloop-rigged longboats, a playful young midshipman at the tiller of each, skipped about the bows of the *Maria*. The boats had been borrowed from a ship of the line, and each one bore across her square stern the name of her parent vessel, even then at anchor in the wide St. Lawrence. Behind the three leading vessels, and filling the gap widening between them and the *Thunderer*, came the gunboats, twenty in all. Six gunboats, including one of Captain Pausche's four, had not yet come up from Ile aux Noix.

Following behind, their sails white against the green north end of the lake and the headland of Windmill Point, at the mouth of the Richelieu, came the supply boats for the fleet: bateaux and longboats and the bobbing canoes of the army's Indian fringe.

The mess pennant fluttered out from the peak of the

Maria, and before Carleton, Burgoyne, and Pringle went below, where the servants had spread their table in the great cabin, thick brown rum was ordered for all hands. A few minutes later, Lieutenant John Starke, ship's captain of the *Maria,* sent up the signal: "Put out cook fires; make ready for battle!" Aboard the *Thunderer,* Lieutenant William Houghton, Fire Master, Royal Artillery, worked the bellows of his furnace in disregard of the order; *his* fire was for hot shot to serve to the Rebels aboard their own craft.

The British fleet, a bone in its teeth, drove south on the lake, past Ile LaMotte, around Point au Roche, and into the ten-mile stretch of water that would take the vessels past Cumberland Head, with the gut between the Hero Islands on their port side. A longboat was dispatched to poke into the gut, in the off chance that a Yankee lay lurking there.

All eyes were searching the big bay behind Cumberland Head, and as the fleet swept by, the Head and Crab Island were pointed out as the hiding place of a French fleet, seventeen long years before. The rugged cliff and pine-serrated ridges of Valcour Island were rising fast on the starboard bow. Captain Thomas Pringle sent a midshipman to the port rail with a glass, ready to search the protected bay at the southern end of South Hero Island — a likely place to hide a fleet.

Pringle's chart marked a ledge to the south and east of Valcour Island. As a deep-sea sailor feeling cramped in a shore-girt lake, he had asked Lieutenant Starke for a little port rudder and a more easterly course, when suddenly he thought his eye caught a flutter of white behind the southwest corner of the island. An instant later, from the *Maria's* deck a schooner showed full and clear, coming out of the bay with all sails set, on a parallel course. She was followed closely by a tall-masted sloop. Immediately, they were identified as the two vessels captured by the Americans at St. Jean the year before. Quietly, the *Maria* swung on a gently curving course, calculated to head off the Yankee vessels, and Captain Pringle ordered up the signal to engage.

On board the *Carleton*, Lieutenant James Richard Dacres, late of HMS *Blonde*, ordered hard a-starboard, and sent his sailors into the rigging to hurry the setting of the sails on the new course. To Dacres, "to engage" meant to drive for the enemy, and his officers and crew (all of them from the *Blonde*) carried that ship's honor with them on board the *Carleton*.

Behind the *Carleton*, the *Inflexible*, carrying full sail, bowled on past the handy schooner, her crew struggling to spill the wind and slow the momentum of the heavy ship. Her new rigging stretched and groaned as Lieutenant Schank, her captain, tried to maneuver her, fearing that every strain he applied above deck would shiver a green mast or spar. The *Inflexible* was two miles south of the island before Schank got her around, to face the new problem of beating upwind for the first time in this fine-looking but as yet untested vessel. From his position, he could look in behind the high shores of Valcour Island, where he could now see the whole American fleet. He was still trying to count the enemy sails when he was forced to order the *Inflexible* about on the other tack.

It was close to ten o'clock in the morning when His Majesty's Ship *Maria* found the Continental armed vessels *Royal Savage* and *Enterprise* trying to break out from behind Valcour Island. This, in effect, had been an enticing movement planned by Benedict Arnold that morning at eight o'clock, when warned by the guard boat that the British were coming. Following Arnold's orders, the decoy vessels came about, once the British were committed to their turn, and went beating back in behind the island.

Now there came over both fleets that quiet time of waiting out the long, dragging minutes, when the steersman grips harder the spokes of the big wheel, and young gunners in the waist look to the older men to see what outward show of courage is lacking in their own stance. The marines retie around their bodies the lines that secure them to the rigging aloft, and the captain has eyes only for the enemy ahead.

On board the *Carleton*, nearest to the island and to the two retreating American vessels, the midshipman of the watch stepped forward, grateful for the action, and turned the glass on the binnacle. A bell was struck sharply, four times. The tableau on deck had not changed, as the half-hour glass was turned for half-past ten; the sand made a growing pyramid in the bottom of the double bell-shaped glass.

The *Enterprise* was gaining distance from HMS *Carleton* on a long reach to the western shore, while on the other tack the *Royal Savage* was driving, heeled over, for the bluff point on the inside corner of the island. While Dacres was watching her and gauging the range, the big schooner caught a cross draft off the cliffs, and for a second she rose up straight, her long boom whipping over, the back sails all aflap. Then slowly her bow swung east, and Arnold's *Royal Savage* drove hard ashore, her masts tumbling on impact. Warned, Dacres fell off a couple of points to give the dangerous headland a wider berth, and ordered his mate at the starboard battery to ready a broadside for the grounded *Savage*.

Around the point sailed the *Carleton*, the seven 6-pounders of her broadside crashing into the wreckage of the American schooner, and the sharp gun smoke rolling back over the quarter-deck. When the smoke cleared, the *Carleton* was behind Valcour Island, with the American fleet stretched in line across the thirty-five-hundred-foot channel from the island to the west shore of the lake. Out of the line, moving under oars that bristled at either side of their slim bodies like the legs of an elongated spider, two vessels were moving to engage the *Carleton*. The waiting was over; the battle was begun.

The crew of the *Carleton* had their hands full. The two galleys (they were the *Washington* and the *Congress*) soon withdrew back into the center of the American line, and the gondolas came out in turns to fire their guns at the Britisher, then quickly withdrew out of range to reload. Dacres fell, senseless and badly wounded, at the first broadside from the American galleys. The very young Mr. Edward Pellew had him carried to his cabin, as the after guard was about to throw his body overboard for dead.

Pellew found Mr. Brown, the first mate, already in the cabin. Dazed, Brown was holding his shattered arm while the surgeon, preparing for amputation, snipped at the tattered sleeve that still covered it.

Pellew hurried back on deck. Though still in his teens, he was now the captain of HMS *Carleton*, her crew, and the fate of both in the battle around him. He had no time to give to anything but his ship.

When the *Maria*'s signal to engage went up, and the turning movement scattered the capital ships, the little gunboats dropped their square lugsails, set their oars in the locks, and with the midshipmen giving the stroke, rowed to the lee shore of Valcour Island where the water was smooth and the going was easy. On this course, the twenty gunboats gained on the *Carleton* and followed her, like a pack of hounds, around the point into Valcour Sound. There they suddenly discovered the *Royal Savage*, a wounded, broken quarry, canted on the shore, her crew struggling with the rigging that snarled the gun deck. Houndlike, they pounced on the dying thing, and with joyous shouts, each gunboat

coming up joined the jostling pack to loose one more round
into the stricken schooner. Nor were the gunboats alone:
HMS *Loyal Convert* joined them at their snapping and
even sent a boarding party to the *Royal Savage*, where the
boarders had the satisfaction of turning her guns on the enemy fleet, before they were driven off the American deck
with their few prisoners.

Into the welter of British gunboats rowed their flotilla
captain, shouting, screaming, and flaying about with words,
dragging the gunboats back, heading them off, and gradually turning them onto the real quarry, at bay down the
Sound. Slowly he sorted out his boats, first directing them
to support the *Carleton* in her fight with the two galleys
moving toward her out of the American line; then, as the
battle developed, spreading the line across the Sound, to
engage targets of choice with the gunboats' heavy 24-pound-
ers and long 12-pounders, rowing up to within range to fire,
then dropping back to reload. The guns fired on, through
the midday hour and into the long afternoon, each side
seeking a conclusion in telling damage to the ships and men
of the enemy. The American fire was from grape more than
from round shot, and this, under seven hundred yards'
range, the British found galling. Prudently, they soon
learned to gauge that distance from the undulating American line. But often they were caught in too close, in the
smoke that rolled downwind on them from the American
fleet.

One of the boats on the British right, commanded by
Lieutenant Dufais, was probing forward for a target when
a billow of smoke rolled back, exposing a Yankee gondola
well in advance of the line, her bow gun bearing on Dufais's
flank. Dufais was a Hessian, his sailors English, which resulted in a moment's confusion. In that moment, the Yankee's 12-pounder fired. The big iron ball shattered through

the gunboat's bow under the gun carriage slide, deflected aft off a heavy support, and ripped into the gunboat's magazine, where it lay smoldering in a broken keg of powder. In an instant there was a shattering explosion. On his own gunboat further west down the line, Captain Pausche was sighting his gun when the explosion occurred. It was Pausche's gun sergeant who diverted him from his work, pointing out that it was a Hesse-Hannau boat that had been hit. The identification was made positive by the white tape and the red pom-poms at the side folds of the gunners' hats, and Pausche ordered his boat to the rescue. Burning now, and half-full of water, Dufais's boat was drifting out of range as Pausche came up, in company with a Royal Artillery boat, to take on board the twenty-one shocked and grimy survivors. Place was made at the bottom of the aft cockpit for the wounded pilot and the little drummer. There they lay through the long afternoon of cannonading, the sounds of battle all around them as they looked up through pain-filled eyes at the profound blue of the sky and the drifting white clouds.

Two more gunboats were hulled, and dropped back out of the British line to seek rescue for their crews. At four o'clock, HMS *Inflexible* came up and joined the line, but the *Maria*, with her precious load of generals, was inshore at ineffective extreme range. Of the big British ships, only the *Carleton* was forward at close quarters with the American fleet. She, too, was in trouble: half her crew wounded, she was riddled, her sails torn, with two feet of water in her bilge. Her signal for recall was up on the flagship, and Midshipman Captain Edward Pellew was dutifully trying to obey. But she would not come about. Running forward, Pellew recognized a fouled jib, holding her bows up to the Americans. To clear it meant exposure, out on the jib boom, to the full force of the enemy's grape and rifle fire.

It was not a job for an ordinary sailor, and Pellew took it to himself. Slowly he worked his way up the canting spar, as a flurry of shot came searching him from the center of the American line, where the big galley *Congress* lay broadside. Steadily he moved through the tangle of the rigging to the very tip of the boom, where the jib stay gave him a hand-hold so that he could stand upright and work, slashing at the fouled lines that held his jib from coming over. He cleared it, and leaning his little weight against the big sail, by force of will he got the wind into her on the other side.

But Edward Pellew's work was not yet over. Two British longboats, the *Isis* and that from his own *Blonde*, had come up to tow the crippled *Carleton* out, and it was Pellow who went down into the bobstays to pass a new hawser to the boats, when a round shot had cut the first. The *Carleton* came out of the action fighting to the last.

A battery of spyglasses searched the American line from the quarter-deck of the *Lady Maria*. Except for the *Royal Savage*, from which the crew had escaped to shore, and which was now burning herself out amid clouds of steam as the fire reached the waterline, the American fleet was intact. Arnold was in the process of withdrawing his line three hundred yards down the Sound. All the Yankee vessels had been badly mauled, though it was hard through a spyglass to assess the damage. A gondola in the center of the line was definitely down in the water, and another, Pringle felt sure, had a great splinter taken out of her mast. As the British commanders watched, a big American sloop (the vessel nearest the Valcour shore) loosed a gun, its boom coming lazily across the calm evening waters. It was aimed at the shore, where little puffs of smoke told Carleton that his Indians, who had landed during the afternoon, were still annoying the men behind their brush screens on the

Rebel's deck. That American gun also told Carleton that the American line, although wounded, must be treated like the rattlesnakes that, he had been told, decorated the striped flags on Rebel ships: sting yet remained in their fangs.

But morning would be time enough to stamp out the Rebel snakes. For the night, he would let the spirit which the Americans had shown during the day drain out of their wounds. In the morning, he would send in the radeau *Thunderer,* just up and at anchor inside of Petite Ile. To protect her, a longboat was sent to the gunboat flotilla leader with orders to withdraw his cordon of boats from across the Sound, and to rally around the clumsy, venerable, floating battery as a guard.

With the *Inflexible* in the center, the *Lady Maria* toward shore, the heavily hit *Carleton* to the east, and the *Loyal Convert* rowing patrol to the rear of the British line, General Carleton and Captain Pringle felt that the stopper in the bottle was secure. They went below to dine; already it was candlelight time in the sparsely furnished cabin.

In his great cabin on board the *Congress,* General Arnold, too, was dining. He had spent the day pointing his own guns, and he was red-eyed and weary, but content. The loss of the *Savage* was a personal blow to him, for when he moved his flag to the galley, he had not taken the time to move his sea chest, containing all his papers. He could have done with a change of clothing before the captains arrived for the conference to which he had summoned them; but, then, the men on deck were in tatters, too, though he had asked Congress for warm clothing for them. For a mutinous rabble which he had barely been able to hold together for this day, the men had fought bravely and well.

With the coming of darkness, the annoying musket fire

from the pine ridges had stopped, and now the captains—
or the officers representing them — came on board. Each
gave his report solemnly, as if reciting in a dream a catalogue of disaster of which he felt no part, his mind covered
by a merciful shield of blank resignation. Hawley, who had
lost the *Royal Savage*, felt a shame in which he had no
companionship, even when Rice, wet to the waist, sloshed
in to report the *Philadelphia* gone. Late in the action, she
had been holed by a broadside from the *Inflexible* and had
settled down quietly, as if to sleep forever beneath the cool
blue blanket of the lake.

In the crowded cabin there was business to be done, and
it could not wait on the fatigue which these captains could
show only now among themselves. Arnold, who stood before his officers as they in turn would stand before their
crews, was bright with cheer and praise as he built them up
to do his new purpose. Before they left, their true spirit
had been restored by the quick, sharp genius of this leader
of fighting men, and each captain returned to his vessel
with fire enough to ignite his own tired crew to do the will
of General Arnold.

Alone in his cabin, Benedict Arnold carefully drew his
watch from his pocket and with an effort studied its two
black hands. He would take twenty minutes from that
dial, all to himself.

Twenty-one minutes later, he was on the deck. John
Frost, mate of the *Congress*, stood beside him, ready for the
maneuver that would take the fourteen remaining vessels
out through the British fleet. Like Carleton, Arnold in talking to his captains had used the simile of the rattlesnake: not
only how it reared and struck, holding its enemy at a distance, as they had held the British that day; but also, how
it slipped quickly and quietly away at the first pause in the
enemy's attack. Darkness had given him that pause, and

when Pringle had moved the gunboats, it was as though he had removed the bars of a cage. The way now lay clear to the Americans.

Captain Warner would lead in the *Trumbull*, close in along the west shore, hugging the bank; the course would be south, passing the *Maria* port-to-port but well inshore; then away for Ticonderoga, up the middle of the open lake. The rest would follow, guided by that dark-lantern in the center of the *Trumbull*'s stern. Then each in turn would show a dark-lantern to the vessel behind her, until at the end came the *Congress*, who would represent the stilled rattles in the snake's tail. If Arnold had gauged his lake correctly, there would be a fog this night, with a south wind rising in the morning, when the sun came up over the mountains of Vermont, which would drive away the characteristic thick fall mists of Lake Champlain.

So in the night, through the silence of the mist, the Americans slipped by the watching British fleet. There was not a watch boat to see them or to hear the drip-and-plunge as the oars of fourteen vessels rowed past. No watch hailed them from the deck of the *Maria*. It was as if the whole British fleet were fast asleep, from Sir Guy Carleton, Governor General of Canada and Commander in Chief, to the wounded drummer boy of the Hesse-Hannau Artillery Company, feverish in the bottom of his captain's gunboat.

General Horatio Gates, army commander of the northern department, had always controlled the Champlain fleet as a part of his army, thereby excluding any interference on the lake by Schuyler (Commander in Chief of the Northern Department), Washington (the over-all Commander in Chief), or the Naval Board of the Continental Congress. By issuing orders for the fleet to Brigadier General Benedict Arnold, the commander he had chosen, Gates himself also had established the strategic role of the Lake Champlain fleet in the campaign of 1776. The *tactics* for the fleet were the concern of its commander, General Arnold.

By inviting the British to attack the American fleet in Valcour Sound, Arnold had disobeyed his strategic instructions not to "assume a wanton risk," nor to "make a display" of his power. Gates had made the order explicit, in an attempt to curb the vainglory and reckless joy of battle which he knew to be in Benedict Arnold. But the orders of August 7 had not been enough to prevent the impetuous Arnold from throwing away, in a last desperate show of bravery, the fleet which, through so much toil, finally had been put into being. According to the grand strategy, the American fleet, found and built in 1776, was to stay "in being" on Lake Champlain for defensive and offensive campaigns yet to come.

For two months, the Champlain fleet under Arnold had "maintained possession of the lake" and had "prevented invasion by the army of the enemy." The rapidly advancing winter season made it likely, but not altogether certain, that those two months, together with an American fleet still intact, had bought a whole year of time for Gates and the northern army. By bringing on the battle of October 11, 1776, Arnold not only gambled a strategic victory but showed his own limitations as a general officer. Temperamentally, he was unable to resist the temptation to use, while it still remained his to direct, the great tool of war that he himself had done so much to build.

The risk that Arnold assumed on October 11, he paid for on October 13.

Seven miles above Valcour Island lay Schuyler Island, a little mound of green, sticking up out of Lake Champlain under the afternoon shadow of Mount Trembleau. On the morning of October 12, it became a tombstone for three of Benedict Arnold's ships. The *Lee* already was beached and half-sunk on the northeastern shore of the island. Two gondolas were careened over deep water, while their crews chopped gaping holes in their planking, preparing to scuttle them. Four more gondolas, their crews sleeping in huddled groups around dying cook-fires ashore, muzzled the island like piglets. Out on the lake, hovering around at the sea burial of the two gondolas, were the *Congress* and the *Washington,* the latter busy trying to brace a cracked mast. A wind was beginning to stir the low-hanging mist which dulled the thud of axes, as they fell on the wet green planking.

Arnold ordered the *Congress* rowed two hundred yards further away, the better to listen to the northward. The work went on; exhausted men slept; Arnold listened.

The wind came up from the south, as Arnold had expected. It was time to go. Soon Carleton would look into an empty pocket, and the Americans could expect a hot and angry pursuit. To judge from the demonstration of sailing ability given by the British vessels on the preceding day, Arnold's would still be the advantage of wind, if his tired men could be driven again into a rhythmic stroke at the long sweeps. Desperation would give them the beat and numb fatigue would keep it going, down to the very dregs of the barrel at the bottom of which was utter exhaustion.

Carleton discovered soon enough that his sorely wounded rattlesnake had vanished. But his next move assured the temporary survival of Arnold's rear guard of limping craft, and gave a safe getaway to the *Trumbull, Savage, Enter-*

prise, and *New York,* and to that other gondola, doggedly following on the long haul back to Ticonderoga.

Not believing it possible that fourteen vessels could have slipped through his cordon during the night, Carleton reasoned that the Americans must have gone out through the north exit from Valcour Sound. If so, he must pursue them and catch Arnold before he got in among the invasion bateaux, ready at Point au Fer and Windmill Point. If the Americans were retreating, as was likely, Carleton must throw his net across to the east shore. This was done, while he assured himself that the fog did not hide a northbound fleet. Forthwith, he sent the *Maria* charging across the lake, shouting orders to the vessels he encountered, still fogbound in the morning mist. Close to the eastern shore, Carleton had a moment of reprise. A hulk loomed through the mist, and the *Lady Maria* got off a broadside before recognizing it as a rock, white-capped with the lime of seagulls.

When a south wind came up and the fog lifted, to show Carleton the true position of the retreating Americans far up the lake, the British gave pursuit. Pursuers and pursued alike made slow work of the chase, Arnold's weary men hauling their heavy craft into the crests of the oncoming waves, and Pringle's salt sailors, unbearably cramped on the narrow lake in vessels designed for the long reaches of an open sea, darting from shore to shore on tacks that gained them little on their quarry.

Night forced the British ships to heave to, but the Americans struggled on at their oars, fighting the cold sleet and rain that drove against their aching backs, as they bucked the wind-lashed waves for another stroke, and another yard toward Crown Point.

With the morning of October 13 came discouragement for the Americans. Despite all their efforts, they had only come opposite Gilliland's Creek (Bouquet River); their toil had brought them no more than a scant ten miles from Schuyler's Island, which they had left so many terrible hours before. There was little comfort for the wretched fleet in the new wind that had sprung up out of the north. It could only bring the big *Inflexible*, scarcely touched by the battle two days earlier, all the more quickly down on the ragged-sailed, battered ships. The *Congress* hoisted her two big lateen sails, which filled easily and caused her to move forward with careless grace in contrast to the tedious pace of the oars. The four gondolas had hoisted their square sails, which billowed forward in the wind coming over their pointed sterns. The change from oars to sail made little difference in the pace of the shattered *Washington*. Under shortened sail on her patched mast, bilge water streaming from her scuppers as the crew labored at the pumps, gradually she fell behind her sister galley. As the gap widened between the two big American vessels, the oncoming *Inflexible* drew ever nearer. Now, in the dawn, she was level with Four Brothers Island and fast approaching under the tall tower of white canvas piled onto her three masts.

The *Congress*, her four gondolas moving ahead, had almost reached Split Rock, at the entrance to the narrows, when the *Washington* struck her colors. Bravely, she had fought her last fight, but the broadsides from the fresh crews at the *Inflexible*'s 12-pounders were too much for her. Foundering in the waves, one mast gone by the boards, and with the big orange-painted ship in position to rake over her stern, she gave up. Slowly her captain hauled down the red-and-white-striped flag. General Waterbury took it from him and silently awaited the boarding party. On the death of Captain John Thatcher from wounds on October 11, Captain David Hawley, late of the *Royal Savage*, had taken over command of the *Washington*. The loss of two ships

Champlain's Battle at Ticonderoga, July 1609
Cornell University Library

A north view of Crown Point (circa 1759) showing a British radeau
Courtesy of Prints and Photographs Division, Library of Congress

Benedict Arnold and his captains, Valcour Island, 1776
Fort Ticonderoga Museum

The American Fleet 1776. Left to right: *Revenge, Washington, Philadelphia, Congress, Jersey, Lee, Royal Savage;* foreground, *Spitfire, New Haven, Providence, Connecticut, New York, Enterprise, Trumbull*
Public Archives of Canada

The British Fleet, 1776. Left to right: *Carleton, Inflexible,* long boat, *Lady Maria, Loyal Convert, Thunderer*
Public Archives of Canada

Battle of Plattsburg Bay, September 1814, as seen from Platt's Point. Left to right: USS *Eagle*, HMS *Linnet*, USS *Saratoga*, HMS *Confiance*
Kynett Collection, Mystic Seaport, Mystic, Connecticut

Battle of Plattsburg Bay, September 1814, as seen from Cumberland Head. Left to right: British gunboats, USS *Ticonderoga*, USS *Eagle*, HMS *Confiance*, USS *Saratoga*, HMS *Linnet*
Fort Ticonderoga Museum

Louis Joseph,
Marquis de Montcalm

Jeffrey L
Amhe

*Portraits from
Fort Ticonderoga
Museum*

Commodore
Thomas Macdono

Major General
Benedict Arnold

Major Ge
Horatio (

within three days was too much for any man; General
Waterbury, second-in-command on the galley, would hand
over the bright ensign.

Before the *Washington*'s final battle, General Waterbury
had sent away, in the galley's towed bateau, Captain Rice
and sixteen men. When they came up to the *Congress*,
Arnold sent them posthaste to Ticonderoga with an urgent
request that a fleet of bateaux be sent to Crown Point to
row the remnant of his fleet back to the fort.

But this was not to be. The *Inflexible*, with the *Maria*
and the *Carleton*, caught up with the *Congress* in the narrows, where Arnold fought a stiff rear guard action to
keep the British away from the four little gondolas. Time
and again, through the afternoon of October 13, the two
long 18-pound stern chasers which Arnold had trained out
of the transom windows struck home in the pursuing British
vessels. With little room to maneuver, and gusty winds off
the mountains snatching at their sails, the three British captains jockeyed their vessels in an effort to bring a crushing
broadside to bear on the embattled Yankee. None of their
attempts to head, rake, or draw alongside was wholly successful.

Up the gut of the narrows wallowed the *Congress*, as
ungainly under oars as a maternal porcupine; after her
cavorted the three British hounds, barking invective from
the long guns in their bows. During the pursuit at close
range, which continued for four hours, the British gunnery
was good, and more telling than that of the Americans.
Twelve times, the *Congress* was hulled; two iron balls were
embedded in the mainmast, and one had cracked the long
yard. Frost, Arnold's first mate, had been killed. His body
and the bodies of three sailors were pitched overboard in a
hasty burial service of necessity. The wounded were passed
through the open hatch to the cockpit, where, drenched in

gore, the surgeon tenderly cut out a jagged raw splinter, or stuffed a gaping wound with shreds of cloth — cloth cut, as often as not, from his own stained coat.

Out of the stinking cockpit crawled the less seriously wounded, patched enough to go on fighting beside the mad general on the quarter-deck, who roared derision at the British when they missed and doffed his battered hat to the enemy in recognition of a fair hit; a general who pulled at a sheet rope when an extra hand was needed there, while at the same time he seemed to be kneeling beside every wounded man, to speak a word of encouragement. In battle, Benedict Arnold was neither general nor soldier; he was a flag, a rallying cry, a white plume, for which men fought as for an emblem dearer than life itself.

Step by step through the narrows, the *Congress* fought the three British vessels. Where the lake widened at Highlander's Bonnet, the Britishers prepared for the kill. With room to maneuver as a team, the two schooners bore away westward in an encircling movement, while the *Inflexible* turned to come abreast of the *Congress*, to sink her with crushing broadsides, or to drive her on shore. Pressed more and more closely in to the eastern shore, Benedict Arnold accepted the inevitable, and with a last effort made the most of it. The soundings he had taken in August gave him knowledge of a small teacup of a bay, three miles above the Bonnet. There, if he could yet make it, he could drain the last dregs of time needed for a final gesture of defense and defiance.

The *Congress* was last into the bay, with only minutes left in which to carry out Arnold's order to his gaunt and haggard men, for their mauled and leaking ships: "Spill out the cannon; then beach and burn the hulls."

This done, the men stood for a moment in silence, each one with a small, pitiful bundle of clothing under his arm, as they watched the flames lick up the rigging, and, in a last blaze of defiant glory, consume the flag at the masthead.

Far out on the lake, the British vessels were still maneuvering in an attempt to get up into gun range of the bay. To the American men on the shore, the English ships seemed to be of a strange and different element. It seemed to them unreal that they, too, had once been sailors, whose whole world had been under tall white clouds of canvas, within the narrow confines of a crowded deck.

The Year That Was Won

The sun had not yet dropped behind the western mountains, nor had the pall of black smoke lifted from the vessels afire in the little bay, before a courier in a fast canoe was on his way to fetch the British army waiting at the northern end of Lake Champlain. All night the paddles dipped, and all the next morning, until, at three o'clock in the afternoon of October 14, the aide landed at Point au Fer, waving the captured colors of the *Washington* for all the cheering advance guard to see. The soldiers embarked at once, General Nesbit's 1st Corps following close behind General Fraser.

Although the lake was now theirs, its wind and its weather were against the British. Butting against headwinds, or forced to seek shelter ashore for men and stores, the bateaux of the army took six days to make the voyage to Crown Point.

Not daring to enter the narrow lake south of the Point without a friendly army along the shore, the proud British fleet could only stand and wait upon the weather, each new day of southerly winds blunting the keen edge of the British thrust to Ticonderoga and the Hudson River.

For both fleets, the days of waiting were days of tidying up after battle. On the English side, there were recriminations; on the American, courts-martial and reorganization. Captain Pringle's conduct of the battle, and his unaggressive use of HMS *Lady Maria*, with Carleton aboard, became the subject of open criticism among the captains of the other vessels and among the Royal Artillery officers who had fought the gunboats so closely in Valcour Sound. Later, when Pringle's report of the battle was made public, the captains of the *Inflexible*, the *Loyal Convert*, and the *Lady Maria* signed a repudiation, which was little less than a thinly veiled accusation of cowardice. Perhaps an even more trenchant cause for discontent in their squadron command after such a great victory was the paucity of prizes. His share in such prizes represented the fulfillment of a naval officer's hopes for a comfortable retirement and a decent old age. The value of the captured vessels was appraised by a "Prize Court," which apportioned the money among the officers and men concerned in the capture, according to the degree in which each one had participated in the action. A fair apportionment was determined on the basis of the captain's official report. The discontent among the officers of the Lake Champlain squadron arose from Captain Pringle having permitted the American fleet to escape, as the result of an inadequate blockade; his not having pursued keenly enough on October 12; and further, they claimed that, in trying to beat up into the bay after Arnold's five vessels (which obviously were burning), he had let go a schooner, a sloop, a row galley and two gondolas — five good prizes. When the contents of Pringle's report became known, indignation in the fleet boiled over. In it, he had inflated his own bravery and control of the battle into a large share of the prize money for the captured *Washington*, as well as for the *Lee* and the *New Jersey*, recovered from Schuyler's Island.

In this dispute, military justice and admiralty fair play took their immutable course. Pringle was promoted to post captain, and died a vice-admiral; Dacres, of the *Carleton*, who had taken the report to London, became a post captain within five years, and vice-admiral in 1805. Lieutenant Schank turned his attention to inventing, and did not attain to a captain's rank until twenty years later; while Starke and Longcroft (with Schank, co-signers of the repudiation) disappeared from the Royal Navy List down that dead end to a naval career that service in the Lake Champlain squadron was to become.

Among the Americans, Benedict Arnold emerged from the Battle of Valcour Island a hero; others did not. Four men were court-martialed for declaring that they would not fight with the fleet when the British came — which they hoped would be soon. The charge was mutiny and the sentences were lenient: flogging for three of the accused, and for the fourth, an officer, humiliation and disgrace.

One James Butterworth, of Arnold's fleet, was condemned to be shot for a breach of the 27th Article for the Regulation of the Continental Army: "Trafficking with, and Harbouring, Receiving, and Protecting an Enemy." After five weeks' imprisonment in the cells at Ticonderoga, Butterworth received a pardon from General Gates, whereby military justice triumphed. The 27th Article did not carry the death penalty.

Horatio Gates and Benedict Arnold tidied up the fleet and repaired the defenses at Ticonderoga. Like so much trash found in a corner, the defeatists and unregenerate malcontents were swept out. The sick were provided with women's care, and went to the hospital at the southern tip of Lake George for cure, recovery, and rehabilitation, after which they returned to their regiments.

When General Waterbury and the other prisoners from the fleet were returned under a flag of truce, they were hurried through the American camp as though infected with smallpox. The generals feared the contagion of defeat, and infection of the good will that General Carleton, before releasing them on parole, had implanted so studiously in the prisoners from the *Washington*. No chance must be taken with the temper of the soldiers who stood at Ticonderoga, their backs to the Hudson River gateway.

Enemy troops were at Crown Point. Their advance guard and their Indians prowled the American picket line. Lake Champlain was merely a boat pond for the British fleet.

A log boom was stretched across the lake, from the low ground north of Ticonderoga to Hand's Cove on the eastern shore. Behind the boom, Benedict Arnold again waited to receive the enemy. The boom was guarded by the guns of three veterans of Valcour Island: the *Revenge*, *Enterprise*, and *Trumbull*, synchronized with the land battery in the redoubt. Taking her place for the first time in the American battle line was Captain Chappelle's galley, the *Gates*. With her was Skene's old schooner, now the *Liberty*, which had been on a run back to Ticonderoga for supplies and so had missed the action of October 11–13. The Americans' position was one of static defense. It was to serve as a deterrent to British naval attack, leaving no room in which to maneuver and offering a poor risk for a slugging match, even with the big guns and howitzers of the *Thunderer*.

The Americans waited, but the English did not come, either by land or by water.

At Crown Point, the British were waiting for a decision at a high-command level. Burgoyne, the dashing cavalry general, was for attacking; Carleton, the staff officer, was in a turmoil of indecision from the standpoint of logistics. The lateness of the season, imposed on him by the summer's naval race, gave him pause. It was past the time when a conservative commander should be laying up his naval vessels against the impending freeze. Already, the effect of the autumn winds and storms was felt on the long supply line to St. Jean. The slow passage of the bateaux fleet could maintain only one brigade, in addition to the advance guard at Crown Point. Carleton could neither stock-pile supplies nor concentrate his main force at the forward position at the Point. With his five hundred and sixty bateaux — which last summer had seemed so many! — no practical logistic timetable could be worked out. The three brigades camped at the northern end of Lake Champlain might as well be mounting guard at Buckingham Palace, for all the effect they would have on any attack that Carleton could launch that autumn of 1776 against the Americans at Ticonderoga. Reluctantly, General Carleton came to the conclusion that his campaign was over for that year, its high-water mark the victory of October 11–13 and the crest of the wave of his advance, the ruined forts on Crown Point.

The attrition of idleness attacked the British army at Crown Point. Burgoyne sailed away on the prize *Washington*, bound for England and the division lobbies of the House of Commons, where he was a member. On October 30, Captain Scott of the *Thunderer* took advantage of a favorable wind to set out for St. Jean. Gallant young officers took to visiting the nearby *habitations* in search of a pretty face, nor did they inquire too closely into the political views of their hostesses, so long as these views were not too apparent.

Of all the fleet, only the small boats kept their interest in the enemy. Of these, the most active was a longboat commanded by young Midshipman Pellew. Patrolling to the south one day, toward a point where he could see the distant fort, Pellew surprised an American boat and gave chase with a free heart. From his place at the tiller bar, he soon saw that he was gaining on the other boat, and he called a faster stroke to his sailors, who responded with a will. He would have caught the boat, too, had not the American officer in the stern swung 'round on to a rowing bench, and pausing only long enough to pluck the tight black stock from around his throat, pulled on an oar. The race led Pellew to shore, where he landed so close behind the Yankees that they escaped only by leaping into the shallows and dashing to the forest. Pellew captured the American boat, taking from it, as a souvenir, the officer's discarded stock. From other articles found in the stern, this was identified as the property of Benedict Arnold!

The last foray on October 28, when three English boats, each mounting a field gun on its carriage, ventured as far as Three Mile Point and loitered there all day, brought the campaign season to a close. One of the boats came close enough to draw fire from a battery covering the boom, and the *Gates* took her maiden shot at the British, in company with the *Trumbull*. Five days later, the English had left Crown Point, and the Americans went into winter quarters.

The winter of 1776–77 was a very severe one in the Champlain Valley. Snow had fallen as early as September 26, covering the decks of the American boats behind Valcour Island, awaiting the arrival of the British fleet. On November 1, a heavy snow squall had powdered the baggage which the British had piled on the shore at Crown Point in preparation for their departure the following day. The big snows were to come early that winter.

On December 10, 1776, the lake froze over on that long stretch from South Bay up to the deep, wide waters above Crown Point. The next day, the Pennsylvania men who were building a hut village at the old French lines west of the fort were racing and playing on six inches of smooth, hard ice in the creek below their camp. A soldier named Turner wandered off while drunk and fell asleep under a pine tree, where he froze to death; what was presumed to be his body, much mangled by wolves, was found the following spring.

In view of these early prospects of a harsh winter, Colonel Anthony Wayne, who had been left in charge, set to work to make a snug garrison out of Fort Ticonderoga and Mount Independence.

Wayne, a thirty-one-year-old Pennsylvanian, had under his command three battalions from his own state and one each from Connecticut, New Jersey, and Massachusetts. As an efficient officer soon to be made brigadier general, he expected (and was therefore able to avert) serious outbreaks of sectional feeling. He did this by keeping his rough Pennsylvanians and the Jersey men on the Ticonderoga side of the lake, leaving the dour New Englanders to carry on their own ancient doctrinal disputes side by side on Mount Independence. Wayne's particular concern was to forestall the rotting of morale among the men left idle to fend for themselves in the hut-and-tent village at the old French lines. Unless measures were taken in advance, disease of epidemic proportions was to be expected among the weather-bound troops crowded into fetid barrack rooms.

The men called Wayne everything from "nit picker" to "mad Anthony," and cursed him roundly and explicitly each week, as they worked to turn out smartly for his Sunday dress parade. But they kept their franchise as members of the human race, and their curses grew habitual rather than pointed as they became accustomed to being shaven, and began to feel odd if their hair was not combed out, queued, and powdered. Men went voluntarily to the regimental tailor to have an elbow patch sewn on to a worn rifle shirt, while the rumor that new wool hats were coming from Philadelphia stirred the units to rivalry — quite out of proportion to the warmth expected — as to who would be issued the new headgear when it arrived.

Twice weekly, the tightly closed barrack rooms and huts were fumigated by burning tar or pitch. A regimental officer supervised each mess to see that no meat was fried; all meat had to be boiled in soups, and flour for dumplings was provided twice a week.

Wayne's campaign for a garrison kept healthy through cleanliness was inaugurated with threats, and these were carried out. The daily parole and countersign usually took the form of a challenge, such as "Philadelphia?" calling for the reply, "Pennsylvania," or other easily associated geographical or proper names. Wayne, however, instituted a series of combinations of words designed to make the men think. Thus, "Military?" brought the reply, "Discipline"; "Courage?" — "Conduct"; "Exercise?" — "Health"; "Disobedience?" — "Cowardice." "Liberty?" was "Happiness," while "Honor?" meant "Virtue."

Drink and women plagued the colonel in his campaign to save the men from themselves and to protect the safety of the northern frontier, vulnerable to a winter attack by a sled-borne army. Drink was a question of stealth, and a game of hide-and-seek between the men and authority. It was not at all a moral issue; rum was issued liberally to men on sentry duty, and the much-damned "Dress-up-like-a-soldier" parade each Sunday was accompanied by an issue of rum as an inducement to make the effort. But drunkenness made shambles of the barracks, or took the men across the bridge to the other camp for an interregimental, interstate religious war.

Such women as were in the army presumably had husbands, and in fact, they often did have a succession of husbands, new ones accruing to them as the old ones faded away. Company or regimental loyalty was equally strong in the breasts of the women and in the men who provided the husbands necessary to keep the loyalty of a cheerful washerwoman. It was in this capacity that the women served, and it was for this that they drew their rations. Wayne's greatest trouble lay in the huts of his own Pennsylvanians, for in the barracks a closer control could be exercised. He understood his own men, and appealed to them, wisely avoiding an accusation against any specific female, but citing the duty of a company washerwoman to keep the men clean and decent, not to render them unfit for duty. To dampen the high spirits of the women, Wayne provided plenty of wood and water and all the laundry they could do, with an alternative of being drummed out of the regiment.

Though the word "washerwoman" had a leer to it when drawled by a Yankee or garbled by a Pennsylvania Dutchman, the women in the army were invaluable, especially in the hospitals. As a whole, they were moral and were devoted to the men they followed to such harsh places as Ticonderoga, suspended at a wilderness crossroad between Albany and Montreal. For any soldier to insult a woman, or to offer money to "entice" any female, was a court-martial offense.

As work kept the washerwomen out of mischief, work also was made for the men, so that they would be grateful to seek their blankets at the sound of the evening gun.

A committee from the Continental Congress, bundled in greatcoats and swathed in scarves, came to Ticonderoga on the last lap of an inspection tour. Tight-lipped and uncommunicative, they went away to write a report favoring the northern army, and outlining the work to be done in order to secure the frontier at Ticonderoga.

The works which they proposed and which the Congress

sanctioned were taken from a list prepared by Colonel Jeduthan Baldwin, who already had started on the program. Barracks had been erected on Mount Independence, and plans for hospitals were being drafted; the commission had been particularly shocked by conditions existing in the medical department. Blockhouses and gun platforms were to be built, and for the days when wind howled around the scaffolding and tools fell from stiffened fingers, inside work was outlined: 1000 hand barrows, carriages for 100 cannon, new ash handles for all the old tools that were needed now, or that would be needed by the new regiments expected to arrive in the spring.

The commissioners looked over the six vessels of the fleet, the schooners and the sloop having been hauled out of the water and decked over. The *Gates* and the *Trumbull* were hedged around with piles, and served as barracks for a detachment whose duty it was to keep the ice cut away from the hulls. Close by lay the gondola *New York*, a little shack built amidships as a home for the sergeant's guard who were its maintenance crew.

Plans for the fleet had changed since Benedict Arnold had left in November for Albany and a new command in New England. Without the prodding of the fiery brigadier general, staff thinking had shifted from offense to defense. The lesson of Valcour Island was interpreted as an overwhelming case for the big ship-of-war, such as the *Inflexible*. It was irrelevant to speculate on the striking force in the eight row galleys that Arnold had wanted, and that Gates and Schuyler had begged for. Sail had defeated oars on October 11, 12, and 13, 1776. It was useless to point out that oars had saved the entire fleet during the nocturnal escape out of Valcour Sound, or that the American *Congress* had outmaneuvered the three British sailing ships during the precious hours of her rear-guard action.

There was to be no naval race on Lake Champlain in
1777. Ticonderoga, Mount Independence, and the landing
at Lake George would be defended. The lake navy of the
Americans would be used as a boom defense on the lake
just north of the fort, and two floating batteries should be
built to increase the fire power out on the lake. A bateau
service should be set up to relieve gunned vessels of any
transport duty. This transport corps should have a strength
of four hundred and sixty-five men divided into fifteen companies, each with its own overseer.

Behind the boom, which had been reinforced with piles
driven upright into the mud bottom of the lake, and even
behind the line of vessels, cribs would be sunk across the narrow passage between the high cliff at the extremity of the
Ticonderoga Peninsula and the escarpment at the northern
end of Mount Defiance. This obstacle would prevent the
big British ships from getting to the supply route south to
Skenesborough and Wood Creek — something neither the
boom nor the fleet was wholly expected to do. To protect
the main supply route the length of Lake George, Colonel
Jeduthan Baldwin was ordered to complete and strengthen
the barbette battery on Mount Hope, a mile west of Ticonderoga, which dominated the portage road between the
two lakes.

Work on the cribs was not begun until the ice on the lake
was at its thickest and the days of winter were lengthening
and warming toward the spring thaw. Each crib was a
basket of heavy logs, built up on the ice to a height greater
than the depth of water below it. Rocks were dumped into
the basket so that, when the ice around it was sawed out, the
rock-filled basket, still in an upright position, sank to the
bottom. More rocks were then dropped into the crib, until
it was deemed to be firmly anchored against the tremendous

pressure of the floes to be expected with the break-up of the ice.

On March 9, 1777, ten cribs had been cut in without mishap, and in celebration, Colonel Baldwin gave a dinner party at which, among other guests, were two ladies. The next day the last two cribs were successfully put in place. By March 13, the ice was too weak to hold a team of horses, and the work of hauling stone was rushed ahead by men with wheelbarrows. Even so, on March 26, one of the piers fell to pieces; soon after, the bottom fell out of another, and the ungainly thing rose partially out of the water. Baldwin recovered the second, but the first one had to be replaced by a floating caisson when the lake became free of ice.

All bets as to the day the ice would go out were paid by April 12, and at the boatyards, bateaux were soaking out their dried seams to the accompaniment of the spring banter among the men at work in them with bailing scoops. With the open water came the threats of raids by British boats. The boom was floated back in place at the Jersey redoubt on April 12, only six days before American rangers sighted four British vessels six miles north of Crown Point.

Invasion was imminent as the American garrison emerged from its hibernation. There was a last round of dinner parties before the ladies who had graced the officers' mess slipped off up Lake George. From their bateaux, they waved handkerchiefs to the disconsolate officers who had escorted them to the landing in one last gay excursion. Now, with the increased tempo of the work, less and less frequently would little groups of officers be strolling off down the Hubbardton road behind Mount Independence for an evening's congenial drinking at "The Scotsman's."

General Wayne's promotion had been announced in February, and the last of the old camaraderie that he had worked so hard to build died with the arrival of the new regiments, who proved a ragged-looking, undisciplined lot. Soon General Wayne was ordered elsewhere, and the Scot, Arthur St. Clair, the new stars of a major general on his epaulets, returned to take command of the defense of Ticonderoga. He had less than a month's time, and less than half the troops he needed, to meet the invasion with any hope of stopping it.

On the lake, St. Clair had the five vessels and the gondola remaining from Arnold's fleet of the previous year. No floating batteries had been constructed. Only the log boom barred the lake, together with the obstructing cribs which now, with interspaced pontoons, served as a heavy bridge. This bridge seemed a formidable barrier, beside which the old footbridge appeared very flimsy. Surely this obstacle would stop the British fleet: the *Thunderer*, the *Lady Maria*, the *Carleton*, the new ship (as large as the *Inflexible*, or larger), and the other radeau, which was called the *Land Crab* and was a towering castle floating on the water. Arthur St. Clair had good intelligence reports from Canada; he knew what was coming against him.

General St. Clair had arrived at Ticonderoga on June 12, 1777. He came in the late afternoon, when the dominating bulk of Sugar Loaf Mountain cast a grateful coolness over the wide basin south of the peninsula, where a few regimental bateaux were fishing in the shadow of the mountain. That same evening the main body of Burgoyne's Anglo-German army was making its first camp a few days' journey up the Richelieu River, on its way to Ticonderoga and Albany.

Johnny Burgoyne Moves South

The year 1777 began auspiciously enough for the English and German soldiers who remained in Canada. Billeted by regiments in Montreal and in the neighboring towns and villages, all elements of the army entered into and shared the life of the *habitants*. With a minimum of military duties, the men made themselves useful around the farms and in the thick-walled Canadian houses which were their winter homes. Montreal, where the young Lady Maria Carleton held court and where local hostesses saw, in well-placed young gentlemen, opportunities for gaiety not enjoyed since the chevaliers of Montcalm's army had been there, gave the officers a social season as unusual as it was unexpected in a provincial capital.

From as far away as Sorel, officers with a pair of fast horses could travel the sleigh road marked out on the St. Lawrence for a moonlight skating party at Montreal, and still be back in time to take the morning parade. Only a few thought the ice could be used to better advantage for an expedition against the Americans, isolated at Ticonderoga. For the most part, these few were embittered Tories, who on their own initiative made an occasional ambush against travelers on Lake George.

All was not cheer, however, for the British army in its winter quarters. Harsh punishment, quickly imposed, was meted out to the soldier who trespassed on the good will of the *habitant*, guarded so zealously by General Carleton. Most of the trouble resulted from clashes between the King's troops and the German mercenaries. The latter, lacking the Britishers' sense of humor, grew morose in the alien climate and became victims of an epidemic of self-induced melancholia, from which several died.

The army wintering in Canada awaited only the return from London of General John Burgoyne, who would bring with him additional regiments. Early in May, exuding all his winning, courtly grace, Burgoyne came up the ice-free St. Lawrence on the British frigate *Apollo*. His time at home had been well spent in Parliament and in the offices and parlors of influential ministers of the Crown. On at least one occasion, he had been seen riding in the Row, deep in conversation with His Majesty, the King.

Lieutenant General Burgoyne returned to Canada as commander in chief for the 1777 campaign, superseding Sir Guy Carleton. The situation was embarrassing for both gentlemen, but Burgoyne's tact in victory was exceeded only by Carleton's generous co-operation. The former brought with him news of Guy Carleton's knighthood, and of the gracious permission of George III for Carleton to assume the title before the formality of an investiture.

Burgoyne tarried in Montreal only long enough to pick up the reins of command and to explain his plan for the invasion. This plan had been proposed in London to Lord George Germaine, colonial secretary in the cabinet of Lord North, whose ministry directed the army in putting down the rebellion in the Atlantic colonies, and had been accepted. The army in Canada was to be divided: the lesser part, under the experienced leadership of Barry St. Leger, would advance on Albany by way of the Mohawk Valley; Burgoyne, with the main body of the army, would swoop through the valleys of Lake Champlain and Lake George and would reach Albany by way of the upper Hudson River. In Albany, the reunited army from Canada would be joined by the army from New York, under General Howe. So confident was the ebullient Burgoyne that he brought with him a replacement lieutenant and some recruits for one of Howe's regiments, guaranteeing quick delivery.

Everyone connected with the army felt so optimistic that no one hurried; they all drifted forward on the irresistible tide of Burgoyne's confidence. The festivities of the winter carried over into the preparations for the campaign, everyone planning and giving advice with enthusiastic strokes of a rose-colored brush. Even the four hundred painted Indians, led by the old white-bearded devil, St. Luc de la Corne, and the nefarious Langlade, seemed in the camp to be like actors in a water pageant. The rhetoric of Burgoyne's speech of exhortation to the men was fine enough for a midsummer's masque, and as dramatic. So was the proclamation of amnesty and friendship that he sent to the colonists in New York — before he sent the Indians. Philip Skene, who was returning to Skenesborough with Burgoyne, told the general of the welcome he would receive from the honest farmer folk of New York and the Hampshire grants, awaiting liberation from the yoke of Whig democracy.

In the wings, as comic relief before the curtain rose on Burgoyne's regatta and water extravaganza, stalked the Brunswick Dragoons, stiff-legged in their enormous boots, their waxed mustachios bristling, long queues hanging down their backs, and at each man's heels, clanking like a fetter, a monstrous sword in a metal scabbard. Unfortunately, the dragoons had no horses, but Skene assured them that these could be procured from grateful settlers down the line of march.

Sir Guy Carleton, accompanied by his lady and his court,

came to St. Jean to see the embarkation ceremony. It was well worth the journey, as the spectacle had been designed and staged by Burgoyne, in whom the dramatic instinct was never suppressed. That the cast far outnumbered the spectators concerned the impresario not at all. The whole elaborate performance was calculated to impress the actors themselves, rather than the few townspeople of St. Jean, a scattering of farmers whose plowing was done, and here and there a Yankee spy.

A pre-dawn hurry and bustle had stirred the camps of the departing regiments. Now, with the sun well up, the ranks stood in idle resignation to the army's creed: "Hurry up . . . and wait." Packs, rolled with blankets, dragged on the backs of the waiting soldiers, and the trenchant whispered comments of slum-bred British privates died out in painful immobility. Leather crossbelts as heavy as horses' harness cut into the men's shoulders, while the Germans, like cattle, kept their rigid ranks under the tongue lashing of mustachioed sergeants. The June sun was hot on the thick blue coats of the gunners, who blinked in the glare from the polished brass of their pieces.

At last, with the morning well advanced, a staff officer strode importantly onto the field at the water's edge, and orders snapped and crackled like musket fire in an ambush, as company after company stiffened to attention. The massed bands blared out, and to their music General Carleton and General Burgoyne, accompanied by all the general officers of the army, strolled down to the pinnaces at the edge of the river.

Out on the water floated the fortresslike *Thunderer*, her masts bare, her crew manning the bulwarks, their arms folded, rigidly at attention. As the band's gay air came to an end, a hush fell on the general officers, who turned and faced the big radeau. There was a flurry of red silk on the high quarter-deck as four heralds flourished their trumpets and blew a royal fanfare out over the river and above the motionless parade. Then, slowly rising up to the masthead, climbed a large silken flag, all reds and blues and yellow gold. As it reached the peak, a wind stirred out the folds to show to all the Royal Standard of England. Never before had the Royal Standard been flown, save over the person of His Majesty. The awesome moment passed, and Burgoyne led the troops in a rousing "Three cheers for the King!" Carleton, in his viceregal capacity as governor general, acknowledged the salute. Three cheers were then given for His Majesty's allies, a salute which was acknowledged by General the Baron von Riedesel, in command of Burgoyne's Germans. Farewells were said and the generals embarked, leaving only the governor's party on shore to wave them out of sight toward Lake Champlain and the enemy. Behind Carleton, cannons boomed a measured salute and the massed bands played gay tunes from the London music halls, as the regiments marched to their waiting bateaux. Then, one by one the bands fell silent, as they, too, filed off to their embarkation points.

General Fraser and his advance guard had not waited for the official embarkation but had sailed the day before for Ligonier Point, near the Four Brothers Islands. With him, Fraser had taken the four hundred Indians, who had no place in the pretty play enacted at St. Jean but would be useful in a rush across a tilled acre to the door of an isolated cabin.

Each of the thirty officers of Major Acland's grenadiers embarked with half of a Cheshire cheese, a parting gift of their commander's wife. This addition to their luggage made more difficult the already crowded conditions in their bateaux, a situation which they endured in holiday spirits. Those commanding the artillery boats were more fortunate:

these boats were larger and more commodious, and, as their complement was less, a degree of privacy could be arranged in the stern.

The bateaux anchored at dusk, and the men went ashore to make camp in the woods. The officers joined in regimental or company messes around blazing campfires. Occasionally, a band would strike up somewhere in the camp, and the music carried out across the water to where, with sails furled and lights showing in the wide open windows of the after cabins, the British fleet lay at anchor.

Up ahead of the main army, the Indians danced their boasting dances and celebrated the taking of their first prisoners — two scouts seized on the Onion River.

By day, everyone took to the water in a long cavalcade of boats, with the bark canoes at the point and the sutlers' boats bringing up the rear. The latter were piled high with goods and wares, on top of which were perched the women in bright colored skirts and shawls.

In front of the ragged tail made by the straggling line of civilian craft sailed the transports. These were the proud warships of 1776: the *Lady Maria, Carleton, Loyal Convert,* and *Thunderer,* and the American prizes *Washington, Lee,* and the gondola *New Jersey.* The prizes were now rigged to the English taste. There was also that relic of the old French wars, the absurd-looking box-on-water now called the *Land Crab.* Lashed and braced on the decks of these vessels was the train of cannon intended for the siege of Ticonderoga — a mighty assemblage of one hundred and twenty-eight guns, mortars and howitzers. In the holds were piled boxes of shells of nine different caliber, and barrels of powder enough for the saturation bombardment of the American fleet and field works.

Up forward, leading the trim columns of bateaux which carried the two divisions of the army, HMS *Inflexible* rode abreast of her slightly larger consort, the new *Royal George*. Each of these towed parts of a large log boom, which was designed to bar the narrow lake between Crown Point and Chimney Point. Of all the British fleet, these two vessels and the twenty gunboats of the Royal Artillery were the only ones ready to give battle, should the remnant of Arnold's fleet sail out from behind the boom across the lake at Ticonderoga. On his flagship, the *Royal George*, Captain Skeffington Lutwidge, Pringle's successor as Commodore of the Lake, felt confident that in such an event his two sloops-of-war could handle the six Yankee vessels.

The progress of the great regatta was leisurely rather than slow. There seemed ample time to enjoy the beauty of the season, the great lake in its broad valley, and the companionship of good comrades. To a certain extent, the pace was regulated by the progress down the west shore of the fifteen hundred horses of Burgoyne's transport, which would be needed at the portage from Ticonderoga to Lake George, and again from Lake George to Fort Edward on the Hudson River. It was ten days before the army arrived at Ligonier's Bay, (Willsboro Bay), the advance guard being at the Bouquet River, only three miles ahead.

At four-thirty in the morning of June 23, the army was to move again, with the advance guard to proceed boldly to Crown Point. But when the bateaux rounded the Point, a gale struck them and they were forced back. The advance guard did better: they battled the waves as far as Button Mold Bay, but suffered the loss of two bateaux, which were swamped. The *Loyal Convert* tipped over and was righted only by cutting her two masts. A pet fawn was washed overboard and drowned, in spite of every effort to save her. The storm continued through the next day, with violent thundershowers and a thick fog which caught the main body of the fleet while still below the narrows. On that day, however, the light infantry, grenadiers, and the 24th Foot, advancing despite the weather, stormed ashore at Crown Point — only to find it in ruins and empty of defenders, unchanged since they had left it eight months before.

On June 26 and 27, the army arrived at the Point and unloaded the transports, though the heaviest siege guns, which were on the two radeaux, had not yet come up. While the army waited for the big guns, the *Inflexible* and the *Royal George* were towed up the lake to Putnam's River, both shores being secured as far as that point by the advance guard of British and Germans. Carefully planning each move, Burgoyne slowly advanced his troops. On July 1, 1777, the army was in a position to invest the American positions on the Ticonderoga Peninsula and on Mount Independence. The plan of advance was up both shores of the lake, Major General Baron von Riedesel's Germans on the east, Major General William Phillips' English on the west, and the heavy guns of the fleet on the lake between them. At Three Mile Point (named for its distance from Fort Ticonderoga), the enveloping movement from east and west would begin, holding the Americans in a bear's embrace while the big cannon mangled the helpless victims.

On July 2, the enveloping movement began. The first and second days of the battle moved according to plan. There was no reaction from the Americans, other than a small play by the artillery in their vessels and water batteries, directed against Lieutenant Colonel Breymann's advance guard of Germans on the east shore. Over on the right, one man and an artillery horse of General Powell's brigade were killed.

The third day, detecting a certain softness to the American left, Burgoyne developed his right wing by bringing across the lake General Gall's brigade of two German regiments and extending his British division, under Phillips, around to the sawmill, thus firmly establishing his position across the road to Lake George. On Mount Hope, the American position fell. The guns in the floating batteries were brought ashore, for it was found that the lake was too low at that time of the year and that the clumsy craft were in constant danger of grounding.

At a conference of the British generals on the evening of July 4, considerable excitement was caused by the report of General Fraser's advance corps artillery commander. This officer, Captain Ellis Walker, a gunner with twenty-two years' commissioned service, that day had scouted a way for cannon up the back face of Sugar Loaf Mountain to its summit, which overlooked the whole American position. British artillery on the mountain would make both Ticonderoga and Mount Independence untenable by the Americans. Walker was called in and given orders to install a battery of 12-pounders on Sugar Loaf. The mission was to be carried out with the utmost secrecy. It is difficult to understand how the Americans, or Abercromby and Amherst in 1758 and 1759, could have neglected the dominating feature of the entire tactical situation.

That night, two 12-pounders were moved around the perimeter of the British right wing, and at sun-up the barrels, wheels, carriages, ammunition, powder, and tools were assembled among the trees at the foot of the long valley that swept eastward up to the top of Sugar Loaf Mountain. Walker led the way, marking the way for the brush cutters to follow. Teams of horses, which could be used for part of the road, were ready and harnessed. The men waited, having no idea of the toil in store for them when the horses would falter and manpower would be called upon to drag the heavy pieces up the last steep incline.

In the afternoon, Walker and his survey party stepped out from the trees and stood triumphantly looking down on the American position.

The two forts were laid out like a plan. Each battery was marked by new-turned earth, and men could be seen moving about the guns. A company of riflemen crossed the floating bridge, which Walker noticed was now on the south side of the pier bridge, over which a mounted officer was coaxing a nervous horse.

The American fleet lay at anchor on both sides of the lake barrier. Bateaux lined the south shore of the stone fort, over which flew the Rebels' "Liberty Flag." To the north floated the American log boom, anchored at the big Jersey redoubt, which was out of range from the mountain top. Further to the north, Walker could see the British vessels and bateaux anchored in position or tailing off up the silvery lake on the supply line to Crown Point.

As Captain Walker was looking down on the panorama before him, the carriage and wheels of his Number One gun arrived at the summit. Under the direction of a red-faced, panting gun sergeant, the sweating crew fitted the wheels to the axles. A few yards off to the west, a man in shirtsleeves fell to with drill and hammer, cutting an eyebolt into the hard rock. The ring of his hammer was sharp and clear and made a musical sound in contrast to the dull booming of cannon, drifting up out of the valley.

Looking through his telescope, General St. Clair had seen Captain Walker and his group soon after they stepped out onto the bold summit of Sugar Loaf Mountain. He had recognized them immediately as artillery officers, and when the gun carriage was rolled up beside them it merely confirmed his fears. Through his glass, he saw the final tableau of the fall of Ticonderoga: a gun on the mountain, up which a gun could not be carried!

St. Clair ordered a secret evacuation of the American position for that night of July 5.

"The World Turned Upside Down"

Surgeon James Thatcher was awakened about midnight, to
learn that the American army was in motion and that Fort
"Ti" and Mount Independence were to be abandoned at
once. His orders were to collect the sick and wounded, with
as much of the hospital supplies as possible, and have them
loaded on the boats and the bateaux at the shore.

Somehow, during the next three hours, Thatcher rounded
up men out of the confusion of the night and set them to
work carrying his wounded and bed-sick on to the boats.
He himself toted cases of medicines down to the shore,
where he tended his patients, then hurried back up the steep
climb to the hospital, where other patients required attention
and other medical supplies awaited transportation to the
boats. Before three o'clock in the morning, Thatcher made
his last trip to the deserted hospital. All the patients had
gone except for one man, who lay dead on his pallet of
straw; the surgeon covered the man's face with a blanket.
In his own quarters, Thatcher hurriedly packed a small box
with his personal effects and returned to the landing. The
bateau with his medical stores was waiting for him; it was
the last boat to leave Ticonderoga.

The transition from moonlight to dawn was almost im-
perceptible on the morning of July 6; it was the birds that
woke Thatcher — his second awakening that day. Their
early song seemed to fill the forest, which compressed the

lake into a stream filled with southbound boats. Men from
Colonel Long's New Hampshire regiment were at the oars
of Surgeon Thatcher's boat, in the stern of which was a
group of sleeping women. Their men were marching with
the main army, overland to Skenesborough by way of the
hamlet of Hubbardton.

In the retreat up Lake Champlain there were two hundred
bateaux, each one packed with stores and crowded with men
and women. Four armed vessels led the bateaux up the
channel through the marshes, flushing wild duck from
their nests and ungainly blue herons from off their fishing
grounds. At the very rear of the long procession came the
galley *Gates*. Behind her, the birds dropped back into their
accustomed places, complained for a moment, and were
silent.

In this order, the refugee flotilla rowed on to the old
shipyard at Skenesborough, where, by the middle of the
afternoon, all had landed.

At first light, three deserters entered the British lines
bringing news of the American withdrawal. Suspecting a
trap, a patrol probed forward over the old French trenches,
and on entering into Ticonderoga, the tale was confirmed.

Immediately, every drum in the army beat the call to
arms, and the whole British camp was standing to.

The grenadiers and light infantry moved out at once for
the bridge leading to Mount Independence. They crossed
in single file, for, though the bridge had been partially
destroyed, the job had not been completed. On the west
shore they encountered the bridge guard, lying dead drunk
beside two loaded cannon, a match burning slowly in a
bucket. The Yankees had finished off a keg of Madeira during their long night watch.

Hardly had the last grenadier gone over when the British

gunboats were at the bridge, tearing away planks and towing off the pontoon between two piers. Within thirty minutes, Colonel Baldwin's lake barrier had been broken through widely enough to permit entry of Britain's two largest vessels.

Three of the American vessels had been run ashore north of the bridge and had been scuttled; that left three of the larger vessels somewhere up ahead. Not trusting the *Inflexible* or the *Royal George* to the narrow lake and marshes to the south, Commodore Lutwidge sent the *Carleton* and the *Washington* in pursuit, and with them, ten of the swiftest gunboats. He was sure that the *Washington*, in any case, could navigate the shallows: she had been launched at Skenesborough.

The channel to Skenesborough Basin, at the foot of the last falls of Wood Creek, turned east out of the very northern end of South Bay. It ran for a mile, close under high cliffs on the north and a double-humped hill on the south, then turned abruptly south into the wider marsh-fringed reach and the ample pool below the falls. It was rather like a rabbits' warren, with its tight, long approach through the brambles to the home nest — snug, roomy, and safe.

Captain John Carter of Burgoyne's artillery, at the head of his flotilla of ten gunboats, burst into Skenesborough at five o'clock that afternoon, ferrets among the rabbits. Surprise had been complete. The British boats, joined by the *Washington* and the *Carleton*, bombarded everything in an orgy of destruction. Bateaux were sunk or blasted on the shore; great gaps were opened in the log stockade by the heavy round shot, fired at close range; and beneath the falls, the *Gates*, two sailing vessels, the gondola *New York*, and an experimental bomb boat were caught with guns run in and secured, while two hundred barrels of powder were being unloaded from their holds. Two of the armed vessels struck their colors at once; the other three blew up in a crashing explosion that rent them asunder, tore them to bits, and scattered remnants far and wide over the mountain and the shipyard where the American Lake Champlain navy had come to birth.

By five o'clock, Surgeon Thatcher had seen most of his patients off for Fort Anne by way of Wood Creek. He had been invited to share the meal of a French family living in one of the four tenant houses still standing at Philip Skene's seat, and he was there when the first shell from Captain Carter's British gunboats landed. It struck the wall of the Frenchman's house, which it penetrated, shattering the dinner table at which the little company had gathered. Thatcher ran out into a scene of complete confusion: shouts came from the bateaux, yelling from the stockade, and from the sawmill where the Fort Anne road climbed up around the falls came the long, high, piercing scream of a woman's cry: "Indians!" For an instant, stiffening fear crippled the Americans, then, as the dreaded cry was taken up, terror drove the refugees into heedless, unreasoning panic.

At the top of the falls, Colonel Long was snatching soldiers out of a mob of fleeing people in an attempt to get together some kind of a rear guard. Thatcher was half a mile down the road when the ships blew up, and Benedict Arnold's brave fleet was gone from Lake Champlain in a big black cloud, billowing up out of Skenesborough.

~~~~~~~~~

The headlong American retreat from the Ticonderoga positions and out of the Champlain Valley not only gave Burgoyne a notable success, but it gave him time not scheduled in his itinerary. Like many another tourist, he took this added time as a windfall to be squandered in rest and relaxation, rather than as an opportunity to press on toward the wonders and adventures in the next valley.

On the afternoon of July 6, General Burgoyne arrived at South Bay with his staff, three regiments, the *Royal George* and the *Inflexible*. By nightfall he was in Skenesborough, politely having delayed his arrival in order to give a member of his staff, Major Philip Skene, time to go ahead and prepare Skenesborough House to receive guests. The victory dinner was such a success, and Squire Skene was such a genial host, that John Burgoyne lingered on for eighteen days in the ample stone mansion. Even then, he seemed reluctant to leave the Champlain Valley.

The day after their arrival, the 9th Regiment was sent down the Fort Anne track to contact the enemy. Near Fort Anne, they met the New Hampshire Continentals, and in a brisk skirmish, the British captured the American colors and bore them back in triumph to Skenesborough: contact made, mission accomplished.

General Fraser and General Riedesel, who had pursued the American army eastward from Mount Independence, sent word of their success at Hubbardton, and on July 9 they came out of the awesome forest onto the friendly shores of the lake at Skenesborough. The wounded were carried in later.

With these successes Burgoyne gave over the pursuit, which had been his natural instinct as a trained cavalry officer, and, as befitted a lieutenant general, he turned his attention to high strategy.

On the large continental map of the war, Burgoyne's army, while still in the Champlain Valley, threatened not only the Hudson River and New York but the Connecticut River Valley road into New England. To the west, Barry

St. Leger's invasion of the Mohawk Valley, scheduled for early July, would also prevent a general concentration across Burgoyne's intended route to Albany.

By toying with problematical strategic time, however, the British general comfortably ensconced in Major Skene's fine house procrastinated in the making of a vital tactical decision: should he proceed overland to Fort Edward by the Wood Creek–Fort Anne road, or should he take the water route on Lake George? The sudden fall of Fort Ticonderoga, the hot pursuit of the fleeing American soldiers, and the rapid breaching of the lake barriers had carried the British twenty miles beyond the turn-off into Lake George, up which Burgoyne had planned to float his army. In Skenesborough, he now found himself eighty miles from Fort Edward, at the head of navigable water if he took the traditional route of armies across Lake George, but only twenty-three miles from that place, over the tree-tops, as the crow flies.

The obstacles presented by each of the routes and the relative time necessary to overcome them — these were the questions on which Burgoyne must balance his decision. On Lake George, the Yankees had a sloop, four gunboats, and a fort at the southern end of the lake. On the overland road, at best no more than a track, Colonel Hill of the British 9th Foot had reported flooding in many places, bridges out, and felled trees effectively blocking the way. Basing his decision on a favorable report made by engineer Lieutenant Twiss, Burgoyne finally gave the order to rebuild the road for the army's advance to the Hudson.

It took the British and German soldiers five days to claw, hack, and build their way forward through the shambles that the American axemen had made of the road. When at last they stood on the banks of the Hudson River, the month of July had gone by. As the flow of the waters had changed from north to south, so their fortune changed from good to bad. Success, triumph — pleasure, too — all these John Burgoyne left behind him on Lake Champlain.

~~~~~~~

Nowhere in the "world turned upside down" of the song popular in the 1770's was it more topsy-turvy than on Lake Champlain, after General Burgoyne and his army had passed through the valley.

During the five bloody years of the French and Indian War, Britain had fought northward on the lake. Now, Burgoyne's expedition had climaxed three years of bitter struggle for the British, going in the opposite direction. The whole quarrel of the old war of 1755–60 in this region was whether Lake Champlain was a part of the Atlantic colony of New York or whether it was a part of Canada. At last, by right of conquest, England had proved conclusively that the lake was a part of her Atlantic colonies. General Burgoyne turned the atlas around again by leaving Brigadier Powell to administer the territory from Ticonderoga, as an advance post of a Canadian district.

From September, 1777, until the end of the War for American Independence, Lake Champlain was to follow a course of retrogression in historical time that would bring the clock full round and would even turn up old, familiar names and faces from the other side of the dial.

Brigadier General Powell was an austere officer, who assumed his duties at Ticonderoga without compromise. General Burgoyne had left him one British regiment, one German regiment, some Canadians, and the usual complement of engineers, gunners, bateaumen, and quartermaster personnel, together with one hundred Yankee prisoners. The militant Whig sympathies of the latter, Powell graciously consented to ignore to the extent of ordering them on parade for thanksgiving services and a feu-de-joie, in honor of the British success that had contributed to their own capture. Powell looked with neither approval nor disapproval on those of the Yankees who joined in the three huzzahs for King George, and chose to ignore the jostling in the American ranks caused by the demonstration. He worked his prisoners as he worked his own soldiers, and included them in the prescribed issue of rum for work parties. At night, he saw to it that they were locked in a barn belonging to a Mr. Davis, whose fields lay west of the French trenches.

Powell's tenure ended when Fort Ticonderoga was demilitarized by the convention marking Burgoyne's surrender on October 7, 1777. But during the approximately four months of his command, he maintained, improved, and defended his post according to the rigid code by which he lived. He admitted neither humor to flavor, nor rancor to mar, the last days of military life of the "old gray lady of Lake Champlain" — Fort Ticonderoga.

Those last days, however, were not spent in peaceful garrison life. From September 18 to September 22, 1777, the old French fort withstood its closest attack and sustained its defenders under Brigadier General Powell.

Colonel John Brown's attack, before dawn on September 18, carried all the outwork of the west shore defenses, from the landing on Lake George to the walls of the fort itself. At Lake George, Brown had captured a blockhouse, an armed sloop, seventeen gunboats, thirty-two bateaux, officers and soldiers, bateaumen, and twelve sailors of the Royal Navy. At the sawmill, which he approached silently behind the noise of the falls, Brown captured another hundred and fifty bateaux and two brass cannon. It was only just getting light when, advancing toward the French lines, Brown overran Mr. Davis's barn and liberated a hundred American prisoners — including those who had sought favor with their captors by joining in the huzzahs at the victory celebration.

Meanwhile, Brown had dispatched Captain Ebenezer Allen (a cousin of Ethan Allen), with forty Vermont rangers, to take the British works on Sugar Loaf Mountain. It was a swarming sort of attack that Allen led up the steep flank of the mountain, but it carried him with a rush into the blockhouse, against opposition. Of the British who were there, a quartermaster's clerk, his brother, and seven other men escaped by tumbling down the steep northeast face of the mountain. In a leaky boat, without oars, they got away across the lake, as the solemn-jawed Vermonters watched their furious antics from the summit and helped them along with an occasional try at a long shot with their rifles.

Captain Ebenezer's attention was drawn to the short 12-pound cannon that had been captured with the blockhouse. Although neither he nor any of his rangers understood artillery, they *did* appreciate the fact that the Englishmen had not left on the mountain a single gun capable of firing a shell into the forts at Ticonderoga and on Mount Independence. The cannon had been put on the mountain more as a signal gun, and, as such, it had been fired at the onset of Allen's attack. Its warning had come too late to arouse resistance to Colonel Brown's sweep, but it had alerted the Regiment Prinz Frederick, on Mount Independence, in time to repel Brigadier General Jonathan Warner's column of Massachusetts militia, making its approach along the Hubbardton road. The Germans were aided in their defense by a fierce cannonading from HMS *Carleton* and from the *Lady Maria*, at their anchorage south of Mount Independence. Though ineffectual in itself, this drove the militia into defensive positions.

Brown's attack was by no means an isolated raid on Ticonderoga. It was the most successful arm of a three-pronged attack on Burgoyne's supply line, co-ordinated from Pawlet, Vermont, by the fat, affable, and extremely able General Benjamin Lincoln. John Brown, with an intimate knowledge of Ticonderoga and the lake, had planned the raid after the American success at the Battle of Bennington, but his original idea had grown into an attack in strength on all the British forwarding points between Ticonderoga and the Hudson. It was a general's command, although Lincoln chose to remain in distant Pawlet with a reserve force of a thousand men, ready to exploit any real success on the part of his subordinate commanders. Brown was given command of the main effort, as much because of his ability as an old hand at woods ranging as out of deference to his having proposed the scheme. Warner's attack on Mount Independence, with five hundred none-too-reliable militia, was planned as a diversion to aid Brown. Colonel Woodbridge was given the third task, that of raiding Skenesborough (which he found undefended), and Fort Edward (where he found no boats — not even those buried secretly and decently beneath headboards in the military cemetery).

The plan which brought Colonel Brown to the walls of Fort Ticonderoga on the morning of September 18 caught General Powell by surprise. Powell's soldiers were scattered among the many posts which, with an inadequate force, he was required to man. Even with only three hundred and fifty men of the 53rd Regiment, Powell's main position in the old fort was strong, while from the Germans over the rebuilt bridge he received word that they, too, could hold their position. Captain Longcroft and Captain Schank held the lake with their vessels. Powell's military experience recognized the attack against him as a raid in force, which would wither with time. He also knew that St. Leger's soldiers, unsuccessful on the Mohawk, were coming up Lake Champlain in response to Burgoyne's urgent call for reinforcements. He could not ascertain whether Brown, too, knew this, but he ordered up from Crown Point the *Loyal Convert* and the supply fleet she convoyed, in a night move designed to give Brown the impression that St. Leger had arrived at Ticonderoga with a big force.

For four days Brown and Warner lurked outside the forts, penning the British inside their walls. On September 22, General Lincoln sent word to both forces to rally to Gates, who, on September 19, had stopped Burgoyne's advance at Stillwater, near Saratoga. Warner left straight away, taking most of Brown's prisoners with him. Brown waited only long enough to destroy the two hundred boats he had captured, drive off the horses and oxen, make a bonfire of all the carts, and send into the fort a parting shot which killed two privates of the 53rd Foot as they were crossing the Place d'Armes. Then he, too, departed, leaving a shambles for the meticulous General Powell to set aright.

At the Lake George landing, Colonel Brown had saved from destruction a naval force with which he intended to attack the two British posts on Lake George: Diamond Island and Fort George, each held by two understrength companies of the 47th Foot. Brown's flagship was a three-gun sloop, its escort three British-built gunboats and fourteen assorted bateaux, which would serve as transport for the bulk of his force of four hundred and twenty soldiers. Tagging along in his own boat was Terry, the sutler, a mean little man who had given up soldiering in order to make a profit out of the war.

Running into bad weather, Brown headed his flotilla in behind the shelter of Sabbath Day Point. There the men, glad to be out of their open boats, made windbreaks of boughs along the edge of the cleared land, and, with their feet to their little fires, slept through the night. By morning the anger of the waves had abated, though a steady wind blew up from the island-choked narrows between the two massive mountain chains that tighten in the waist of Lake George. During the second night, which bad weather forced Brown's expedition to spend camped once more on the shore of Lake George, Terry slipped away. Although tired out from rowing, cupidity transformed fatigue into energy that carried the sutler and his boat's crew to Diamond Island, in time to warn the British garrison (for £10/13/0 cash) of the approach of the Americans.

Sir Guy Carleton's main reason for having put the fleet back on a war footing, and for supporting General Powell's positions from Ticonderoga to the Hudson, was to aid Burgoyne in scrambling back to his former lines of communication. To an old staff officer such as Carleton, this was the only solution to Burgoyne's problem, after he had been stopped by Gates in the defile at Stillwater. When Burgoyne's army did not come back, Carleton found himself in a position of imbalance. Not enough troops were left to him in Canada to maintain a long salient down the Champlain Valley, with a strong garrison at its farthest extremity. With winter coming on, Carleton would have to pull back, as he had done in 1776. He gave the necessary orders to evacuate Ticonderoga and all posts south of that fort. For this move, the fleet would again act as transport for all stores and equipment, after which the vessels would go into winter quarters at St. Jean. Captain Samuel Greaves, Royal Navy, could see to it.

But unfortunately, Captain Greaves could *not* see to it: he had walked up too boldly to a sentry who had imbibed too freely, and, because of his blue navy coat, he had been shot for a Yankee. The surgeons amputated his left arm and carried him back to his cabin on board the *Inflexible*, where he lay recovering from the brutal shock of the operation. Hurriedly, Commodore Skeffington Lutwidge was recalled from Canada. All the large vessels had already gone to Ticonderoga, and Lutwidge was forced to make the trip up Lake Champlain in an open longboat, in a cold October rain, each soaking, icy drop of which warned of the coming of winter and the great freeze. The commodore arrived on November 1 to reassume command at Fort Ticonderoga.

By the time he had thawed out in the cabin of the *Inflexible*, Lutwidge had written his first order. It was to the captains of the *Royal George, Washington, Loyal Convert,* and *Land Crab* at Point au Fer. He had passed them northbound, loaded with provisions and under orders from the stricken Greaves to unload at Point au Fer and return immediately to Ticonderoga for reloading. Lutwidge was changing these orders: the vessels were to make their way to St. Jean, unloading into bateaux at the shallows on the Richelieu if necessary, and at St. Jean they were to go into their winter moorings. Under no circumstances were they to attempt another passage on the lake, at the risk of being iced in far away from a friendly base, where they would be easy prey to marauding Vermonters.

The weather was now so forbidding that Lutwidge, with a vigor that refuted any possible accusation of laziness, applied himself to the loading of the six vessels remaining at Ticonderoga. If he gave a thought to the displeasure he had aroused in General Carleton, he feared more the wrath that the Lords of Admiralty would heap upon him if the Lake Champlain fleet became frozen in. For four days he lay off Ticonderoga, harrying the stevedores and lightermen and his own crews at their labors. Finally, on November 4, he could wait no longer, and he moved the whole fleet up to Crown Point. The army be damned! If they wanted to save their precious guns and provisions, they could send them up to Crown Point by bateau. Lutwidge was right, of course. At Crown Point he had deep and wide water to the north, while at Ticonderoga he had only a shallow, narrow passage which a north wind would plug, like a stopper in a sherry decanter.

The *Maria* and the *Thunderer* were sent on to St. Jean that same evening. The *Lady Maria* was loaded with the sick and with provisions. The *Thunderer* had been loading with ordnance stores, when urgency required that she take on board another hundred and fifty of the sick. Hay was pitched over the hard boxes of cannon shells and the casks of powder, which, with the provisions, made a gigantic bed to receive the blanketed invalids and their attendants and female nurses.

On board the *Inflexible*, Lutwidge waited one more day to take on some brass guns that made up the last load out of Diamond Island and Fort George. Then he, too, sailed north, in company with the *Camel* — yet another of those humpbacked covered arks, relics of Commodore Loring's fleet, that had been commissioned at St. Jean during the summer. The *Camel* carried artillery stores, mostly powder under cover; the *Inflexible*, provisions and Captain Greaves, now out of danger, the morbid fever gone from the stump of his arm.

When he took the *Inflexible* north on a course set for the narrows, with a good wind filling her sails, Lutwidge had little to fear for the safety of the two vessels he had left behind. In all probability the *Carleton*, ever the best sailer of the entire fleet, would catch up with him before the

Inflexible passed the Onion River. Now, her hold and her deck laden with a variety of heavy stores, the *Carleton* waited only for the last of the sick to be carried on board from the hospital.

The *Lee*, which rowed as handily as she sailed, would wait to accompany the army as a flagship for Brigadier Powell.

For three days, the *Lee* waited. Then, on the morning of November 8, the regiments embarked: red-coated British from the Ticonderoga side, blue-coated Germans from Mount Independence. Lines and columns formed quickly under directions from the navy-manned gunboats already on the water. No one wished to tarry; everyone wished to leave the two bare headlands, so somber now under a milky sky that veiled a cold, copper-colored sun. General Powell stepped quickly aboard the *Lee* from the pier in the little cove, just north of the place where the Ticonderoga end of the Americans' big bridge had been anchored. He nodded to the officer at attention in the stern and ducked into the little cabin aft. Lieutenant Stowe gave the signal, and a gunner touched his match to the vent hole of the signal gun. At the report, the whole flotilla moved as one; every oarsman had been poised, waiting to be off.

The *Lee* fell in behind the bateaux, and for a few minutes Stowe was busy setting up sail and making signals to the lubberly soldiers in the bateau ahead, who were making a poor job of setting their own patched square sails. When all was squared away, the Royal Navy lieutenant glanced momentarily astern to where two boats, the last of his convoy, were pushing off, one from each shore. They were the engineers' boats. Twiss was in one of them; Stowe did not recognize the other man. They had just ignited the fuses that would end the life of a great fortress. The explosion would shake the very dead in their graves — and there were so many, many dead, buried forever in the graves at Ticonderoga.

Lieutenant Stowe, R.N., looked away to stare at a lake covered with sails and ships and living men, going away from the old fortress. When the explosion came, he did not look back.

Brigadier General Henry Watson Powell stayed below in the small, dark cabin.

The Prevailing Wind

Suddenly, with General Powell's abandonment of Ticonderoga in November 1777, Lake Champlain and Lake George again became a long, deserted road through a vast and desolate wilderness. There was no army post between the small blockhouse at Fort George, manned by erratic American militia, and the low, island-like Point au Fer, guarding the mouth of the Richelieu River. The few settlers who had lived between these points, mostly on the Vermont shore, moved southward into New England or northward into Canada, according to their political sympathies. For with the withdrawal of the army posts went the security of order and discipline, and the whole fair territory of the lakes lay open to marauding bands; nor were the marauders far behind Powell's retreating army.

Ebenezer Allen, confirmed as captain by a militia commission and followed by a wild band of Vermont rangers, caught the British rear guard breaking camp at the mouth of the Richelieu. In a lightning swoop, Allen led his men out of the woods and, in full sight of the boats on the lake, swept up forty-nine prisoners, slipped back amongst the gray trunks of the trees — and was gone.

For five years, until the War for American Independence was won, bands of Indians — or Tories — or Whigs — roamed the valley. Settlers who returned to their lands in hope of gathering a harvest fell prey to Indians from Canada.

Shelburne was raided by a party that came up the lake on skates, and was stoutly defended. An old man and two boys were taken prisoners from the grazing land around the village of Orwell. Bristol was raided; Brandon was attacked. Vermont organized her militia and made Ethan Allen, returned from his captivity in England, its general. Late in the year of 1778, a big war party remembered the old war trail of the Algonquins: up the lake to Burlington Bay, on up the Winooski River, over the mountains to the headwaters of the White River, and down that river to Connecticut. Now, in 1778, the war party raided, burned, and took thirty prisoners at Royalton. In 1704, the raid on Deerfield, Massachusetts, had netted one hundred and eleven prisoners.

As the clock turned back on Indian raids, so did it turn back, too, on the expeditions that took the Lake Champlain highway to the towns along the Hudson and the Mohawk.

Sir John Johnson — shades of his father! — led an expedition on Lake Champlain. For a Johnson, it was a wrongway journey, starting in Canada and aimed at the Mohawk Valley; but then, the world was "turned upside down." The Johnsons were in exile in Canada, their Mohawk Indians with them. Along the Mohawk River now lived the stolid Whig Dutch. The great Iroquois Confederacies were all but broken, the Nations scattered. Johnson Hall remained standing, square and graceful on its green hill, and buried nearby by a faithful Negro slave was the Johnson family plate. Sir John wanted his silver, as a part of the new dignity he was building in Canada for his family.

Six hundred men accompanied him. They were British regulars and Tories from the Mohawk, recruited into Johnson's own regiment, the "Royal Greens," and into that of his father's overseer, "John Butler's Rangers." There were two hundred Indians, followers of Joseph Brandt (Thayen-da-ne-gea), himself a member of the Johnson family by Indian marriage, and upbringing at Johnson Hall.

Sir John and his expedition were escorted by the vessels of the British Lake Champlain fleet, which, under its commodore, the recently promoted Captain William Chambers, during all the five empty years made periodic cruises in strength on the forsaken waters. At Crown Point the raiding party disembarked, to travel westward out of the Champlain Valley to the headwaters of the Sacandaga River, which flowed out of the dark Adirondacks near to Johnson Hall.

Chambers withdrew his ships into the center of Bullwagga Bay to await Johnson's return. At this uneasy anchorage off a deserted shore, an alert watch was kept from behind the anti-boarding nets. Slow matches glowed in their little wooden buckets beside the loaded cannon, and iron flare-baskets were ready on the quarters. At night, the watch below slept easily only because of the reassuring calls from the boat watch, circling and listening in the outer dark.

Nothing appeared during the days and nights of Chambers's vigil. All was silent and barren around the sweep of the wide bay shore. Then came the signal that the raiders had returned, and the fleet moved in to re-embark the troops.

It had gone well for Johnson, and aboard the flagship, with Crown Point falling astern, Sir John, in his travel-stained green coat, stood laughing as forty of his soldiers spilled his crested silver plate out of their knapsacks at his feet.

Too far astern, now, for the British to see them, men stood on the shore below the walls of burnt-out Fort Amherst. Captain Harder's pursuit, all the way from Albany with two hundred militiamen, had been only a few hours too late. Johnson and his silver "got clean away."

In the great struggle for independence, they were trivial

— the vicious raids that whirled up and down the Champlain Valley like little hurricanes between 1777 and 1782 — as trivial as the raid for Sir John Johnson's family silver. Few British regulars were stationed in Canada, and General Washington's veteran Continentals had gone on to other battlefields after they had thwarted Burgoyne's great strategic plan at Saratoga. The uneasiness on the frontier from the Great Lakes to the Connecticut River held back the march of the settlers and kept the militia, with their few Continental officers, alerted by continual musters, pursuits, and forays.

To watch and to guard the doorways at the southern end of the Lake Champlain corridor, Adiel Sherwood, a captain of Continentals, sweated out a dull occupation of Fort Anne with seventy-five idle militiamen, whom he had given up trying to make into soldiers. Two companies of Colonel Warner's Green Mountain Rangers, with eighty militiamen, occupied Fort George, and Captain John Chipman kept his Rangers out on watch at the post Robert Rogers had pioneered, overlooking Crown Point and Fort Ticonderoga.

Over in the old "Hampshire Grants," since 1777 called Vermont, in a declaration of independence directed at New York but including Canada, General Ethan Allen held a militia line from Castleton and Pittsford to the ridges of the Green Mountains, the eastern horizon from Lake Champlain. Through the Vermont line messengers passed to and from Canada in a desultory negotiation between the Green Mountaineers and the British government in Montreal regarding possible statehood in Canada. These talks, which indifferently kept the frontier quiet, were not so much the result of a warm loyalty to England as they were an attempt to threaten the American Continental Congress into admitting Vermont to the Union as a fourteenth state, thereby

THE PREVAILING WIND 257

nullifying New York's claim to the eastern shore of Lake Champlain. Vermont's armed neutrality was neither forgetting nor forgiving, and held firm to its convictions in self-sufficient independence.

~~~~~~~~~~

Such was the new nation's state of readiness in October 1780, when high policy pushed open Britain's door to the lakes, in a brief diversion and an unheeded show of force intended to draw attention to the northern frontier, with its waterline poised at the back of the Atlantic states.

The new governor general of Canada, Sir Frederick Haldimand, welcomed the order to show force on Lake Champlain. His own negotiations with the stubborn, procrastinating Vermonters would be forwarded by the army's occupation of Ticonderoga and Crown Point. With an army and a fleet on his western flank, General Allen would be forced to decide for loyalty.

London's reason for activity on the lakes was even more far reaching than the wish for adding a new province to Canada. The American hero, General Arnold, had sold out: he was in contact with General Howe, and for a commission as brigadier general in the British army he would turn his coat, and by treachery, give up the important American position on the Hudson River highlands at West Point. This was to take place in October. Haldimand's thrust for the upper Hudson would implement Benedict Arnold's treason, by threatening another attempt at cutting the American colonies in two.

Though Arnold's plot was discovered and his treachery in regard to West Point aborted in late September, Haldimand's expedition was carried out.

Eight vessels of the British fleet, with twenty-six bateaux, sailed from the advance base at Point au Fer with fifteen hundred regulars, Loyalists, and Indians aboard as a striking force. At Crown Point they were seen by American Rangers, who hurried back to Captain Chipman at Fort George. The scouts did not wait long enough to observe and report that a party of four hundred men had detached itself from the fleet and was taking the western valley route, nor did Chipman warn Fort Anne of the British advance, which carried the ships and troops in to a landing at the southern end of South Bay. There Major Christopher Carleton, nephew and brother-in-law to Sir Guy, disembarked the troops under his command.

On October 10, an unsuspecting Fort Anne, low in ammunition and even lower in determination, capitulated on command to the overwhelming force of the British. With all the assurance of an ambling bear, Carleton turned to the American fort at the head of Lake George, which he attacked on October 11. In Captain John Chipman and the eighty-seven Rangers of Warner's regiment, waiting for him in Fort George, Carleton stumbled into a hive of stinging resistance. The British killed twenty-eight of the defenders before the remainder, wounded and exhausted, surrendered to them.

With new-found respect, the English approached the last objective of their raid: Fort Edward, where Colonel Henry Livingston was in command of a weak garrison force. The caution of the British major was no match for the cunning wits of the American colonel, who dispatched to intentional capture a resourceful messenger, bearing an exaggerated statement of the numbers defending Fort Edward. Taken in by the ruse, Carleton skirted wide of the post at the Hudson River end of the long portage, limiting himself to a rampage of fury directed against the small communities of Kingsbury and Queensbury, and the sawmills along Wood Creek, which he burned. He then rejoined the fleet and returned to Crown Point, reaching there on October 25.

At Crown Point, Major Carleton waited: nothing happened. The western valley raiders came back, after a spiteful attack on the settlement at Ballston. General Allen rallied the Vermont militia at Castleton and awaited developments. Commodore Chambers worried about his fleet and the advancing season.

At last, with a brisk wind up from the south, the British sailed to Canada. Many winds had blown the British up and down Lake Champlain in the years since 1775. But the south wind blowing up from the Atlantic colonies in 1780 was new, and fresh, and strong. Undeniably, it was the prevailing wind.

IV

The American Lake

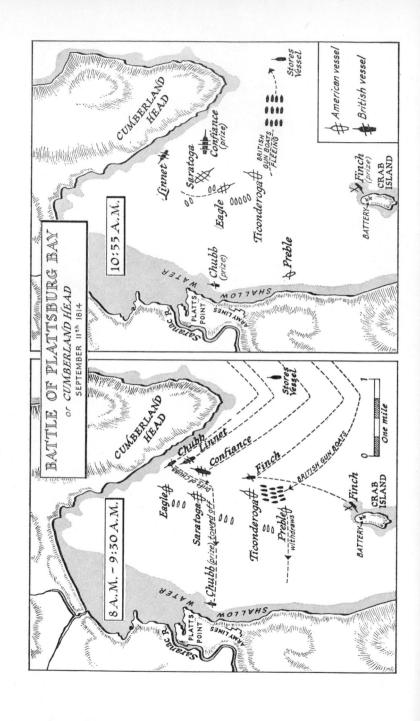

BATTLE OF PLATTSBURG BAY
or CUMBERLAND HEAD
SEPTEMBER 11th 1814

10:55 A.M.

CUMBERLAND HEAD

Linnet
Saratoga
Confiance (prize)
Eagle
Chubb (prize)
Ticonderoga
Preble
BRITISH GUN BOATS FLEEING
Stores Vessel
Finch (prize)
CRAB ISLAND
BATTERY
SHALLOW WATER
ARMY LINES
PLATTS POINT
Saranac R.

American vessel
British vessel

8 A.M. – 9:30 A.M.

CUMBERLAND HEAD

Chubb
Linnet
Confiance
Finch
Eagle
drift of Chubb
Saratoga
Chubb (prize) towed off
Ticonderoga
Preble withdraws
BRITISH GUN BOATS
Stores Vessel
Finch
CRAB ISLAND
BATTERY
SHALLOW WATER
ARMY LINES
PLATTS POINT
Saranac R.

0 ____ 1
One mile

The U.S. Navy on Lake Champlain

At Portland, Maine, on October 5, 1812, Lieutenant Thomas Macdonough turned his back on the sea. For three days he rode westward along mountain trails; the fourth day's riding was down a winding river valley, where, as the high Green Mountain ranges were left further and further behind, the farms became more numerous and appeared to be more prosperous. At nightfall Macdonough reached Burlington, Vermont.

Next day, he assumed command of the American fleet on Lake Champlain, as he had been ordered to do by President James Madison. With Lieutenant Macdonough, the United States Navy came to the lake, and nowhere in that proud young service could a more typical and a more exemplary officer have been found.

Born in the year that the War for American Independence was won, Thomas Macdonough secured his midshipman's berth in 1800. The war with the Barbary pirates followed quickly after the vigorous little naval war with France, and Macdonough sailed with the squadron bound for the Mediterranean. The very birthplace of sailing ships and sailing men, this ancient sea received the fledgling United States Navy with scorn and derision. The American sailors resented this unfriendly attitude, especially the supercilious mien of the sneering English, and during these years the American eaglet developed many of the qualities of a bantam cock. The American officers kept their honor filed to the hair-trigger cock of a dueling pistol, and Midshipman Macdonough himself was not above a brawl — or a formal duel — when he thought that the American Navy had been slighted.

Afloat, the Americans were as pugnacious as they were when on shore. The twenty-six gun frigate *Philadelphia* ran aground and was captured while chasing a Tripolitan vessel into the harbor of Tripoli itself — a bold misadventure which covered her skipper with official honors, rather than with condemnation for the loss of his ship. The cutting-out expedition, which burned the captured frigate under the very guns of the Bashaw of Tripoli's fortress, gave the American Navy what England's greatest sailor, Lord Nelson, deemed to be "the most bold and daring act of the age."

Young Thomas Macdonough missed the first of these exploits. The *Philadelphia* was his ship, but at the time of her loss, he was taking a prize into Gibraltar. He was with Captain Stephen Decatur on the cutting-out expedition, and was of the party which swarmed over the bows of the *Philadelphia*, charged with firing the berth deck and the forward storeroom. For his work that night, he was commended. Later in the year 1804, Macdonough — still with Decatur — won another commendation for his part in the gunboat attack into Tripoli Harbor.

Macdonough returned from the Mediterranean a lieutenant, and a naval officer who had fought at firsthand against the impressment of American sailors into the British fleet — a principal cause of the War of 1812. In Gibraltar Harbor, Macdonough had boarded a British launch to retrieve a sailor pressed from an American merchantman, and, in the British captain's own port, had defied him to protect the man.

But promotion was slow in a navy that turned out officers

faster than Congress could — or would — turn out ships, so Macdonough gained a leave of absence, and sailed in merchantmen in the West Indian trade until America's second war with England broke out in June of 1812.

Under the motto, which was run up into flags — "Free Trade and Sailors' Rights" — the United States Navy went out to fight, and the war hawks on land sent wearied old generals to rattle sabers on the northern frontier. Macdonough returned to active service with the navy as commander of a gunboat flotilla, on guard and convoy duty in Portland Harbor. In this post, there was little prospect of gaining promotion through valiant action and virtually no opportunity to augment, with prize money, a lieutenant's meager pay of seventy-four dollars a month — and Thomas Macdonough wanted to marry Lucy Ann Shaler!

The presidential order came to Lieutenant Macdonough as a windfall of opportunity, although it meant exile from the salt sea. Promotion would come as he built his command into a fleet, and the expectation that once again Britain would push open the Lake Champlain water gate meant action and prizes, both of which, in turn, meant more money. That night of October 9, 1812, therefore, there arrived in Burlington, Vermont, an ambitious and conscientious young officer of the United States Navy, with training and experience in the best traditions of the navy way, and spurred on by personal as well as patriotic incentives.

Macdonough wasted no time. Having decided upon his shore quarters in Burlington and settled into them, he went over to call upon the army commander across the lake at Plattsburg, New York. It was a beautiful sail. As he set out across Burlington Bay and around Lone Rock Point, the whole sweep of the high Adirondacks was spread out in a panorama over his port quarter, the high peaks capped with snow, the lower slopes all red and gold in full autumn foliage. As the boat angled north across the lake, the Green Mountains reared up behind the deep Vermont shore, appearing more sweeping and graceful than the tumbled peaks on the New York side. Soon the pine-covered bluffs of Valcour Island detached themselves from the shore line beyond, and the new commander on Lake Champlain could see and appraise the tactics of his predecessor, and of the British enemy of thirty-six years before. Beyond Valcour, Macdonough passed Crab Island, where the French fleet had tried in vain to hide; then he sailed into Cumberland Bay.

Lieutenant Macdonough's call upon General Henry Dearborn was the courteous gesture of a newcomer, of equal stature in command but very junior in rank, toward a venerable gentleman of high rank and great distinction. From the old hero of the Revolutionary War, who, as a major of the Continental line had won a brevet at Saratoga, the young naval commander learned that an American thrust to the north was planned along the Champlain Roadway into Canada. It had, in fact, been scheduled for the summer just ended, but the plan had never been carried out. The navy's role on Lake Champlain, as envisaged and applied by the army while it controlled the ships, was one of transportation. Macdonough's instructions from the Navy Department were to take control of the war vessels on the lake, and as a naval commander, he intended to use those vessels as fighting ships and not as transports. With orders to this effect, and having paid his respects to the aged general, he left Plattsburg for Whitehall (as Skenesborough was now called), to continue his inspection tour and to familiarize himself with Lake Champlain.

On this tour Macdonough saw a busy lake, filled with shipping of every description. There were bateaux, scows, gondolas, and all types of sailing vessels, the largest of which he judged to be of about 75-ton burden. He saw, too, the big 120-foot steamboat *Vermont*, the second such boat of her type in the world. She was tied up at one of the many landings along the shore, having suffered one of her frequent breakdowns. Later, Macdonough was to inspect her more closely and to consider the question of steam versus sail. In the narrows, he sailed within hailing distance of a fast sloop flaunting a Spanish flag. He was informed that she was the *Saucy Fox*, owned by the unofficial admiral of the lake, Gideon King, and King's absent partner, John Jacob Astor, and — conveniently under a neutral flag — she was engaged in the fur trade with St. Jean.

The appearance of the shoreline did not impress the young naval lieutenant as it had awed the old army commander in Plattsburg, who had known the lake thirty years before. In 1783, when Macdonough was born, not a settler had dared to build his cabin on the shore of Lake Champlain. On the Vermont side, Ethan Allen's Onion River Company had suspended operations for the eight years of the war, and the few pioneers had withdrawn southward during the bloody Indian raids of the previous five years. On the west shore, poor William Gilliland had returned to find his once prosperous estate in ruins, the houses and mills burned to the ground and the fields run to alder patches and nettles. Gilliland died broken-hearted, demented over his losses. Philip Skene, the other great landowner on Lake Champlain before the Revolutionary War, had forfeited his American holdings by his loyalty to the Crown, and from all the wreck of his estates, gained recompense from his own government for only one eight-gun topsail schooner, the *Liberty*, and for two gondolas.

It was a wholly new community that Macdonough now saw spread up and down the Champlain Valley. During the few years since his own birth in snug Delaware, twenty-five thousand people had come to Lake Champlain. Already, he had seen two of its four new cities: Burlington, with two thousand inhabitants, and Plattsburg, with three thousand. Now, as his craft turned out of South Bay, he was about to see Whitehall, the transfer point for goods of every kind, brought up over the wagon road from the Hudson. In fact, there was talk of a canal to connect Whitehall with the Hudson River by way of Wood Creek.

Whitehall was the army's main supply base for the six thousand regulars and militia who made up General Dearborn's command. At this busy port, Lieutenant Macdonough expected to straighten out the question of a transport fleet in relation to his own ships-of-war.

In October 1812 government vessels on Lake Champlain were divided among the treasury, the army, and the navy.

First, there was the revenue cutter, the *Fly*, which in the days of the embargo on Canadian goods had fought the bloody little battle of August 3, 1808, against the *Black Snake*. In that battle, Captain Farrington had lost two of his revenue men, killed before he could board and capture the smugglers' vessel.

The army maintained on the lake a fleet of six transports and two armed vessels: the sixteen-gun *President* and the sloop *Montgomery*, carrying seven long 9-pound cannon and two 18-pound carronades.

At the time Macdonough took command on Lake Champlain, the navy owned but two sloops on the lake: the *Hunter* and the *Bulldog*. Both of these vessels were in such a sad state of repair as to be unfit for active service. They were tied up in shallow water, where their tired hulls could rest on a solid bottom, which at least kept the water from the captain's cabin and the gun deck. The *Hunter* had been purchased by the navy from its owner, Gideon King, who had the best of the bargain — as was "the King's way." The former owner of the *Bulldog*, too, had made a good thing out of his deal with the government, but what Macdonough particularly resented was the English ring to the name: the *Bulldog!*

On the army's dock at Whitehall stood Thomas Macdonough, commander of a navy without a single ship afloat. As a result of his interview with General Dearborn, he had secured the reluctant transfer of the *President* to the navy command. Now, he only awaited the return of that vessel to Whitehall so that he could formally take over from the army's lake transport command the vessel and its crew.

In Macdonough, the *President* found her master, and she learned "the navy way" from a man who had himself learned it from such men as Bainbridge, Decatur, and Charles Stewart. With his pennant at the masthead, Macdonough turned the vessel around so fast that the crew had no time to take their dirty linen ashore to the washerwomen of their choice. They sailed for Basin Harbor in the narrows, where the *Hunter* and the *Bulldog* were at rest. There Macdonough expected to meet Lieutenant Sidney Smith, USN, who had been in command during the summer. From what Macdonough had learned of the U.S. Navy on Lake Champlain, Smith was either indolent or incompetent, or at best was incapable of action because of lack of funds and lack of co-operation from the army. Smith turned out to possess all three of these characteristics, to which was added that of resentment at being superseded by another officer. He was brave, however, and under supervision he could carry out orders.

Together, the two lieutenants, with the help of Jairus Loomis — an old sailor and captain of the *Bulldog* — got what water they could out of the holds of the two dilapidated sloops, and, with extra pumps rigged and working steadily, they set sail from Basin Harbor for Whitehall. The *President* hovered anxiously in escort.

Back at the army's docks, Macdonough arranged with the local shipbuilders to overhaul the two sloops completely, with the object of making them seaworthy. In addition, orders were given for gunports to be cut and decks reinforced, so that when they were launched again in the spring, each one could carry eleven instead of seven cannon. Macdonough also gave new names to the sloops: the *Hunter* became the *Growler*, and the *Bulldog* was given the more appropriate name of *Eagle*.

With this work in hand, Macdonough sailed north for Burlington. Already people were talking of the ice. Winter was soon to come, and Macdonough's job afloat would have to wait the April thaw. He sent the *President* into dock in Shelburne Bay. Then he went on leave.

The leave was a busy one. He fulfilled a growing religious consciousness by seeking confirmation in the Episcopal church, where, a few days later, he and Lucy Ann Shaler were married. And during his honeymoon, he found time in New York to secure fifteen ship carpenters to work on his sloops at Whitehall.

The thaw came early in 1813, ending the protracted stay in Burlington, where the young couple found themselves the center of local and navy society.

Shortly after the *President* was afloat once more and the wooden snow-cover removed from her deck, her new carronades came up by barge from Whitehall, where these heavy hitting cannon had arrived during the winter. Within a few days the *Eagle* and the *Growler* joined the flagship, now at the navy dock in Burlington Bay. These two ugly ducklings raced each other into the bay like two shining black colts, let loose in pasture on a sunny morning. Caulked tight below and under new suits of sail, with their guns run out and the red-and-white gridiron flag snapping at their peaks, they now looked like navy ships. As he watched their arrival from the window of his office on the hill above the bay, Macdonough noted with approval that, whatever his shortcomings, Lieutenant Smith could handle a ship — too recklessly, perhaps, but in the American Navy there were no courts-martial for boldness.

The time had come again for Lieutenant Macdonough to go to sea. He sailed in April with all his fleet, unquestioned master of Lake Champlain. The *President* had twelve guns and Lieutenant Smith's *Growler* had eleven, as did Sailing Master Jairus Loomis's *Eagle*. In addition, Macdonough had two gunboats of two guns each, and had chartered a small sloop, the *Wasp*, to serve as dispatch boat. At the time of sailing, the sloop was being mounted with five small cannon.

Against this maximum armament of forty-three guns, the British had three single-cannon gunboats, and three more building at their shipyard at Ile aux Noix.

From South Bay to the mouth of the Richelieu River, Lake Champlain was an American lake. Army transports sailed at will; no port or place, from Whitehall to Swanton, was denied the American fleet; trading vessels went about their business undisturbed. "Commodore" Macdonough, who in seven months had put a navy on Lake Champlain, was prepared and able to carry out the orders he had received from the Secretary of the Navy: "Upon no account are you to suffer the enemy to gain ascendancy on Lake Champlain."

In June, Macdonough lost his whole fleet of capital ships. He had spent the month of May breaking in his new crews. These were stranded men from the small boats off the coast of Maine, who, moved by a wave of patriotism (and by recruiting blandishments), had joined McCobb's militia regiment, and like Macdonough, had marched inland to Lake Champlain. Now, proving that they were not soldiers and never would be, they had volunteered again, and, for the feel of an oar instead of a musket in their hands, they had signed on as seamen in the lake navy. As soon as the men's "X" had been affixed to the Articles, Macdonough put out upon the open lake. There, undisturbed and alone, he and his executive and training officer, Lieutenant Raymond Perry, taught the men the difference between hauling in lobster pots and jumping to a boatswain's whistle on a Yankee man-o'-war.

But before the green men from Maine had mastered the teamwork of their watches, the *President* had run aground. She struck on one of those offshore rocks which lie unnoticed beneath the surface during the time of year when Lake Champlain is swollen with the melted snow from two mountain ranges. In working off, several of the flagship's ribs cracked ominously. The damage that Macdonough feared had been done to the keel which was covered in bilge water from opened seams. Plattsburg was nearby, so the *President*, with her two sloops, put in there. The damage to her hull was found to be severe.

On June 2, word came that the British gunboats were raiding the shore above Ile LaMotte. With the *President* out of action, Macdonough sent the *Growler* and the *Eagle* to drive the English back into the Richelieu, and then to watch the mousehole. Lieutenant Sidney Smith, who was in command of the two sloops, arrived at the mouth of the Richelieu River in the evening of June 2 and began his cat-like watch. By dawn, his patience was exhausted. With a strong south wind over his stern, he ducked into the mousehole with the *Growler*; Sailing Master Loomis followed dutifully with the *Eagle*.

At Ash Island, six miles down the stream, the channel narrowed from three-quarters of a mile to less than four hundred yards. There Smith sighted the three English gunboats. He chased them all the way to Ile aux Noix, where the three scared mice turned on their pursuers. They would have beaten the Americans back to the hole, had Smith and Loomis been able to drive against the wind, still blowing strong from the south. Caught and outgunned by the heavier cannon of the three British boats, the two Yankees fought as best they could, in constant danger of being driven aground every time they turned crossways to the stream in order to bring a broadside to bear. The gun duel had not been long engaged when a new discomfort attended the harassed Americans: musket fire from both shores began to nick the sides and plop into the rolled hammocks which lined the high gunwales of the *Growler* and the *Eagle*. The fire grew in intensity as more and more British soldiers were hurried up from the fort at Ile aux Noix. Though the muskets had little killing effect at that range, the raw American seamen hesitated to expose themselves at the open gun ports, as they had to do in order to load and ram home the shot when the carronades were run inboard after firing. It was even more discouraging to see their own well-aimed shots fall short of the English boats.

Perhaps it was fury that kept the Americans at their work during the long hours of the fight. They grew heedless of the big shot from the long 18- and 24-pounders, which ripped through the rigging overhead or ricocheted with a screaming whine over the water close outboard, sometimes striking in a bitter shower of splinters torn from the new planks of the gunwales.

As the men from Maine, and their shipmates from the navy's big frigates, grew warm to battle, they "melded" into a crew, heeding no harm to themselves while the guns needed serving and the flag still flew at the peak of the gaff. In all the fury, only one American sailor was killed; eight men aboard the *Growler* were wounded enough to go below; and by eleven o'clock that morning, Loomis had eleven wounded men lying in the cockpit of the *Eagle*, just forward of the helm where he was standing. All the *Eagle's* port battery was shotted and run out, each gun captain behind his piece, waiting only for the swing-around of the vessel to bear so that he could give the adjustments for elevation and line. From a gap in the line of hammocks, a midshipman called "Shot!" Loomis turned his head and caught a glimpse of a puff of smoke rolling back over the bow of one of the gunboats. Then, in her turn, the *Eagle* moved slowly around. Starting from the bows of the ship, gun crews sprang into action as the commands of the gun-pointers snapped out in a wave, lapping along aft. Loomis was on the point of flinging an order over his shoulder to the helmsman when the British shell struck. It hit hard, just below the gun deck. Loomis had felt the punch of a 24-pounder before, and he took the shock on his sea legs. But he was not prepared for the crash that followed. The big round shot had passed through the width of the boat between decks, ripping three whole planks out of the starboard side, below the waterline. With the sound of water rushing in below and the deck already beginning to list under his feet, the sailing master gave his order to the helmsman: "Steady as you go!" In the narrow river it was only a moment before the *Eagle* found bottom and, with a jar and a shiver, settled into the mud. Stunned and bewildered, the men fell silent, as Sailing Master Jairus Loomis ran down the bright flag of fifteen stars and fifteen stripes in a signal of surrender. He had no other choice.

Out in the channel, the *Growler* fought on, but only a few minutes' more fight was left in her. The shot racks beside the guns were empty, and little round shot remained in the locker below. Fifteen minutes later, a 24-pound ball struck the *Growler*'s mainmast, and an order from Lieutenant Smith sent sailors flying to the belaying pins, to drive them out and drop the sails before they carried away the weakened spar. With bare poles, the *Growler* became unmanageable, and, at the mercy of wind and current, she drifted in to shore. Helpless, out of ammunition, but with a good fight under his belt, Lieutenant Sidney Smith struck his colors, and with one hundred and twelve men from the two ships of his command surrendered himself as a prisoner of war.

Alarms and Excursions

Lieutenant Sidney Smith's loss of the two sloops, added to the accident to the *President*, upset completely Macdonough's carefully calculated arithmetic of naval armament on Lake Champlain. In May 1813 the ratio of American to British guns had been a most satisfactory forty-three to three; by the second week in June, the ratio tabulated out on the American commodore's scratch pad at an alarming seven to twenty-eight, in favor of the enemy.

The British had wasted no time in refloating the *Growler* and the *Eagle* — now known, respectively, as the *Shannon* and the *Broke*. With these two vessels and the gunboats, the British naval commander on the Richelieu, Captain Daniel Pring, was quite willing to venture out onto the lake and do mischief to the Yankees. Neither did Macdonough waste time in restoring a more equitable ratio between the two fleets, both of which, in a certain bitter sense, he had created.

The *President*, with the two gunboats, had been sent to Burlington, where naval carpenters were now repairing the structural damage to the sloop. Macdonough secured from the army the loan of the nine-gun *Montgomery*. The soldiers were now thoroughly alarmed for the safety of their transports, and, expecting momentarily an invasion from Canada by six thousand redcoats, they were only too glad to relinquish their naval pretensions to a sailor. The *Mont-*

gomery joined the *President* under the bluff at Burlington, where it was to undergo conversion to navy standards.

Casting about the lake for a likely vessel to purchase, Macdonough came upon a 50-ton sloop, named the *Rising Sun*. She had been built by Eggleston, who had designed and launched from his slips on the New York shore both the *President* and the *Bulldog/Eagle/Broke*. Macdonough liked the lines of the sloop, and he bought her from her owner, Elijah Boynton of Burlington. Before she was recommissioned as the *Preble,* in honor of the commodore of the Mediterranean squadron during the Tripoli War, several changes were made. The mast, which appeared so stumpy to Madonough's Chesapeake Bay–trained eye, was replaced by a tall spar with a distinct rake aft, so that the vessel had the look of a Baltimore privateer. Seven long 9-pound cannon and seven long 12-pounders constituted her main armament, with two 18-pound Columbiads for hitting power at close range.

In Macdonough's planned tactics, the *Preble* would be the chase ship, should the *Broke* or the *Shannon* break out of the blockade he intended to keep on the entrance to the Richelieu River. With her longer cannon, the *Preble* could match range with the British gunboats, and could outrange the two prize sloops, which in all probability would still have the same armament of carronades with which they had been captured.

To keep the fleet at sea, Macdonough chartered a small sloop, the *Frances,* as a supply ship. He gave her four 12-pounders and an 18-pound Columbiad. In this service the *Frances* joined the *Wasp*, the latter having proved such a sluggish sailor that her gun rating was cut from five to three, in an effort to lighten her in the bows.

As in earlier wars, from the fleet came the cry for more and more seamen. The captain of the Brooklyn navy yard sent a hundred sailors to the lake. Travel-weary, they arrived in July in company with a group of ship carpenters, who carried their tools, in inlaid and polished boxes, on their backs. The men and the cannon (which Macdonough also had urgently requested) came up overland on the cart road from Troy, on the Hudson River, passing through Cambridge and Salem, New York. The horses strained into their collars up a long grade on the dry, dusty road, breeching back as they picked their way down a rocky hill on the way to Whitehall, where boats were to have been waiting to take over the load. At Granville, however, they were waved on into Vermont and the long road to Burlington, on the east side of Lake Champlain.

That summer of 1813, the water in the lake was so low that the docks stood out over mud flats, like wobble-kneed centipedes, and fish floundered in shallow pools left by the receding waters of the marshes below Ticonderoga.

Even these hundred salt-water sailors were not enough to man the ships, and in July, Macdonough told General Thomas Parker that two gunboats would have to be laid up until crews for them could be found. But the army did not respond by opening its ranks to navy recruitment, as Macdonough had hoped when making his threat; it was too much concerned over meeting the expected land invasion. Few of the merchant sailors on Lake Champlain came forward to volunteer. They were landsmen, anyway, and fair weather sailors at best; and as gunners, they were "squirrel shooters"! Macdonough was more fortunate in young boys of good family who eagerly sought midshipmen's berths on his vessels. The officers came overland from the big ocean, as had the commodore himself, bringing with them a hard core of salt-encrusted sailing masters, boatswain mates, and master gunners.

In July 1813 Macdonough's commission as master commandant came up from the Navy Department. The promotion did not affect his earlier appointment as commodore, but it not only gave him increased pay and seniority, but broke through the hedge of "lieutenant" into the fields where were nurtured "captains," the navy's highest rank.

On the army side of the Lake Champlain defenses, one commanding officer followed another, on each of whom the newly promoted master commandant paid a call at the headquarters in Burlington. General Dearborn was returned to staff command. At the behest of his political friend John Armstrong, the Secretary of War, plump little James Wilkinson came up from Louisiana to make a grab at glory as commander of all the northern armies of the United States. At the order of General Wilkinson, Colonel Isaac Clark was replaced on Lake Champlain by a Virginian, General Thomas Parker. In less than thirty days, he in turn gave way to the influential United States Senator from South Carolina, General Wade Hampton.

The effort of each of these officers was to concentrate the whole military force at Burlington. There, on August 2, more than four thousand American soldiers — dragoons, artillerymen, infantry, and militia — overflowed the camps and jostled the sailors in the waterfront taverns.

So imminent and terrible was the expected invasion by the British that the citizens of the town mustered a home-defense force, calling themselves by the definitive name of "Burlington Corps of Exempts." The people of Plattsburg, on the other hand, with no troops to protect them, put on a peaceful mien to face the invasion. According to the proclamations from Canada, private property would be respected.

Intelligence reports became somehow confused with cook-house rumor, as they passed from desk to desk at the headquarters of the rapidly changing American generals.

Of the six thousand redcoats expected by the Americans, Colonel John Murray had only fourteen hundred at Ile aux Noix to mount the invasion in which he was loath to disappoint them. In addition to his soldiers, Murray had a most eager naval captain, Daniel Pring; and they had been joined, quite unofficially, by a very congenial naval type, one Captain Thomas Everard, of HMS *Wasp*, who had come to see naval action amid mountain scenery. Together, the three men planned the raid — the conciliatory raid — and, as the intelligence reports came in to British headquarters, they seemed to have every prospect of success.

They crossed the international boundry on July 30 with HMS *Shannon* and HMS *Broke* (Everard in temporary command), three gunboats, and forty-seven bateaux. The following morning the British troops were landed at Plattsburg, where, for twenty-four hours, they indiscriminately destroyed government and private property, and went as far as two miles inland in order to burn a deserted American blockhouse covering Fredenburg Falls.

On August 1, Colonel Murray and his friends parted company about ten o'clock in the morning. The soldiers rowed back to Canada, stopping along the way to burn a house at Cumberland Head and a store at Chazy Landing. Before Murray left, it had been decided to detach two gunboats filled with soldiers to Swanton, on the Missisquoi River, where there were other military barracks and stores, from which American troops had been pulled back to Burlington.

With his guest, Captain Everard, Captain Pring sailed the sloops and the remaining gunboat from Plattsburg to Burlington, for a look at the American fleet. Perhaps they could tempt a part of it out to fight!

Tacking against a south wind, which, as long as it held, was assurance of a hasty retreat, Pring and his little squadron approached Burlington about half-past two in the afternoon on August 2. On a line between Shelburne Point and Lone Rock Point, and about a mile and a half off the navy dockyard, the *Broke* dropped her mainsail, backed her main topsail, and came up slowly into the wind, hanging there on her jib. Following the maneuver of her sister vessel, the *Shannon* took station astern, within hailing distance. The gunboat tagged along behind, like a little brother eager to please. Gun crews hurried to their stations, marines lined up on deck, and there was chattering among the group of skinny little powder boys, quickly silenced by the boatswain. Captain Pring was at the port taffrail, on which, steadied by his extended left arm, rested his long brass telescope. His left hand carefully slid the eye tube forward and back until the prisms came into focus.

The sound of church bells ringing the alarm over the town, but without urgency, could be heard on the British decks, cleared for action. In the circle of his glass, Pring could see the three American vessels tied up at their docks. One of them, the *Preble*, was without her mast; the other two showed bare spars. There was much activity on board the vessels and on the dockside, and Pring guessed that crews were busy rolling big guns across the decks in a shuffle that would bring a long 18- or 24-pounder to bear on his vessel. On the waterfront loomed the government warehouses, large and tempting, just waiting for a torch.

Pring moved his glass up into the town, sprawling over a hillside that was crowned by neat church steeples. Squads of blue-coated soldiers hurried down the streets toward the waterfront. He was giving the town a scare.

Suddenly, he heard the unmistakable sound of a round shot striking the water. He looked questioningly at his first lieutenant, who pointed toward the high bluff above and a little to the north of the American fleet. The shot had been in line. Pring's eye returned to the glass, which he quickly sighted on the bluff. All its summit was raw earth, and, as he counted the thirteen embrasures, two of them belched out white smoke. He straightened up to watch for the fall of the shot: again both were short, but the line from the bluff to the *Shannon* was true. With respectful admiration, Pring concluded that such shooting, which on the first three rounds compensated so accurately for the south wind, was directed by an experienced gunner working with trained cannoneers.

The gunner was Lieutenant Sylvester Churchill, a recent graduate of the United States Military Academy and an artilleryman, who was trying to coax a little more range out of his two 24-pounders from the battery he had positioned on the bluff. Though the American guns fell short, they kept the British vessels well out in the bay and discouraged any bombardment of the town by the carronades on the former Yankee ships.

The threat to Burlington lasted only twenty minutes; then the two English captains sailed away. During the remainder of their cruise the *Broke* and the *Shannon*, followed by their gunboat, showed Captain Everard the mouth of the Bouquet River, a distant view of Split Rock, and the Four Brothers Islands. They also captured four small sailing vessels.

In spite of his efforts to make haste, Macdonough had been caught unprepared. A scratch crew of sailors and army artillerymen took the two gunboats out in belated pursuit, but they soon returned. Scarcely a shot from an American vessel had been fired at the interlopers.

It was another three weeks before the American fleet was ready, and it was September 6 when Macdonough finally sailed. By then, he rated his three sloops at twenty-eight guns, and he had four gunboats. The British still could muster only twenty-five guns, unless the gunboats on the ways at St. Jean had been completed.

When Macdonough sailed for Plattsburg, he had aboard two hundred and fifty seamen, recently arrived with their officers from New York. General Hampton had relented, too, and had given him some soldiers to serve as gunners and marines.

The purpose of the cruise that began on September 6 was to find and engage the two British sloops and the three gunboats, reported to be out on the lake north of Cumberland Head. Macdonough found them, but they ducked back into the Richelieu River before the Americans could come up to them. Having demonstrated his mastery of the lake, Macdonough returned to Plattsburg — and a disagreeable interview with General Hampton.

The senator-turned-general had received from the Secretary of War orders to attack St. Jean on the Richelieu, and he wished Macdonough, with his big boats, to accompany the army into Canada. Macdonough declined to do this, on the ground that his orders from the Secretary of the Navy were quite specific in confining the fleet's activities to the lake, not including the river. In order to encourage an aggressive spirit among junior officers in the navy, Sidney Smith had been exonerated for the loss of the *Growler* and the *Eagle;* but Macdonough, as the senior naval officer on the lake, already had created two fleets, and he did not want to lose the second where he had lost the first. The two officers parted, Hampton to write a letter of complaint to the Secretary of War, after which he went off to Canada, to wander timorously about for several weeks south of the St. Lawrence. Eventually he drew off his four thousand American soldiers after a clash at Chateaugay with four hundred French Canadian *voltigeurs,* led by Lieutenant

Colonel Charles de Salaberry, an officer more intrepid than the senator.

The military activities of the autumn of 1813 kept Macdonough's vessels on the water long after the time normally considered safe for putting them up for the winter. As late as December 4, the American sloops and gunboats were standing by, on the alert, in Burlington Bay.

On that day, Captain Pring led out six gunboats to raid storehouses on Cumberland Head. A watchboat came in with news of the raid, and Macdonough put out at once with all his fleet. Rounding Appletree Point, the Americans could see the distant smoke of the burning buildings. Around the point, the sloops met the full force of a northwest wind, which, in the long reach of thirteen miles of lake, had kicked up a heavy sea of spume-flecked blue waves. Fearful lest the enemy should again escape before the big guns of the sloops could come up, Macdonough put his lieutenant into the *President*'s longboat, with orders to take the gunboats and keep the British engaged until Macdonough himself could come up with the bigger ships.

In the rough waves the transfer from the *President* to the longboat was a hazardous undertaking. The commodore could not tarry a minute, and the change from boat to gunboat was a wild leap into outstretched arms, as the stern bench of the *President*'s boat dropped away from under the lieutenant's booted feet. So it was that Lieutenant Stephen Cassin arrived aboard his flotilla leader all of a heap, with her commander in the narrow space under the feet of the tillerman.

Macdonough had been glad to see Stephen Cassin come up from the coast. They had known each other in the Mediterranean, ashore and afloat. Now, ten years later, when Macdonough sent Cassin ahead with the gunboats on the bleak December waters of Lake Champlain, he knew he had given the job to a reliable officer.

The thirteen-mile row was a torture to the men at the sweeps, and almost as bad for the gunners, shivering in inaction beside their long 12-pounders at the bow. The American sailors dug their oars doggedly into the wild water that seemed to swoop under the searching blades. Cassin stood high in the stern of his boat, wet through by the flying spray, shouting encouragement to his own oarsmen and waving on the other gunboats, challenging them to try to pass him. Fighting for every yard, the little flotilla drew on Cumberland Head. While the Americans were still a mile away, the British boats put out from shore — big boats with guns fore and aft. Cassin and his men expected them to stand and fight, in which case it would be a slashing cutlass battle. In these boats, in this sea, there would be no gunnery duel, and Cassin knew that as firearms the pistols stuck into his wide leather belt were sodden and useless.

But the English boats did not wait; instead, they turned north for Canada. The pace began to tell on the Americans: more and more frequently a sailor would miss his pull at the oar, and the rhythm along the whole bank would be broken by the runaway shaft. It was the unevenness of the race that put the weariness of discouragement into the Americans' stroke. The larger boats of the enemy had twice the sweeps of Cassin's small boats, and the men who plied them were fresh and rested after the congenial work of a successful raid.

Gradually, the white ensigns at the stern of the British vessels drew away from the tiring American gunboats. Cassin finally gave over the unequal race and ordered his four boats into a defiant watch line, across the narrows between Cumberland Head and South Hero Island. There

Macdonough caught up with Lieutenant Cassin, who had done all he could; the Englishmen had not stayed to fight.

Two days before his thirtieth birthday, Master Commandant Thomas Macdonough laid up his fleet for the winter and went home to Lucy Ann — to make plans for the year 1814.

The Frigate *Saratoga*

Early in the new year of 1814, Charles E. Darling, President Madison's Secretary of the Navy, sent his instructions to Master Commandant Thomas Macdonough.

In his office at Burlington, while the snow feathered down on his hibernating vessels, Macdonough studied the instructions that were to guide him through the next summer's campaigns. Basically, they were unchanged from those of the previous year: he was to dominate the lake, and he was advised to be cautious only when assuming responsibility for connecting waters. If by "connecting waters" the Secretary meant the Richelieu River, Macdonough could still command this river by guarding the outlet from Lake Champlain.

Reading further, Macdonough found with satisfaction that he was authorized money and credit with which to hire workmen for building the full-rigged ship which he alone deemed necessary. Specifically, he was directed to build either one such ship or fifteen gunboats.

For years Congress and the paper-shuffling sailors in the Navy Department had advocated gunboats for defense. A mass of figures and logical facts supported the dry land forces of the navy in their argument that, in the harbors of the United States, gunboats were superior to ships. The fact that seventy-five gunboats cost no more than one frigate of the United States' biggest class, and carried almost twice as many guns, was a favorite argument during the budgetary discussions in Congress. But when a seaman like Macdonough was given discretionary power in such a matter, as was the case in Darling's orders of January 28, 1814, he would choose a ship — even for the waters of a lake as cramped and narrow as Champlain. A ship provided a steady platform for the guns, which a gunboat did not; a ship could take punishment that would sink a gunboat; and, as for the argument of economy, it would take two thousand sailors to man a fifty-gun flotilla of boats, with three officers to each boat, as against a crew of four hundred and fifty on a forty-four-gun frigate. Macdonough, who had commanded gunboats at the start of the War of 1812, chose to build a ship.

He called to his clerk to bring the rough drawing to him, and, with the edges of the paper weighted down by the souvenirs on his desk, Macdonough studied the plans and specifications. The *Saratoga* — already he had chosen that evocative name — was to carry twenty-six heavy guns. This was her primary requirement, and her lines and dimensions were those of a flat-sided, shallow-draught gunboat. On Lake Champlain, Macdonough did not require the speed and maneuverability, or the range of operation incorporated with weight of broadside, that were so exquisitely designed into great American frigates such as the *Constitution* and the *Constellation*. Three tall masts and a full set of canvas would carry the *Saratoga* to any place on Lake Champlain where a battle could be enjoined. Her lines were flat, with little sheer or rake, and she carried her batteries low on the water, where they could best play on the enemy's vulnerable waterline.

Macdonough had selected, too, the place where he would build his lady. Of all the communities on Lake Champlain

and on the waters connecting with it, that best suited for a
naval shipyard was Vergennes, Vermont. Burlington or
Shelburne, Plattsburg or Essex — these were towns too exposed to raids from the lake, and they would be among the
first objects of a land attack. Whitehall, in addition to being crowded with army shipping, was too well guarded by
the long marshes, which, under a persistent south wind, or
in a drought such as that of 1813, were shoal water.

Vergennes was situated seven miles up the Otter River,
twenty-one miles below Burlington; it was defensible by
land and from the lake; and it was on the overland supply
route up which the naval stores would come. Moreover,
the community of Vergennes offered a group of enterprising industries, located close to their source of raw material.
There were eight forges, a blast furnace, an air furnace, a
rolling mill, a wire factory, a gristmill, a sawmill, and a full-
ing mill. Most of these would be useful to Macdonough in
the building program that he had in mind.

During the winter, navy headquarters were moved to
Vergennes, and with them went the shipwrights and carpenters, officers and sailors, leaving only a caretaker staff
at Shelburne, where the vessels of the existing fleet were
laid up.

For his *Saratoga*, Macdonough now needed a builder.
Among the shipwrights and carpenters sent up from New
York the previous summer, two brothers, Adam and Noah
Browne, had stood out as masters of their trade. Macdonough invited the brothers to his office and unfolded his
plans. As the craftsmen studied the drawings in silence,
Macdonough took their measure. After a few searching and
pertinent questions, the Messrs. Browne finally agreed to
launch a twenty-four-gun vessel within sixty days. The
three men then sat down to bargain. Time and cost were

the only points open for discussion and argument, as all three were driven by the common motive of patriotism and necessity. Slowly, Macdonough went up in the number of workmen to be allotted to the job; as reluctantly, the builders whittled down the number of days and weeks required to complete the vessel. At last, the brothers looked up from their whispered calculations, and the elder of the two gave his final estimate: forty days from tree to water, at eighty dollars a ton, for a twenty-six-gun ship. Macdonough quickly multiplied seven hundred and thirty-four tons by eighty, and came up with a satisfactory $58,720.00. Figuring the cost of fifteen gunboats at $4000.00 each (the government estimate), this showed a saving of more than $1200.00. The Brownes' figure was agreed upon, and the three men, all now determined to see the *Saratoga* afloat, shook hands.

On March 2, 1814, one hundred and ten men set out to cut the trees and saw the planks and adze the timbers for the ship. On March 7, the Brownes laid down the keel of the *Saratoga* on the shore of Otter Creek.

With his big gun carrier now on the ways, Commodore Macdonough faced up to a decision he had been postponing for some time: did he dare to commit the navy, and his own position on the lake, to a steamboat?

When first he had explored the town of Vergennes and its shipbuilding facilities, a steamboat was under construction there. She was then not much more than a frame, and to his sailor's eye, the engines appeared only a pile of pipes and tanks (called "boilers") and hardware. Having examined this curiosity, he had gone away; but he had not forgotten. A few days later, he returned and seized the vessel for the United States Navy. Work had gone ahead on the hull, until it had come to that moment when the boilers and the firebox and the mysterious engine had to be lowered in, and the deck beams and planks laid over them.

For five years, the steamer *Vermont* — the second steamer in commercial service in all the world — had maintained a schedule on the lake. Macdonough had seen her, but more often than not she had been tied up to the shore while her machinist tackled the recalcitrant engine with curses and a spanner. All along the shore Macdonough had seen woodpiles, which, he was told, were fuel for the voracious mouths of the *Vermont*'s boilers. In order to carry a pay load, frequent stops were necessary; otherwise, she looked like a floating woodpile for her own consumption.

Reluctantly, with the image of the *Vermont*'s faltering engines in his mind, Commodore Macdonough gave the order which converted the hull at Vergennes from a steamboat to a two-masted schooner. On Lake Champlain in 1814 the risk was too great, and the responsibility for putting the United States Navy into steam was too heavy for a very junior master commandant.

So it was a schooner, not a steamer, christened *Ticonderoga* that was launched into Otter Creek during the winter of 1814. She was a well-found, seventeen-gun vessel of 350 tons, with a few extra braces deep in her hold, and, below, a boiler cradle indicative of her intended character.

As the evenings of March drew out, stretching the days to spring, to the thaw, and to the closing campaigns of the War of 1812, work was reaching a climax in the shipyard at Vergennes. Since the *Ticonderoga* had gone down the ways, scarcely a day seemed to go by without a navy launching. In addition to the ship and the schooner, Macdonough had ordered the building of six large gunboats, with which he could pursue down the Richelieu River in relative safety.

One by one, the vessels kissed water in the bowing, bobbing dance of a launching: the *Allen*, the *Burrows*, then the descriptively named *Borer, Centipede, Nettle,* and *Viper.* As the builders finished them, they were poled down the creek to lie, together with the *Ticonderoga*, awaiting the arrival of their guns from New York.

On the big *Saratoga*, activity continued until late each night, as the Brownes went around lighting torches, trying to get one more hour's work out of their carpenters, so they could start a new job next morning. Adam and Noah reckoned that, if the weather held, they could keep their word to the commodore by April 11. On the tenth of April, they went together to Macdonough's office to report that they would launch her next day. On the morning of April 11, the *Saratoga* was christened and launched, and by afternoon the frigate was alongside the wharf and sheers were rigged for stepping the three lower masts. Adam and Noah Browne had built their ship with five days to spare; as craftsmen, their word had been made good.

Though all the vessels were now launched, their ordnance had not yet arrived from Troy. The early thaw had made a mire of the roads, and the warm April rain and churning hooves of the teams had kept them deep in mud. Messengers came up from the south, the bellies of their horses thick with wet mud, to report that guns and anchors for the *Saratoga*, with cables and rigging and sails, were on the way. Macdonough could do nothing but wait, and prepare defenses for the unarmed hulls that composed his navy.

On April 2, the ice had gone out of the northern end of the lake. Macdonough assumed, therefore, that the British fleet had been water-borne before the *Saratoga* was launched. With an enemy fleet on the lake, his vessels at Shelburne and at Vergennes were subject to attack. The army could protect the *President*, the *Montgomery*, and the *Preble*, as well as the four gunboats at Shelburne, which could be moved the very day that the ice left the bay. At

Vergennes, the vessels were in danger of a determined raid by the British, with a blockship, which, if sunk in the narrow mouth of Otter Creek, would effectively bottle up the American fleet for weeks to come.

General Wilkinson was as greatly concerned as was Macdonough, and on a visit to Vergennes in mid-April the commanders of the two services went out to the mouth of the river and selected a site on the north shore for a battery of naval guns. On his return to Burlington, Wilkinson sent five hundred troops to Macdonough, to build the battery and to provide a guard on the boat basin.

The alarm came early in the morning of May 11. A messenger from Burlington, riding hard, arrived at Macdonough's headquarters just before dawn. The urgency of the knocking at his door had the commodore out of bed and reaching for his pistols before the man found breath enough to call up to the open window that the British were out. A new brig and two sloops, with thirteen gunboats, had anchored the night before in the lee of Providence Island. As he pulled his riding boots over his blue overalls, Macdonough dispatched a servant to rouse his officers in their billets around the town. He finished dressing in the kitchen downstairs, where the exhausted messenger was washing down bread and cheese with ale, black as molasses. While the man refreshed himself, he told the rest of his message: General Alexander Macomb was sending fifty artillerymen in light wagons, to help the sailors man the battery — called Fort Cassin — at the mouth of Otter Creek. They would be in Vergennes by dawn.

A midshipman appeared, dressed to dirk and pistols, but with his hair still rumpled. Macdonough sent him to meet the cannoneers and lead them to the fort by way of the track west from Ferrisburg.

Stephen Cassin burst into the room, heard the news, and was off by the creek road to his battery.

Before the others arrived, Macdonough learned from the messenger that the brig was of a size with his own *Ticonderoga*, and that she appeared to have eight gun ports to a side. When the man referred to the two British sloops as the *Chubb* and the *Finch*, Macdonough looked up questioningly. But the messenger was a dragoon, and all he could tell of the British ships was that they had a wide orange stripe around their sides.

Captain Pring seemed in no hurry to attack. All that day he stayed in the bay between Providence and South Hero Islands. On May 12, he loitered off Burlington, and in the afternoon of May 13, he was sighted off Essex, New York, where he looked over the Eggleston shipyard. He could see no activity there.

Early in the morning of May 14 Captain Pring drew near to the mouth of Otter Creek. He saw the new earth and the fascines of Fort Cassin, from which he made the deduction that he had come upon the lair of the Yankee vessels. He moved into range, and for an hour and a half he bombarded the new fort. Cassin's seven 12-pounders, mounted on ships' carriages, replied shot for shot during the long cannonade, and the Americans succeeded in driving off every attempt by the British gunboats to dash in for the creek. A British shot, coming in through an embrasure, struck a gun carriage and injured two artillerymen. Otherwise, the shots from the *Linnet* and the two sloops (identified by Cassin as the *Eagle* and the *Growler*, refitted and once again renamed: the *Chubb* and the *Finch*) fell harmlessly into the earth walls of Fort Cassin. With several gunboats damaged, Pring finally withdrew to the north.

Crowding up onto the parapet together, soldiers and

sailors as one cheered their own success. Two ship's boats, their painters cut by near misses and trailing over their bows, drifted unmanned out near Diamond Island. Urged on by more cheers, Cassin sent out two officers — a soldier and a sailor — in a rowboat with crews to bring in the drifting boats. They were the first American prizes of the naval war on Lake Champlain.

The British vanished toward Canada. It was several days before Macdonough heard that, on his northward passage, Pring had detached three gunboats up the Bouquet River to raid the flour mill, and there had very nearly lost all to a local militia.

Finally, on May 28, Macdonough warped his two new vessels around the tight bends of Otter Creek and gained the open lake. Standing north for Plattsburg under a spread of canvas that had not been seen on Lake Champlain since the British *Inflexible* and *Royal George,* the *Saratoga* and the *Ticonderoga* swept down the lake. Near Juniper Island, the trim sloop *Preble* fell into position astern, and the three American men-o'-war sailed on to Plattsburg Bay.

Macdonough Anchors His Fleet

During 1812 and 1813, the winds of war had stirred only desultory little whirlwinds around the Champlain Valley. The huffing and puffing of ineffectual American generals had blown down scarcely a tamarack in the Canadian forests north of the border. No force of strength in men or in command had developed along the Richelieu River, or in the flat wooded prairie from Montreal to Rouse's Point, seriously to challenge the Americans' right to the old warpath of the nations — the Champlain gateway to the land. In the two sailing seasons of the war, the naval commanders on the lake had scarcely tested each other's strength.

Thomas Macdonough inherited all the problems that had confronted earlier military leaders who had sought to build a navy on which to ride northward to victory. Winthrop, Johnson, Amherst, and Arnold — all had felt the weight that now rested on the shoulders of Macdonough. They, too, had created war fleets from the standing timber of the forests bordering on Lake Champlain. They, too, had been compelled to wait for men and materials to make the long journey from the distant Atlantic coast. And in the increasing complexity of advancing civilization, the demands of the vessels each had required — canoe, whaleboat, row galley, and now, in 1814, full-rigged ship — kept pace with communications to hand.

Daniel Pring, British commander on Lake Champlain but

in actual fact master only of the Richelieu River, suffered under stifling official neglect. Britain's military efforts on the northern frontier, in 1812 and 1813, had been directed on land to the Niagara Peninsula and the western end of the Windsor Peninsula, and, afloat to Lake Erie and Lake Ontario, where they were met by the full strength of the Americans. Early in the war, when Sir James Yeo had been sent out from London to command all of England's inland fleet, Captain Pring had been dismissed, almost summarily, to the naval backwater of Lake Champlain. At the time of his appointment, which was also the time of maximum war against Napoleon, Sir James had been the only British naval officer ashore. He was in London, undergoing a court-martial for the inglorious loss of a ship! In Canada, while Sir James built his huge ships on Lake Ontario but would not fight them, Pring (who was not a Yeo man) fought against both official inertia and the Americans.

Yeo's naval policy — a large fleet of ships in being on Lake Ontario — fitted the tight defensive policy of the man who was responsible to London for the over-all prosecution of the war from Canada. Since the days of Murray and Sir Guy Carleton, the governor general of Canada had always been a military man, with the duties of commander in chief. During the War of 1812, that double responsibility reposed in Sir George Prevost. The son of one of those Swiss soldiers of fortune, who, by founding the 60th Royal American Regiment of the British line in the 1750's, had become so closely associated with British North America, Sir George Prevost had won his baronetcy in 1805 for his stubborn defense of the island of Dominica. After that date, promotion came to him for merit on the civil side, rather than for his military achievements. He was appointed governor general of Canada in 1811, and when war broke out on Canada's southern frontier in June of the following year,

Britain found herself with a commander in chief in a situation far beyond his military capacity. Sir George's reluctance to take the offensive, either on his own two western frontiers or in the Lake Champlain Valley, was an admission of his own lack of self-confidence. For two years, Prevost kept his civil dignity intact by assuming the familiar armor of inactive defense.

In 1814, events in Europe forced him onto the offensive. On April 11 of that year, Napoleon Bonaparte abdicated the throne of France, and a great hush fell over Europe. From Cape Trafalgar to the Baltic Sea, soldiers and sailors were coming home. In the quiet of peace only the rustle of papers was heard, as monarchs and chancellors, ambassadors and ministers gathered up their notes and documents to join in that polite but vicious struggle that was the Congress of Vienna.

Only in London was the government distracted by the rattle of an unconcluded war. With Bonaparte safely on Elba, Lord Liverpool's Tory government could now focus on England's two-year-old struggle with the United States. What it saw was neither pleasing to itself nor salutary at the approaching Congress. Consistently, British ships on the remote seas had been outfought by trifling American frigates. On the distant Canadian frontier British armies and land-locked navies had failed to gain a conclusive victory, or had been defeated. Lord Liverpool and his ministers set in motion measures finally to conclude this unwelcome war.

Their method was in the most approved style of power diplomacy. In the summer of 1814, the British foreign minister, Castlereagh, sent his commissioners to Ghent, where an American commission was waiting, to bargain an end to the War of 1812. But the attaché cases of the British commissioners were empty. In them were no conquered territories to be released for a ransom, no occupied cape or island to be ceded back in return for an advantageous trade agreement.

Before the commissioners set out across the Channel, the British soldiers who would implement their talks with victories for England had sailed for North America. The army that Lord Liverpool chose to send was the most formidable in Europe. It was the Duke of Wellington's Peninsular Army, which for six long years, from Lisbon to Toulouse, had fought Napoleon's greatest marshals and finest troops and had defeated them. Intact, indomitable, and invincible, the stolid regiments boarded their transports. Though they sang "A troopship was leaving Marseilles, bound for old blighty's shore," and though they deserved home more than any other soldiers in Europe (save possibly the remnant of the French army), they had one more war to finish before they got the final stand down. So they sailed, disheartened at the westward course of the transports, but Wellington's old soldiers still.

Four thousand men went to Bermuda, bound for Washington, to carry out Lord Liverpool's high policy of cowing the United States government by burning its capital city. Twelve thousand troops went to Prevost in Montreal. With them came orders to the reluctant governor to invade south through the Champlain Valley and to seize American territory.

Even with such positive orders and such a world-renowned army, Prevost still could find reason to hesitate before following Burgoyne's trail. In his indecision he grasped at the same straw which in 1776 had brought failure to Sir Guy Carleton: he entered into a naval race with the Americans. To help him, he called upon Sir James Yeo.

Where ships were concerned, Sir James thought in large terms. The vessel which the English built on the Richelieu River in the summer of 1814 was a 1200-ton, 36-gun frigate.

In tonnage and armament, she equalled the United States Navy's *Constellation* class, and was by far the largest and most powerful war vessel to sail on Lake Champlain. At her launching on August 25, she was christened the *Confiance*, a French name in keeping with Sir George Prevost's policy of conciliation toward French Canada.

The fault of the *Confiance* was that it had taken too long to build her, and as her size and broadside were intended, like Wellington's "Invincibles," to awe the Americans, no secrecy was maintained regarding her specifications.

With information and time, Macdonough was able to retaliate by building the brig *Surprise*, a good reply to British confidence. The shipbuilders of Vergennes contrived to build the *Surprise* within a space of nineteen summer days, between July 23 and August 11. She was a 500-ton vessel and carried a main battery of twelve short 32-pound carronades, augmented by eight long 18-pound cannon. On second thought, Macdonough changed her name to the *Eagle*, and, with Lieutenant Robert Henley in command, she joined the battle fleet in Plattsburg Bay.

The spring and summer had been busy for Commodore Macdonough and his American fleet. Though Captain Pring had not come out since his sortie in May, a constant watch was kept on the Richelieu River. But the fleet's main job in preparation for Prevost's invasion was in co-operation with the army. For Macdonough that job had become a congenial one.

In 1814 General George Izard was the army commander in the Lake Champlain pass. He was an engineer officer whose skill could not be denied, nor could it be hidden under the covering of superannuated generals and political favorites that blanketed American military operations at the beginning of the War of 1812. The vigor of George Izard, and of other assertive officers who rose to high command, soon restored the morale of the regular army to the great traditions of George Washington's Continentals.

In such an atmosphere Macdonough and his naval officers felt at ease, and co-operation between the services was natural and unstrained. General Izard expected the blow from Canada to come down the west side of Lake Champlain. To counter it, he moved the army from Burlington to Plattsburg, where he set to work fortifying the Saranac River line and Cumberland Head. Under Macdonough, the fleet convoyed the soldiers across the lake, and then went to work helping with the defenses and running supplies into the bay, or down the lake to the forward posts on the Canadian border.

All ranks worked cheerfully in preparation to receive the invaders. In their pride of commander and of regiment, the soldiers anticipated with professional curiosity the coming match against Wellington's veterans. The sailors, speculating on their approaching encounter with the *Confiance*, leaned confidently against the tree of navy tradition.

But the first blow to fall on General Izard and the American forces on Lake Champlain did not come out of Canada. It came from the south, in the form of an order to General Izard from the Secretary of War. The general read the order with astounded incredulity; it was fantastic. Taking with him four thousand regular troops, he was to go "at once and with all speed" by way of Lake Champlain, Lake George, Schenectady, and the Mohawk River, to reinforce General Brown's two thousand regulars at Fort Erie.

Reading the order in Plattsburg in late August, Izard could find neither rhyme nor reason in it. There was no question of Arnold-like treason in the document. Armstrong's bungling interference in past campaigns had been too consistent for ordinary villainy to be indicated in this, the most monumental blunder in a career star-spangled with stupidities.

Izard read the order again: its wording left no room for doubt. There was no phrase that would permit a delay, not even a delay long enough to meet Prevost. As an army officer, he could only protest — and obey.

On August 29, General Izard and the bulk of the army sailed from Plattsburg to implement Secretary Armstrong's emphatic order. At Ticonderoga, the troops were disembarked to take the Lake George route. When General Izard thought to look back, already the trail had closed in behind him; he could no longer see the waters of Lake Champlain.

At Plattsburg, Izard's friend and fellow in the U.S. Army Corps of Engineers, Brigadier General Alexander Macomb, was far too busy to think of himself as abandoned to a forsaken cause. In the time left to him, Macomb had to consolidate his men and his resources into a tight defensive perimeter, and then make his stand within it. For his main post he chose Platt's Point, between the lake and the southward bend of the Saranac River, with detachments to watch the upper crossings on the river. To resist Prevost's invasion with fifteen thousand troops, Macomb had a meager army of forty-seven hundred men; his regular soldiers numbered fifteen hundred effectives, eight hundred invalids, and six hundred noncombatants. At General Izard's summons, some five hundred Essex and Clinton County militia had turned out, while Vermont's governor, by law not allowed to order his militia out of the state, had contrived to supply the balance of Macomb's army with volunteers. In order to make use of every man, the convalescents were given posts in the three forts guarding the neck of the point, while the sick were sent to Crab Island in the bay, where they were to man a two-gun battery if they were able to do so.

Of the navy, General Macomb asked only for protection on his eastern water flank, and this protection Commodore Macdonough was ready, able, and eager to give. For two years he had been building ships and men into an entity as a fleet. Now, in the first days of September 1814, he made the final adjustments and preparations to use to its best advantage the weapon he had forged.

Four American men-o'-war — the *Saratoga, Eagle, Ticonderoga,* and *Preble* — rode at their anchorage in the hook formed by Cumberland Head, providing a hard right fist for the army ashore. Six large gunboats and four smaller boats of one gun each, their names commemorating American sailors who had lost their lives in earlier naval action, were at their moorings close under the guns on Platt's Point, ready to row out and take their places in the American battle line.

In number of guns and weight of broadside, the American fleet and that of the British expected to come against it were about equal. The British crews were of unknown quantity, though probably outnumbering the American sailors, and it could be assumed that they were experienced sailors and gunners serving under able professional officers. In quality Macdonough's officers were a match for the enemy, and through their training together and their cohesion the Americans could equalize any disparity in numbers.

On board Macdonough's flagship, the *Saratoga,* which he himself would command, there were two hundred and forty men. Under the master's mate and the marine sergeant, they had been trained aloft and on deck and were now able sailors and competent marines. Aft on the quarter-deck, the commodore had a trustworthy first lieutenant in Peter Gamble. When illness had beached Raymond Perry, to whose efforts the highly efficient level of training throughout the fleet was due, Gamble had taken over as lieutenant. The *Saratoga*'s sailing master was a modest old saltwater sailor named Peter Brum. As onetime pilot of the steamboat *Vermont,* Hugh Ferris could be relied upon to pinpoint every rock and shoal on Lake Champlain, should the coming battle develop into a chase. Even Macdonough's clerk, James Sloan, who was a bookseller by trade, had begged permission to stay on board for the battle, and with the purser, had trained as a gun number. At the beck of the commodore, there would be a group of eager young midshipmen in fast-rowing boats who would carry messages during battle to other vessels of the American fleet, should this be necessary.

The captains and first lieutenants aboard the other ships, however, could be relied upon to work together instinctively and without further orders. This mutual understanding was the product of a common heritage in training, and of a familiarity grown out of friendship. Stephen Cassin was captain of the *Ticonderoga*. Macdonough and the long-nosed Cassin had been shipmates during the Tripoli war. John Stansbury was Cassin's number-one officer on the *Ticonderoga*. He had come to Lake Champlain in 1813, on being promoted out of a midshipman's berth on the forty-four gun *United States*, where he had been a shipmate of Stephen Cassin's brother. While serving on the *United States* Stansbury had acquitted himself with distinction during that frigate's fight with the *Macedonia*.

Similarly close to each other, and to their commodore on Lake Champlain, were the two senior officers aboard the *Eagle*. Her captain, Robert Henley, was a Virginian who, at seventeen, had been highly commended for bravery, and who had lived up to every expectation of him. Lieutenant Joseph Smith was Henley's choice for the *Eagle*'s second-in-command.

Only in the case of the *Preble* did Macdonough give specific orders to restrict and restrain her captain. This was not due to any lack of confidence in Lieutenant Charles A. Budd, but the *Preble* was very small, and, with only thirty men on deck, she was particularly vulnerable to a boarding party from a British gunboat. Macdonough's own gunboats would give her some protection during the battle, and instructions to this effect already had been given to Lieutenant Francis Mitchell, the commander of the American gunboat flotilla. Each of the other nine gunboats was commanded by a senior midshipman, a sailing master, or a master's mate. Among them there was a healthy rivalry on which Macdonough could depend for aggressive action, when and where it was required when the approaching battle developed.

Strategic considerations forced Macdonough into a defensive position which in no way reflected the temper of his sailors or the readiness and strength of his vessels. Once more, as in 1776, a strong British army with a great fleet was descending out of Canada to force the Champlain Valley, as the gateway to the Atlantic seaboard. And once more, effective naval strategy appeared to Macdonough, as it had appeared to Benedict Arnold, when he placed his little fleet in behind Valcour Island: the attacking British ships, riding on a strong north wind, would be forced to give up the advantageous weather gauge in order to come up to the Americans, sheltered behind a land feature.

For Macdonough to attack the British ships in the open lake north of Cumberland Head would be to take a foolish risk. The traditional and favorite tactic of the British navy was the long-range gun duel, for which their ships mounted the long guns. Conversely, the American ships were armed with short, heavy carronades, for the battering, close-in fight preferred by the American navy. This being the case, Macdonough would gain the strategic advantage by forcing the enemy to come up-wind for a slugging match at his anchorage in Cumberland Bay.

Maneuvering this strategic advantage to favor his defense, Commodore Macdonough had time to rehearse and rearrange his battle line so as to have the tactical advantage, too, once the battle was enjoined. Meanwhile, the British army deployed, and the British navy waited impatiently for a wind from the north.

The *Eagle* was the first to move. From her moorings in the open bay, Lieutenant Henley edged her east and a little north toward Cumberland Head, and, when the leadsman at the bow reported the bottom rising, the *Eagle* dropped anchor. Looking westward across the bay, Henley could see as far as the first bend in the Saranac River. He was about four hundred yards from the shore, off Cumberland Head. A British battery there would not give him trouble, in the way that the left of Arnold's line had been annoyed by Indians and light infantry from the shore of Valcour Island. But, close as he was to shore, no Britisher could cross his bows and turn the American line.

Astern of the *Eagle*, Macdonough placed his *Saratoga* in line southwest with Crab Island. The *Ticonderoga* was next in line of battle, and behind her was the sloop *Preble*, with four gunboats off her stern. The other six gunboats, in pairs, guarded the spaces between the vessels.

The British fleet would come with a northeast wind over the taffrail. Clear of the point, the vessels would have to beat up into Plattsburg Bay. In the lee of the gently sloping rise of Cumberland Head, the wind would drop, and the English vessels would lose steerage way and be forced to drop anchor in order to hold their position. This position would be well within the range of Macdonough's big guns.

Riding at anchor, bows on into the northerly wind, it was the Americans' starboard broadside that would be engaged. By rearrangement of the guns on the decks of his vessels, Macdonough would be able to increase the weight of his broadsides. This rearrangement was made by all the captains, who also selected their best-found guns to roll across to the starboard gun ports, which would open the battle.

In the short-range fighting which was expected, many of the guns would be hit and disabled, and up and down the engaged line the cannon would fall silent one by one, until one ship or the other lay helpless, at the mercy of her enemy. When this happened, unless the opposite battery could be brought to bear, a ship was lost.

With time for preparation, Macdonough anticipated the eventuality. If he trussed his ships completely in a cradle of anchors, a trained crew could wind its ships around, end for end. He gave orders for this to be done.

Macdonough rowed out with the two longboats, the kedge anchor slung between them, and from his gig supervised the laying of the *Saratoga*'s winding anchor. At a point ahead of and well off the starboard bow, he dropped the anchor, which was secured by a loose cable to the starboard quarter. Off the port bow, in relatively the same position, a second kedge anchor was dropped, its cable also coming overside on the starboard quarter. This accomplished, Macdonough had himself rowed under the *Saratoga*'s counter, where a best bower was being lashed, with a long reach of cable running the length of the vessel down the port side, and in at the port hawsehole to the capstan.

All anchors in place, Macdonough ordered a practice run of the maneuver. At the bow, the bow anchor was taken in and secured (in battle it would be cut free). On an order from the quarter-deck, the stern anchor dropped with a splash into the bay; at the same time, its cable was bent around the forward capstan, and to the lead of the chantyman's song and the clicking of the wooden ratchet the crew began their measured march around the capstan. By the stern, a crew was hauling in the kedge anchors. Slowly, in the calm water, the *Saratoga* moved around, her stern making an arc to starboard. When her stern was in line with the starboard kedge, the order was given to haul in on the port kedge anchor by the stern. With every heave, the big vessel moved further around until she had changed end for end. All three cables were then secured.

The maneuver was practiced once more while Macdonough rowed ashore to consult with General Macomb. The two American commanders exchanged intelligence: the previous night Macdonough's watch boat had seen part of the British fleet at Ile LaMotte, where the men were landing supplies and erecting a battery; according to Macomb, the British army had passed through Chazy, and he expected contact to be made the following morning, September 6.

Macdonough returned to his flagship, having first secured the general's promise to beat his personal band for volunteer powder boys for the *Eagle*.

On the morning of September 6 red-coated infantry were seen marching toward Plattsburg, along the beach at the head of the bay. Macdonough sent some gunboats to harass them. In spite of the mounting south wind, gunfire could be heard inland, where Major John Wool's advance guard was falling back before the right wing of the British army. Mistrusting the wind, Macdonough ordered his gunboats back; it was no time to risk the loss of even a gunboat, with the entire British fleet expected on the next north wind.

But Sir George Prevost was not yet ready. The inexplicable transfer from Plattsburg of General Izard and four thousand soldiers had thoroughly alarmed the British commander in chief. Suspecting a trap, he moved with even more than his usual hesitancy. On September 1 he had crossed the American frontier in force, but it took him five full days to advance the nineteen miles to Plattsburg. Wellington's veterans were disgusted; their spirit had been weakened by the detour to North America, and, without their Iron Duke to drive them, they gladly fell out beside the road and brewed their *cha*. Their brigadiers, accustomed to obeying Wellington's orders, subsided into inertia under their new commander in chief. From force of habit, they waited for orders — orders that did not come. Under Prevost, all the instinctive and ingenious resources of the wise old soldier for self-preservation asserted themselves.

While Sir George was stifling his army by his ineptitudes, Sir James Yeo was showing a belated interest in the Champlain fleet. With the launching of the *Confiance* on August 25, Yeo saw an opportunity to do a favor for a friend, and at the same time to offer an additional snub to Captain Pring. On September 2, Captain George Downie arrived at Ile aux Noix to take over command on Lake Champlain and to hoist his commodore's flag on the new frigate. Pring was left in command of the brig that he himself had built. Downie was a mature man, a senior captain in the British navy. He was under a great handicap on Lake Champlain, where he was unfamiliar with the lake, unknown to the men, and a stranger to the ships with which he was to rush into battle.

The *Linnet*, under Captain Pring, and the *Chubb* and the *Finch*, commanded respectively by Captains James McGhie and William Hicks, were ship-shape and battleworthy. The same was true of the twelve gunboats, but these were manned by uncertain crews of Canadian militia. Downie's own flagship was unfinished, and her crew had been made up hurriedly of drafts from ten different British warships then in the St. Lawrence River. The shipwrights were still aboard the *Confiance* when Captain Downie took her to Ile LaMotte to join Pring, with the rest of the British fleet, at the base being established in LaMotte Passage. There he discovered, to his consternation, that his guns lacked the flintlock mechanism for firing. A fast cutter was sent back for the forgotten box. Before the boat returned, the wind had shifted to the south; it was the same September blow that had caused Macdonough to call back his gunboats enfilading the beach. The wind blew without let-up for five days.

His fleet held by the wind at Ile LaMotte, General Prevost accepted another delay. His regiments were in position and his siege train was approaching the north side of the Saranac River, but he would not launch his assault until he had British vessels on his shore flank. The fire from Macdonough's gunboats on September 6 had taught him caution. Prevost waited in position for Downie's fleet to attack the American ships at anchor in the bay. When that battle had been joined, he would order the assault across the river. At last, events had pushed the reluctant general up to the turning point of his timorous career.

Macomb was as nearly ready as he ever would be, both in his fortifications and in the morale of his soldiers. Macdonough was ready, his crews going quietly about their work on his ships.

On September 8, the wind still hard out of the south, Macdonough had himself rowed ashore. He sought out the general and found him where Macdonough had hoped he would be: at Fort Brown, intently studying a British rocket battery at the neck of the big salient made by a southward bend in the river. It was to discuss this very battery that the commodore had come ashore. Macomb handed his telescope to Macdonough, who noted at once that the battery was oddly constructed, being without embrasures. Above the brown earth walls there was a row of cone-shaped objects, slanted almost imperceptibly toward Platt's Point. These objects were war rockets. Though they were unfamiliar to him, Macdonough guessed these to be of the largest size, with a reported range of two thousand yards. As he watched, the high fur-crested cap of a rocket battery gunner appeared, and its owner, a red-faced man, leveled a spyglass in the direction of Fort Brown. The commodore restrained an urge to wave his hand.

From this battery, the rockets could not reach the American ships on the other side of Plattsburg Bay. But these new weapons were highly mobile, requiring only a two-legged wooden trough for launching. Galloping pack horses, led by gunners, could round the north end of the bay and, from positions quickly set up on Cumberland Head, could command Macdonough's fleet. The rocket was a terrible weapon, and, being unfamiliar — its snarling rush in flight, followed by a comet's tail of sparks — made the steadiest man uneasy. If one *did* hit on a ship's deck, its heavy charge of powder, in a thin iron casing, burst with the heavy concussion and spread fire high into the inflammable rigging.

Macdonough wanted to have the Royal Artillery rocket battery raided and neutralized; General Macomb agreed and promised an immediate raid. Captain McGlassin, with fifty men, did the job during the night of September 9, and the rocket battery never went into action against the American fleet or the army.

Next day, the commodore visited the vessels of his battle line. He talked with the men, and in the tiny wardrooms he went over the signal codes with the ships' officers.

That evening the wind went down with the sun. Over the Adirondack Mountains, a few long clouds were red as fire. During the night, the wind would rise in the north, and in the morning the British would come on the blast of new cold air out of the ultimate reaches of British Canada.

A Signal Victory

It had still been dark when the midshipman who had the distant watch on September 11, 1814, had arrived on station midway between Cumberland Head and South Hero Island. It was cold in the open ship's boat, and no cloak could keep out the sting of the north wind that blew up the nine-mile avenue from Ile LaMotte. There would be no warmth for the midshipman or for his boat's crew until their relief came out from the fleet — or until the British came.

It was now seven o'clock in the morning. Far down the lake beyond Point au Roche, a big whitecap flashed on top of a wave. The lake was kicking up! Then, in the same place, the whitecap showed again. The midshipman wiped his eyes carefully on the cuff of his coat, blinked, and looked once more. The "whitecap" was a sail; then he saw that another ship was breaking clear of Point au Roche. The second vessel had two masts, both of them under square sail. A third vessel was close behind the second: she was big, with a wide spread of canvas on masts that towered into the pale morning sky.

The British fleet was out in force!

In the bow of the watch boat, the boatswain was fumbling with flint and steel over the touch hole of the 2-pound signal gun. Suddenly warm again, the midshipman alerted the men at the oars for the first long stroke on the race to the *Saratoga* with his news. The 2-pounder coughed its little charge, and a cloud of smoke, snatched from the muzzle, scudded downwind. On board the American fleet, all hands knew now that the enemy was coming.

Prepared and ready, the Americans waited. The few last jobs were done: galley fires were put out; a few water buckets, used for a morning douse, were refilled; sand was scattered on the scrubbed white planking of the deck. In the cockpit of the *Saratoga* the surgeon and his mate moved the table they had fetched from the captain's cabin, so as to catch the light coming through the open hatch. Their instruments were laid out neatly, their blue coats hung precisely on pegs. Carefully rolling up the sleeves of his white lawn shirt, the surgeon raised his head: suddenly, a deep silence had fallen over the ship. Not a footfall nor a whisper came from the deck above. Hurrying up the steps of the companionway, the surgeon saw the whole ship's company kneeling on the deck, their heads bowed in prayer. Slowly, he dropped to his knees, slipping the rakish black *chapeau* from his head. At the breech of a long 24-pounder knelt the commodore, his hands clasped, his face uplifted to the mast top, and his fine deep voice calling out for help, for forgiveness, and for victory. From under a bushy eyebrow, the surgeon noted that the "skipper" had girded himself with a cutlass and a pair of brass-bound pistols, all stuck inside a wide black belt.

Shortly before eight o'clock, the Americans got their first view of the vessels they would fight. Beyond the flat point of Cumberland Head, the three white-tipped masts and the three topgallant sails of HMS *Confiance* glided by above the trees. With this harbinger, the British fleet broke clear of the point: first a sloop, then the brig *Linnet*, finally the *Confiance* herself, followed by a second sloop. A string of signal flags climbed into the rigging of the flagship, and as one the ships of the British line backed sails and came up all standing.

For long minutes the two fleets watched each other — the Americans in position, the British sizing up the Americans while waiting for their own gunboats.

More signals broke out from Commodore Downie's flagship, and, their bows veering slowly up into the wind, the *Chubb* and the *Linnet* beat up into the bay on a course set to cross the "T" of the American line. Getting under way more slowly, the big British frigate set her course for the bow of the USS *Saratoga;* without making much headway, her long bowsprit bobbed knowingly into the chop off the point of Cumberland Head. Behind the *Confiance,* Lieutenant Hicks, in the *Finch,* was gathering in a dozen gunboats to lead them against the *Preble* and the *Ticonderoga,* at the southern end of the American line.

On board the *Linnet,* his feet wide apart and his stance firm on his quarter-deck, was Captain Daniel Pring. He had entered Plattsburg Bay once before, as commodore in a successful raid, with Murray of the army, and with his good friend, Captain Everard. But this Sunday morning it was different: it was ship's work that was to be done. For almost three years, Pring had sought Macdonough, as Macdonough had sought Pring, to stand against each other, sailor to sailor. Now, as the ships drove to engage, Pring was passing by his old adversary on the Yankee frigate *Saratoga* — an adversary who, when the flagships met, would come against a stranger.

Though the *Linnet* and the *Saratoga* were out of range of each other, Pring ordered a broadside from his port battery of long 12's aimed on Macdonough's three-master. In effect, and almost in intent, it was a salute. Seven of the iron shot splashed harmlessly into the water; for some reason, the eighth shot carried to the *Saratoga.* All but spent, it dropped onto the deck and rolled to the port scuppers, smashing a wooden cage in which a gamecock was hidden. In the red rooster was the pride, the hope, and most of the pay of the boatswain's mess. Free, ruffled but belligerent, the bird stalked cautiously across the gritty deck. Seeing no enemy, it flapped up onto the starboard gunwale, and there, across the waters, it saw the great white wings of the British sail. To this enemy, the red cock crowed its defiant invitation to battle.

The *Chubb* began the battle. Close-hauled into the wind, she drove fast to pass the bow of the *Eagle*, which had been firing all during the *Chubb*'s run up into the bay. As the range narrowed, the shots fell closer. A ricochet screamed over the rail, tearing a hole through the big mainsail. Another five minutes and Captain McGhie would have his vessel through the worst of the *Eagle*'s fire. The *Chubb*'s port battery of short 18-pounders was coming in range. McGhie gave the order to fire. The sloop reeled, and acrid powdersmoke whipped back over the captain. When the smoke cleared, a midshipman, stationed in the bow with a leadsman, came to McGhie with word that the bottom was rising to the lead and shoal waters were ahead. McGhie acted instinctively, slamming the rudder hard over in a turn away from the menace inshore. The mainsail went slack, the big, heavy boom lashing back and forth in the confines of the close haul of the sheets. The jib and staysail cracked and whipped as though they would tear themselves loose.

The *Chubb* swung round to port and came to a stop. For a moment there was confusion, as gunners left their guns to help get the sloop again under way. As she lay, the *Chubb* was abeam of the *Eagle*. For the time being, McGhie considered his position safe from the Yankee's full broadside, so it came as a surprise, crashing just over the deck line, tearing great splinters from the rails, ricocheting off the gun barrels and bowling men over like so many duck pins. Just ahead, there was a splintering crack as the big spar of the boom snapped. The sail split in a long ripping tear; the broken end of the boom fell athwart the littered deck. The *Chubb* was helpless.

The dazed men struggled up out of the wreckage to stare unbelievingly, shocked out of all feeling, incapable of any reaction. In the north wind, the stricken ship drifted to the south, away from the *Eagle*. Soon she would be between the *Saratoga* and the oncoming *Confiance*, masking the *Saratoga*'s fire in the important early moments of battle.

From his flagship, Macdonough saw the *Chubb*'s white ensign still flying from the peak of the jib. He ordered a bow gun to be fired at the sloop and sent Midshipman Charles Platt (from nearby Plattsburg) in a longboat to board and tow her, as a prize, out from between the two battle lines.

The British ensign had been run down before Platt came aboard the *Chubb* to take the surrender from her wounded captain. Every man aboard was a casualty of some sort: six lay dead, sixteen were badly wounded, all the rest were bruised, cut, or stunned.

The *Eagle*, which had brought a full broadside to bear on the *Chubb* by hauling her stern anchor around on a spring to the bow anchor cable, was now engaged with Captain Pring's *Linnet*. In the time it took to reload the *Eagle*'s broadside, and for the stricken *Chubb* to drift clear, the *Linnet* was on the American brig's fore. Having used the limit of his spring on the bow anchor, and with the cables for his winding anchors shot away, Henley could aim only the single starboard bow gun on the *Linnet*. With but one cannon against the Britisher's whole port battery of eight long 18-pounders, the *Eagle* was taking a hard pounding along her crowded deck and through her rigging. Ten of the *Eagle*'s men were dead and heaved overside; a dozen badly wounded men were below. Henley ordered one of the sailors to resand the bloodstained deck.

Tenacity could no longer serve the purpose of the American line. The *Eagle*'s guns could be used to better advantage from another position. Regretfully, Robert Henley ordered the remaining cables cut, and sent the men aloft to make sail. Breaking off her hopeless fight with the *Linnet*, the *Eagle* dropped back out of the American line, to take a station between the *Saratoga* and the *Ticonderoga*. There, with its port battery it could just range on the *Confiance*, and could keep the bows of the hard-pressed *Ticonderoga* clear of attack by the British gunboats. From his new position, Lieutenant Henley saw that both the British *Finch* and Captain Budd's *Preble* were out of the fight.

The *Preble* lay inshore, under the protection of the American army on Platt's Point. Charles Budd had not stayed long in his position. The English gunboats came in force against him, opening the battle with their bow guns from extreme range. The *Preble* fought back with her trifling starboard battery of four long 9-pounders. In weight of metal, the little *Preble* aggregated 63 pounds, against a combined weight of 436 pounds for the twelve British gunboats. But Captain Budd's real danger lay in the boarders whom he could expect to swarm over his low sides, overpowering his small crew of thirty men. His only plan of battle (which he had discussed with Macdonough) was to keep as many of the enemy engaged as possible, for as long a time as possible, and then to retire and save his vessel. So Captain Budd fought his ship with his head, rather than with his feeble armament. Deliberately, he angered the gunboats and enticed them to attack. When he saw that they were losing interest, he dropped back as though he were about to flee. Like a pack of 'coon dogs, the gunboats attacked the "treed" vessel. Captain Budd kept his eye on the *Ticonderoga* and the four American gunboats to the north, now engaged with the British sloop *Finch*. When he saw the battle there develop in favor of the Americans, he hoisted sail, and, like a chattering squirrel, easily eluded the hounds below by leaping to another tree, and bore off out of the battle. His gunners had done well, reporting several hits, and two of the gunboats hit hard.

His Majesty's eleven-gun sloop *Finch* had made straight for the *Ticonderoga* but had failed to get in close enough for her short 18-pounders to strike her enemy with full force. From nine until ten o'clock that morning, the *Finch* and the *Ticonderoga* exchanged broadsides. In that hour Captain Hicks saw his vessel whittled away beneath his feet and chopped down over his head. Great scores, marking the passage of a cannon ball, appeared across the *Finch*'s white deck. The taut rigging snapped with the crack of a rifle; the gaff, half shot away, was held up only by the peak halyard, still intact. One by one the guns were silenced. The mast was hit and, without sufficient support to hold it, bent dangerously to the tension of the jibstay. Hicks heard a shot strike his rudder and saw his tillerman go flying, wild-eyed, across the deck. The man clutched frantically at the broken rail, which gave way; almost deliberately, he fell overboard, where he caught a line and bellowed for help.

The *Finch* was done. Slowly, she drifted southward toward Crab Island. Hicks looked to his men: strangely enough, only two were severely wounded, and these he sent below. As for his vessel, she was only a derelict hull. The ship's boat had been holed by an American shot that had passed astern of the *Finch*. Hicks had cut the boat adrift, and now he could see her, awash, drifting out toward the middle of Lake Champlain. There was no chance of getting away; captain and crew were marooned on board the wreck. If the northwest wind (which was dropping) held long enough, it might carry the *Finch* out into the lake where the British storeship, waiting off the point of Cumberland Head, could send a rescue boat.

Instead, the drift carried the sloop onto Crab Island, where she grounded on a reef. On impact, the delicately balanced mast whipped forward and snapped off, eight feet above the deck. A midshipman scrambled over the tangle of canvas and ropes to retrieve the fallen ensign. With his treasure wet but safe, the midshipman — borne on the shoulders of a seaman — was lashing to the stump of the mast the white flag with its big red Cross of St. George when the two guns of the battery on Crab Island fired. The sick men at the guns were weary, and the shots were wide, but it was futile to take further chances, and Hicks gave the order to strike. From his perch on the seaman's shoulders, the midshipman handed down the ensign to his captain.

On shore, the gaunt Americans cheered. Some of them came down to the water's edge to have a closer look at their prize: HMS *Finch*, formerly the USS *Growler*.

There was no respite for the *Ticonderoga*. Before the *Finch* had drifted out of range, Stephen Cassin had turned his attention to the gunboats which were boring in on him from the south. Four of his own gunboats were keeping the enemy from rounding his stern. The British gunboats came at him in lunges, four to a wave, trying to get at his guns on the starboard quarter and to board at the stern. Twice, they got in close enough to cast their grappling irons, and, twice, the Americans cut away the ropes from the jagged hooks that bit into the gunwales. Once the British were so close that they got a purchase on the *Ticonderoga* with their boat hooks. On that occasion, Cassin himself leaned over the taffrail and discharged both of his pistols into the faces of the wildly shouting crew. They were swarthy Canadians, who crowded forward in their eagerness to gain the *Ticonderoga*'s deck with cutlass and boarding pike. That boat had been driven off by the American gunboats *Borer* and *Nettle*, which rowed in close to spray grapeshot over the open gunwales of the Britisher. Somehow enough of the crew survived the blast of bagshot and musket fire to row the big craft away. As she swung around, she showed the name *Centipede* painted large at her stern. In one of those moments of merriment that come to a man engaged in mortal combat, Stephen Cassin noted that the English gunboat was painted green as a bug. He threw back his head and roared with laughter, looking up to the taffrail on which, a moment before, his lieutenant, John Stansbury, had been standing. He wanted to point out the aptness of the British joke, but Stansbury was nowhere to be seen. Momentarily, Cassin was puzzled; then his attention was called elsewhere. Later, he was to learn that one of the powder boys, coming on deck with his arms full of powder bags, had seen Lieutenant Stansbury run aft and leap up on to the rail, holding a pistol in his right hand. For an instant he stood there, poised; then a cannon ball struck him full in the body. Before he hurried on, the powder boy had seen the lieutenant's body, arms and legs asprawl, go flying over the port quarter rail.

Two more American gunboats had dropped aft from

their station between the *Ticonderoga* and the *Saratoga* and had joined in the fight against the Royal Navy gunboats. To the men on the American schooner, it seemed that the British boats were losing their stomach for the fight. Three of the English boats had been sunk; now the nine remaining boats had drawn off and lay on their oars, a mile away.

It was almost eleven o'clock. Six men had been killed and six lay wounded in the cockpit of the *Ticonderoga*. Midshipman Hiram Paulding looked down at his right hand, realizing that it pained him excruciatingly. As he looked, the pistol in his hand fell to the deck. A wave of nausea seized him, as the pain from his hand surged up through his body. Someone caught him as he fell, and he was carried into the fetid cockpit. For the two hours of the action, when the slow match given him proved useless, the seventeen-year-old Paulding had fired his division of guns by flashing his pistol priming into the fine-grained powder spilled into the vent. Each shot fired had enveloped his right hand in a searing flash of white flame, and as often as not, the buck of the exploding gun had pounded the raw flesh before he could snatch his hand away.

To the north of the *Ticonderoga*, the battle still raged. Three vessels continued to fight: the *Linnet*, the *Confiance*, and the *Saratoga*. On both fleets and in both armies, all knew that the final outcome of the battle would be decided by the duel being fought between the two frigates.

At eight o'clock that morning, Commodore Macdonough had stood beside a long 24-pounder, watching the British vessels deploy into Plattsburg Bay. The *Chubb* and the *Linnet* sailed by, making for the shallow water that protected the head of the American line. He saw the smoke envelop the *Linnet*'s orange side as Pring let loose his broadside. Macdonough did not bother to take cover and was mildly surprised to hear the thump of a shot, dropping on the deck of the *Saratoga*. When the gamecock crowed, he looked toward it, as did all on board the frigate. The laughter and the spontaneous cheer that the rooster's gesture called forth from the men on deck, broke the glaze of pre-battle tension. After that, men moved about and talked quite naturally. To the southeast, though still out of range, the British gunboats had begun a ragged fire on the little *Preble*.

Over the round black breech of the cannon, Macdonough studied the oncoming *Confiance*. At her bows, both anchors were dangling a cockbill from the catheads; obviously, once she was in position on the *Saratoga*'s fore, the *Confiance* was going to drop anchor. Up and down the American line the guns were silent, waiting for Macdonough to open the fire. Carefully, the commodore lay his long 24-pounder on the bow of the *Confiance*. He figured the level and the range, then ordered the piece traversed to port. Stepping back with the firing lanyard in his hand, he gauged the lead of his gun against the slight angle of the enemy approach. At the precise moment, he jerked the lanyard: the flint fell on to the steel frizzen, the priming powder ignited, the cannon roared and bucked. The shot was on its way.

It was a well-aimed shot, but it was lucky, too. It cut the anchor cable as it passed through the port hawsehole. Loose on the open deck with the whole range before it, the round iron ball ripped splinters from the deck and showered them over the sailors at their battle stations. Finally, its progress was stopped by the wheel of the *Confiance*, which it reduced to sticks and slivers.

The first full broadside from the *Saratoga* followed close on Macdonough's opening gun. Its effect changed Commodore Downie's plan of action. Both anchors were lost to him in that broadside, and with his steering impaired he was forced to back his sail and come up all standing. Instead of being across the *Saratoga*'s bows, he was on the Yankee's beam, with only 300 yards of blue Lake Champlain water between them.

Accepting his position, Downie ordered a broadside. For this first broadside, the guns of the *Confiance* had been loaded with two round shot each, and with an extra charge of powder.

With the fury of a hurricane, the wave of hurtling British iron struck the *Saratoga*. She reeled under the impact: men were thrown on the deck and extra shot tumbled out of the racks built into the starboard gunwales. For a moment, Macdonough thought that all the men strewn about the deck were casualties, but soon one man picked himself up, then another. Finally, the voices of officers and gun-captains were raised in shouts for their gun crews to "jump to it." One by one, the cannon were rolled out into their firing positions and reported in action. One gun in the first division stayed back in its inboard loading position: a British shot, coming in through its gun port, had shattered the left forward wheel of the carriage, sprung the side wall, and dropped the short barrel, cantwise, onto the axle. Whole men of the stricken gun's crew had already scattered themselves among the other cannon as replacements for the wounded.

The *Saratoga*'s second broadside crashed out in a volley. After that, the guns fired at will, so that the roar of the carronades dinned constantly around the deck, and men, their teeth flashing white against smoke-blackened faces, shouted at each other in an effort to make themselves heard.

The American frigate received the second broadside high. It ripped into shreds the rolled hammocks stowed along the gunwales. Some of the hammocks caught fire, and a fire-control party dashed forward with buckets and hooks, tearing the white canvas from its bed and dousing water over the flames.

No more did the British shot plunge into the *Saratoga*'s hull. The first heavy broadside of the *Confiance* had loosened the wedge-shaped quoins under the breeches of the British guns, elevating the muzzles. No one thought to recheck the angle, and the *Saratoga* took the enemy's fire on her bulwarks and in her rigging.

As his duties permitted, Macdonough himself sighted the long 24-pounder with which he had begun the battle. On one occasion, when he had bent over to sight the barrel, a large piece of the shattered spanker boom fell across his shoulders, knocking him down. He lay for a moment, benumbed; then, again on his feet, he strode forward to show himself, unhurt, to the crew.

Already, Peter Gamble was dead, his chest stove in by a blow from the quoin of a gun, sent flying in the first broadside.

From the bows, Macdonough saw the *Eagle* making sail to drop back. At the port gangway he found young Midshipman Platt, just returning from the prize *Chubb*, which, after having raised the gridiron flag over the white ensign of the Royal Navy, he had turned over to boats from shore. Macdonough grabbed the boy, and, over the din around them, sent him with the commodore's compliments to Lieutenant Henley, asking Henley to bring the *Eagle* to the *Saratoga*'s stern, to engage the *Confiance*.

So the duel progressed. On board the American flagship, now receiving over her bows a raking fire from the *Linnet*, one by one the guns of the starboard battery fell silent. More and more wounded men were carried down into the screeching hell of the cockpit.

Before his favorite 24-pounder was put out of action,

Macdonough was hit again, this time by the flying head of his own gun captain. The grisly object caught him full in the stomach, knocking him into the scuppers, where he lay gasping and covered with blood. For the second time that morning, the commodore was reported killed. This time, as he struggled to his feet there was a silence on the smashed and debris-strewn deck of the *Saratoga*. Only one gun of the starboard broadside remained in action.

Still on one knee, Macdonough saw that his last carronade was being man-hauled forward to fire once again. Sticking out of the short barrel was a canister shot of grape: in their fury, the gun crew had crammed two canisters in on top of the double-round shot. It was Master's Mate Joshua Justin's gun, and he was making it do the work of four. Now on his feet, Macdonough saw the gun fire. Still dazed, he was surprised to see the piece come free from its carriage and arch back, inboard over the deck. The heavy carronade seemed to pause in midair; then it dropped, straight down through the open main hatch. One long, piercing scream came up from below.

Unless Macdonough could bring the port battery to bear, the *Saratoga* was beaten. Sailing Master Brum reported to the quarter-deck; he was of the same mind as his commodore. Already he had mustered the men to cut the cable of the bow anchor, and to bend the cable of the stern anchor to the forward capstan.

Macdonough ordered all men on deck, except those of the winding party, to seek shelter below during the maneuver. Quietly, the gun crews dropped through the open hatches.

A sailor was sent below to cut the lashing that held the big stern anchor to the transom windows. It splashed overside. The men heaved on the starboard kedge anchor cable, which was wet and cold to their hands. Gradually, the wide stern began to move around, and the bow fell off to port. The wind, which would have helped to swing the broad ship, had dropped, and only brawn and muscle and determination could get the Saratoga around. Slowly, she swung until the stern was pointed directly at the long, orange side of the British flagship.

Having waited for this moment, the *Confiance* loosed her broadside, now much weakened by the telling fire of the *Saratoga*. The round shot and grape swept over the Yankee's stern and rattled down the length of the big open deck, over the backs of the American sailors, who had flattened themselves to receive the raking. Of all those on deck, only Sailing Master Brum was discomfited by the blast: somehow, the clothes were torn from his body, and, but for a few tatters, he was naked in the warm September sun. In one of those incongruous actions that men find important in battle, the old fellow retrieved a stained 'kerchief from the deck and fashioned it carefully into an apron. Philip Brum was a very modest man.

Macdonough himself had cleared the snarl that had suspended his ship midway through the difficult maneuver. More quickly now, the *Saratoga* moved around as the cables were drawn or paid out. At last, all the cables were made secure, and the gun crews scrambled out from below to man the guns of the port battery, intact and now pointed at the *Confiance*. After the stern-raking broadside, the British frigate had hastened to copy the *Saratoga*'s maneuver. Lacking time to carry out the kedge anchors, she sought to haul herself about as the *Saratoga* had done, by a line bent from the anchor cable at her bows, and led around to her stern. She had completed only half the turn when a shot cut the bend, and — without the help of any wind — the big frigate lay in the still waters, her stern to her enemy, completely at the mercy of the *Saratoga*'s full port battery.

On the afterdeck of the *Confiance*, Lieutenant John Robertson stood beside the jury-rigged tiller that had replaced the shattered and broken wheel. He had commanded the flagship since the second American broadside; killed by a cannon hurled off its carriage, Commodore Downie lay dead in his bunk below.

The port battery was a shambles. For it to deliver a four-gun broadside would have been a miracle. It was tantalizing to the lieutenant to see the relatively trig starboard battery, menacing nothing but the British gunboats, drawn off to the east away from the American line.

Aloft, the tall masts of the *Confiance* were scored and splintered to the trestle trees. As he looked up, Robertson saw that two sailors in the cross trees of the mainmast were lowering the body of a red-coated marine by means of a line around the dead man's waist. Everywhere, the new white sails hung in tatters above the deck, and the ends of cut ropes dangled from tilted and broken spars.

Lieutenant Robertson knew that the hull was in no better condition than deck or rigging. For two hours, the ship's carpenters had been below, stopping, with canvas, planks and balks, those holes dangerously near the water line. There were a hundred holes in the port side of the *Confiance*.

Casualties had been appalling: about forty dead were still on board; perhaps another forty had gone over the side; sixty badly wounded, some of them dying, were below in the surgeon's care. Robertson, as well as the crew, were shocked at the news from the cockpit, spreading quickly over the ship: while helping at an amputation, the wife of the steward had been instantly killed by a round shot that had come through the hull. She had been a favorite of the men, and a mother to the little powder monkeys.

Without a chance to retaliate, men and ship had taken all the punishment either could stand.

The *Confiance* struck her colors.

On the *Linnet*, well stationed across the stern of the *Saratoga*, Captain Pring saw the flagship's big white ensign come down. Since driving away the *Eagle*, he had had an hour's steady firing over the bows of Macdonough's flagship. The American commodore had paid him little heed, though Pring knew that his guns were hitting the Yankee often and hard. Now, with the *Confiance* out of the fight, he could expect some serious attention from his old adversary on Lake Champlain. He ordered a boat away to the *Confiance*, to bring back from the commodore a situation report, and any new orders he might have.

Before the boat returned, Pring was heavily engaged with the port battery of the *Saratoga*, Macdonough having continued around on his kedge anchor to bear on the *Linnet*. For fifteen minutes, Pring took the fire of the thirteen heavy guns of the *Saratoga*'s broadside. Valiantly, his own eight 12-pounders answered the roar of Macdonough's guns. When the midshipman returned from the *Confiance*, Pring learned of the frightful conditions aboard her, and learned, too, that at the southern end of the line, beyond the screen of smoke that curtained him off, the fight was over.

Daniel Pring was also told that, by the death of Captain George Downie, once again he was Commodore of the British Fleet on Lake Champlain. The honor was a hollow and a bitter one.

With ten dead and fourteen wounded on board his brig, Pring hauled down the last enemy flag on Lake Champlain.

Two days after the Battle of Plattsburg Bay, Commodore-Master Commandant Thomas Macdonough sat in his cabin aboard the *Saratoga*, writing his detailed report. Before his table was carried back from the cockpit, the bloodstains had been scrubbed away with vinegar. The whole fleet, in fact, had been cleaned up and was again in battle trim. Prize crews had gone aboard the four captured British vessels, and had spruced them up, too. They now rode in line, inside the four American vessels that had beaten them. In a corner of Macdonough's cabin, neatly packaged, were the four British ensigns, ready to go to the Secretary of the Navy with the commodore's report.

The British gunboats had lowered their colors and fled the bay. Macdonough regretted that he had no vessel left, fit enough to pursue them; but without their big consorts they were harmless to the American cause. That cause had now been won.

Instead of attacking on shore while Downie attacked with the fleet, Prevost had waited cautiously to see the outcome of the battle on the lake. When the battle went against the British, he withdrew his whole army back to Canada. Wellington's "Invincibles" were on their way home at last. Though Macdonough could not know it, his battle in the crook of Cumberland Head had decided the outcome of the war. When word of the battle reached Ghent, the British commissioners — on orders from London — conceded to the Americans' demand: *status quo ante bellum*. On Christmas Eve, 1814, the inconclusive War of 1812 came officially to its dreary end.

To a commander of men, the most happy of tasks is the rewarding of the loyalty, devotion, and bravery of his subordinates. Though his back ached from the blow it had received during the battle (Macdonough tried to forget the cause of the big purple bruise on his lower ribs), the commodore worked hard to see that in his report no worthy name would be forgotten. Swords, medals, promotions — the milestones that mark a successful career in the Services — would come to those whose names appeared in the report. For Macdonough himself there would be a captain's commission, and, as a gift from the states of New York and Vermont, certain tracts of land, one of which was on Cumberland Head. But behind the list of the brave was the unwritten list of the dead, gone beyond any possible reward from grateful and obligated governments.

Out on Plattsburg Bay that evening of September 13, 1814, it was only another beautiful day on Lake Champlain that was now drawing to a close. The waters were clear and bright, as they had been before the battle; no wreckage was left to mar the peaceful quiet of the wide bay. Water does not show its ugly scars, nor does it bear the weight of monumental memories, as does the land.

That morning, the second day after he had been killed, the body of First Lieutenant John Stansbury, late of the United States Navy, rose to the surface near his old ship, the schooner *Ticonderoga*. His shipmates lifted the body tenderly out of the water and buried Lieutenant Stansbury in the cemetery on shore. Lake Champlain had rejected its last battle casualty.

The Boats that Participated
in the Battles

THE BARK CANOE

The familiar birch-bark canoe was first developed by the
northern Algonquin Indians. Utilizing the light, strong bark
of the birch trees which grew so plentifully in their hunting
ground, the Algonquin tribes built a craft adapted to their
particular requirements. Living as migratory hunters in a
land which was a vast complex of lakes and rivers, they
needed a carrier of good burden, yet light enough in weight
to be carried easily through the woods from one body of
water to another. They found such a craft in the birch-bark
canoe. This was later adopted, also, by the Iroquoisian
Hurons who came to settle among the Algonquins.

Samuel de Champlain, who traveled long hours and many
miles in these Huron and Algonquin canoes, describes those
he first saw, along the lower St. Lawrence:

. . . (canoes) are from eight to nine paces (pas) and about a
pace and a half broad in the middle, growing narrower toward

the ends. They are very apt to turn over in case one does not understand managing them, and are made of birch bark, strengthened on the inside by little ribs of white cedar, very neatly arranged; they are so light that a man can easily carry one. Each can carry a weight equal to that of a pipe.

The instability of the canoe, remarked upon by Champlain, was due to its being constructed without a keel, the shape being held by the interior bracing. This bracing is mentioned by the Reverend John Cleaveland, writing in 1758, when he describes canoes of a larger type than those, intended for only three men, which were used by Champlain on his trip of exploration in 1609:

. . . After Dinner took a walk down to ye Lake to see the two Birch-Canoes which were bro't in last Night; one is about Thirty-Feet long upon the Edges and Five Feet wide in the Widest Place, the other about Three or four and Twenty long, the outside made of Birch-Bark. The inside cieled with Cedar Clap-Boards thin as brown paper and laid lengthways of ye Canoe upon which crossways of ye Canoe is another laying of Cedar bent to the Shape of Ye Canoe adzed down with young split Willow. They go with Paddles and The largest will carry 20 men. It is so light that four men might lift it up and carry it on their Shouldirss. Their Seams on ye Out-side are patched to make them tite.

In comparison with the birch bark canoe of the Algonquins, the Iroquois bark canoe was a heavy, cumbersome affair. It was little better than the canoe hollowed out of a single log, which had sufficed the agrarian Iroquois until their migration brought them to the Mohawk Valley, and their war parties sought to dominate the Algonquin tribes.

When the Five Nations turned to making bark canoes they followed the method of construction learned from the

Algonquins. The Iroquois, however, lacked two things: an adequate supply of large birch trees, and a skill developed through the centuries.

The making of a canoe was as follows: the Indians having selected from the forest the smoothest-bodied and largest basswood or elm tree, the bark was carefully peeled in one entire sheet, free from cracks or holes. It was then spread out upon the ground, the smooth side downward, and held in this position by heavy stones and blocks of wood placed upon it. The sides and ends were then bent upwards, and retained in this position by numerous small stakes, so driven into the ground as to press against them. Thus, the shape of a boat was given to a sheet of bark which being securely held at every point by weights and stakes for several days until it became thoroughly dried, then retained its form. A few braces and other supports to render it more firm were then added; and the rude craft was ready to be launched and carry its burden over the water.

THE RADEAU

The *radeau* arrived in the Lake Champlain Pass at the very beginning of the French and Indian War, and from that time until the end of the American Revolution, it was a distinctive feature of army transportation on the lakes.

John Dies, a ship chandler of New York City, writing to

General William Johnson on August 19, 1755 (nine days before Johnson's army moved from the Hudson to Lake George), suggests the building of a radeau, tells Johnson how to build one, and outlines its tactical use:

. . . by what Little I Know of the Route you Intend to Take it Seems Cleer to me, that the Enemy will meet you with their whole Force and Polesey where you are to Land, Lett it be near or att Som Distance from the Fort now To Favour your Landing I think the Following Method would be of Greate uce, I would build two or att Least one, Flatt In the Same Mannor as the Ship Carpenter's build their Flatts by which they Creen the Vessels, the Bottoms are made of Squar'd Loggs 8 or nine Inches thick, and as Broad at they Can be had, to Mak the Fuer Joints, and as Long as the Floate is Intended, these are Fastned together by a Square peice of Timber, Notched Down about half the thickness across the Endes of the Bottom Peices, and Pind or or Trunnel'd to Gether, the Sides of this Flott Should be Rais'd high Enough for a Breast work to Cover the Men, with portholes cut In them att a proper height, and allso holes to Run oars out through, In Souch a Floate you might Mount Some of your Field Pecies, Man'd with 40 or 50 Men, it Seems to me a thing of this Sort might be of Servis to Cover the armey when Landing, the Loggs they are Made of ought to be of the Softest and Lightes wood you Can Gett, they are Easey made Tight by Caulking them Inside, as it would be Difficult to turn the Bottum up to Doe it outeSide, and if you should fall Short of Oakom you Can make them Tight By Driveing Soft wood or Tough Bark or Moss In the Joints, you'l Excuse my Troubling you with this Scheame, if you think it wont answer or you wont want it, as it Springs from a Sinceare Desire of your Sucksess and wellfare, as they are made onley of Sq'r Loggs and you have Hands Enough I Dont Doubt but in 2 or 3 Days you may Compleate them.

By May 1756 the English had built two radeaux. On his return from a scout to Fort William Henry, Sieur Perthuis, interpreter to the Caughnawagas (Iroquois living in Canada), reported:

They also saw two boats shaped like flat barges and very wide, ready to be caulked; they judge these are the vessels which the English is to use for the transport of his artillery.

When the radeau *Invincible* was launched on July 17, 1759, this type of vessel, a mobile floating battery, had taken on the additional duty of convoy escort. The radeau was a floating island of heavy guns, mounted ready to fire in defense of the fleet of bateaux which carried troops and baggage. These bateaux, unable to defend themselves, rallied to the radeau if and when attacked.

As soon as General Amherst had captured Ticonderoga and gained a beachhead on Lake Champlain, he ordered his naval officer, Captain Joshua Loring, to build a fleet. Of the vessels that were built, the first to be launched was the radeau *Ligonier*, named for Sir John Ligonier, the commander in chief of the British army. The Ligonier was 84 feet long and 20 feet wide; she carried an armament of six 24-pound cannon.

In the Library of Congress there hangs a "View of Crown Point," * showing in the foreground a six-gun radeau. This is thought to be the *Ligonier*, though it could be any one of the three radeaux used to transport Haldimand's artillery in the concluding campaign of the French and Indian War.

Under oars the scow-like radeau was painfully slow, but under sail before the wind she could make remarkable speed. In his journal, Lieutenant Hadden remarks that the *Thunderer* once sailed ninety miles in nine hours.

The *Thunderer* was the ultimate example of this class of vessel. Built at St. Jean in 1776, she was 91'9" on deck, and 72'0" on the keel. At her widest beam (she was not entirely square in plan) she was 33'6", and she was 6'8" in the hold. Accounts vary as to the *Thunderer*'s armament, as was probably the case when her guns were rearranged for various operational roles, but all agree that she had nine gun ports each side, two cut into the transom, and (according to Pausch's journal) two in the bows. When ketch-rigged, she had mortars firing from mounts on the center line of the main deck forward. Detailed plans of this vessel are in the Admiralty Papers in London.

The last of the military radeaux passed down Lake Champlain in November 1777, when the British abandoned the forts at Ticonderoga and Crown Point:

"The *Maria* and the *Thunderer* are proceeded on towards St. Johns. the former with Provisions and Sick, the latter with some Ordnance Stores and as many Sick as she cou'd contain— about 150 are on board, and it was thought necessary this Vessel should be appropriated for their reception, after taking in a Tier of Shoff and Provisions.

The *Camel*, laden chiefly with Artillery Stores, and the *Inflexible* with provisions, remain here to take in some Brass Guns

* See illustration "A View of Crown Point" following page 210.

brought by Lake George to Portage yesterday, which I expect down in Batteaux this day. The danger of the Vessels being stopped by a Northerly Wind and frozen up at this advanced Season induced me to get them out as soon as possible, and I hope there will now be no danger of the whole Naval Armament being safely laid up at St. Johns.

So passed into history the mighty *Thunderer*, and the *Camel* (perhaps more aptly named), which is presumed to have been a vessel of the radeau type. Towed civilian scows and oil barges have taken the place, today, of the old radeaux.

THE ROW GALLEY

As a type of vessel particularly adapted to naval purposes on Lake Champlain, the row galley in Benedict Arnold's 1776 battle fleet was not an innovation.

In 1759, charged with constructing a fleet to deny the lake to the advance of General Amherst's army, the French naval officer, de la Bras, had built three row galleys: *La Brochette* (The Pike), *L'Esturgeon* (The Sturgeon), and *La Musquelonguy* (The Muskellunge).

When the American army retreated from Canada in the late spring of 1776, a small row galley was building at St. Jean. This vessel was dismantled, its parts transported south to Skenesborough, and there reassembled and launched as the *Lee*.

These, and the four row galleys built for Arnold's fleet during the summer of 1776: the *Trumbull*, the *Washington*, the *Congress*, and the *Gates*, were all of one type, the counterpart of which was to be found in the "xebec" or "chebec" of the Mediterranean Sea. The vessel was characterized by its shallow draft, great length in proportion to its beam, its weather-braving ability, and its maneuverability under oars. These features were deemed well adapted to naval requirements on Lake Champlain, in action against a British navy

traditionally bound by a deep-ocean construction policy: deep draft, full-ended ships which were slow sailers and which required sea room in which to maneuver.

Various rigs were used in adapting the basic hull to Lake Champlain. De la Bras rigged his three xebecs (in 1759, the French used the Moorish-Spanish name for their vessels) as sloops. Arnold gave each of his four row galleys (he used the doubly descriptive name, part English, part Franco-Italian) two lateen sails in the North African manner. When the English took the galley *Washington* a prize, they restepped her two masts and refitted her as a schooner. According to a contemporary watercolor in the Fort Ticonderoga Museum, "New England Vessels at Valcour Bay," the little 43′9″ *Lee* was sloop rigged with a square topsail and no bowsprit, when she was in the American service. When they rerigged her as a prize, the British gave her a bowsprit, as shown in the British Admiralty drawings of the prize: the *Lee*.

From this same set of drawings, preserved among the Admiralty papers of the British Archives, the lines, dimensions, and construction details of the row galley *Washington* have been preserved. These also give us a reasonably accurate picture of the three other row galleys in Arnold's fleet, though it appears from the Fort Ticonderoga watercolor mentioned above, and from a panoramic sketch in the Canadian Archives, that each of these differed slightly from the others. The *Trumbull* and the *Gates* appear to have been sister ships, smaller than the *Washington;* the *Congress* was larger than the other three, as would befit Arnold's flagship during the battle.

In armament, the *Washington* and the *Congress* differed slightly. Both had two 18-pound cannon and two 12-pounders, but where the *Washington* originally shipped aboard two 9-pounders and four 4-pounders, the *Congress* had four 6-pound cannon and two 2-pounders, which brought her weight of broadside down to 88 pounds against the *Washington*'s 94 pounds. Both vessels had eight swivel guns, but the *Washington* carried, in addition, a 2-pounder on a swivel mounting. This comparison of gun power is based on receipts for armament taken on board on October 2, 1776, out of ordnance stores at Ticonderoga. These receipts are on file in the Naval Records Collection of the Naval Records and Library in Washington.

Only three of Arnold's row galleys were engaged at Valcour Island on October 11, 1776; the *Gates* was still at Ticonderoga, rigging, fitting, and arming.

The failure of the row galleys lay not in the concept of their design or in their tactical employment, but in their lack of numbers.

THE GONDOLA

As early as May 3, 1776, the curiously controversial but brilliantly energetic Brigadier General Benedict Arnold had written down detailed specifications of the gondola. May 3 was the day after news had reached the American army in Canada that the British fleet of warships and transports was in the St. Lawrence.

Arnold's note bears the title, "Dimensions for two Gondolas to be built at Chambly," and is signed and dated at that place. The specifications are found in Kenneth Roberts's notes for *Rabble in Arms*, now in the Fort Ticonderoga Museum.

A rough sketch, accompanying Arnold's notes, gives the deck plan. This calls for a fore deck 13' long, with an after width of 13'; a 4' long well deck; a main deck 16' long, which foreward is 16' wide and 14' aft; and finally, an after cockpit 15' long to the pointed stern. It will be noted that the over-all length of the deck diagram totals 48', not the specified 45'.

These, then, are the proportions of a gondola as first envisioned by General Arnold. Eight such vessels were built, and served in Arnold's fleet at the Battle of Valcour Island: the *Providence*, *New Haven*, *Boston*, *Spitfire*, *Philadelphia*, *Connecticut*, *Jersey*, and *New York*. Of these, it would seem that only the *Spitfire*, known to be smaller than the others, was built to Arnold's "Chambly" specifications. The sunken *Philadelphia*, raised in 1935 through the thrilling efforts of Colonel L. F. Hagglund, gives us proof of the exact dimensions of an eighteenth-century gondola. Undoubtedly, the other city-named gondolas of Arnold's fleet were replicas of the *Philadelphia*, differing only in details, as the individual master carpenters differed in their interpretation of the plans provided them. Of greater length than that called for in the "Chambly" specifications, the *Philadelphia* is 54′ long, with a beam of 15′, and a depth of 5′. An after deck 13′ long has been added to the original plan, with a 3′ well deck between it and the main deck.

Gondolas moved under oar or sail. The Lake Champlain gondolas show a tall mast. The main mast of the *Philadelphia* less the missing top mast, measures 35′11″, with a main and a top sail. Here again, the *Philadelphia* gives us the dimensions of these spars, for they were found, water-logged, lying athwart the gunwales, when the vessel was first discovered resting on the bottom of Lake Champlain near Valcour Island. The main yard of the *Philadelphia* is 27′ long, the topsail yard 22′.

The armament of the gondola consisted of three cannon: either three 9-pounders or, ideally, one 12-pounder in the bows and two 9-pounders on the main deck, one firing to port, the other to starboard. In addition, eight swivel guns were carried. On the *Philadelphia* was found a small cannon with a broken yoke which had been used in place of the usual stocked swivel gun.

Each of Arnold's gondolas had a complement of forty-five men to work her guns, man the sweeps, and set the sails. Usually, the men lived ashore, except for the boat guard. But we can imagine all on board, the night before the battle of October 11, 1776, crouching huddled and cold on the crowded deck and in the narrow space below the decks, among the stowed gear and powder kegs. It must have been a long night.

CAPITAL SHIPS AND GUNBOATS — 1814

H.M.S. *Confiance* was the largest warship to be built on Lake Champlain. She was the ultimate in size and power in the naval race which, for almost sixty years and through three wars, consumed the time, energy and resources of the successive commanders on both sides who vied for control of the Lake Champlain water gate. The *Confiance* ranked with the great *Constellation* class of frigates which, on the wide seas, did so much to enhance the reputation of the fledgling United States Navy.

In tonnage, the *Confiance*, 1200-ton, far exceeded the 734-ton *Saratoga*, with which she fought a duel to the death in Plattsburg Bay in September 1814. The disparity in tonnage resulted more from a difference in construction than in over-all dimensions, for the *Saratoga* was built as a corvette rather than a true frigate. A corvette was a frigate-rigged vessel with a low freeboard and no high quarter-deck: she carried her guns on the upper deck. The difference in construction between the *Confiance* and the *Saratoga* emphasizes again the contrast existing up to this time between the Royal Navy and the United States Navy. Where the British were steeped in tradition, the young American navy was free to be imaginative. As Benedict

Arnold, in 1776, "invented" the row galley for use on Lake Champlain, so Thomas Macdonough, in 1814, borrowed the corvette from French naval construction in building his *Saratoga*.

The difference in tradition was shown, too, in the type of guns used by the two capital ships in the Battle of Plattsburg Bay. The main battery of Downie's *Confiance* consisted of thirty-one long-barreled, long-range cannon firing 24-pound balls. Macdonough relied on the hard-hitting but short-ranged carronade, of which he had six 42-pounders and twelve 32's.

As the two capital ships on Lake Champlain in 1814 far exceeded in size any of their predecessors in other wars, so did the gunboats of both sides out-measure the earlier boats of their class. The four larger American gunboats were 75' long, as compared with the 54' length of Benedict Arnold's gondola, the *Philadelphia*, and others of her class.

The naval race did not come to a halt with the cessation of hostilities after the Battle of Plattsburg and the Peace signed in Belgium in December 1814. Left without a fleet, except for the gunboats which had escaped capture by Macdonough, the British built two heavy gunboats in May 1815. Probably these were yawl-rigged. The *Axeman*,

63′10″ long with a beam of 16′2″, was armed with bow and stern guns and a mortar amidships. The *Caustic* was of approximately the same dimensions but with three cannon, each one on a turntable mount, along the centerline.

While the *Axeman* and the *Caustic* spent their lives in the Richelieu River, at the northern extremity of Lake Champlain, the captured *Confiance* and the other British ships, with only caretaker detachments on board, were moored at Whitehall, where, over the years, they faded away.

A List of Books about the
Lakes and their Battles

By deliberate intent this book list is brief, being confined
for the most part to those volumes assembled for working
reference on only two of my library shelves. A compre-
hensive list would include a catalogue of virtually the entire library, as well as a long memory of a lifetime's reading.

Acknowledgment has been made elsewhere of my in-
debtedness to Mr. Stephen H. P. Pell, of Fort Ticonderoga,
and to his two sons; also to Miss Eleanor Murray, Librarian
at the Ticonderoga Museum and, after the death of Mr.
Pell, Editor of the Museum Bulletin. In accordance with
the policy established by its original editor, the contents
of the Bulletin have been based, for the most part, on material
in the Museum itself: the objects in the galleries and the
large collection of books and manuscripts in the Museum
Library. Had other sources not been available, here alone
could have been traced the long history of the Champlain
Pass.

PRIMARY SOURCES

Anburey, Thomas: *Travels Through the Interior Parts of America*, William Lane, Leadenhall Street, London, 1791.

Baldwin, Colonel Jeduthan: *Diary*, Bulletin, Fort Ticonderoga Museum, Vol. IV, No. 6.

Brainerd, John: *Letter to P. V. B. Livingston*, from *Family Records and Events*, by Livingston Rutherford, 1894.

Bull, Epaphras: *Journal*, Bulletin, Fort Ticonderoga Museum, Vol. VIII, No. 1.

Burton, Lt. Col.: *Letter to the Earl of Loudon*, from *Fort William Henry — A History*, by Stanley M. Gifford, Bullard Press, Glens Falls, 1955.

Chaussegros, Gaspard-Joseph: *Diary*, Bulletin, Fort Ticonderoga Museum, Vol. VI, No. 4.

Champlain, Samuel de: *Works*, 6 Vols., English Text by H. H. Langton, The Champlain Society, Toronto, 1932.

Champlain, Samuel de: *Voyages*, Translated by Charles Pomeroy Otis, The Prince Society, Boston, 1878.

Cleaveland, Rev. John: *Journal*, Fort Ticonderoga Museum.

Clinton, George: *Public Papers*, Wynkoop Hallenbeck Crawford Co., New York and Albany, 1899.

Congressional Committee: *Report to the Northern Department, 1776*, Fort Ticonderoga Museum.

Digby, Lieutenant William: *Diary*, with Notes by James Phinney Baxter, Joel Munsell's Sons, Albany, 1887.

Forbush, Eli: *Letter to Rev. Mr. Steve Williams,* Bulletin, Fort Ticonderoga Museum, Vol. I, No. 6.

Gage, General: *Letters,* Bulletin, Fort Ticonderoga Museum, Vol. IX, No. 4.

Hadden, Lieutenant James M.: *Journal & Orderly Books,* Edited by Horatio Rogers, Joel Munsell's Sons, Albany, 1884.

Johnson, Sir William: *Papers,* Edited by James Sullivan, Albany, 1921

Kalm, Peter: *Travels in North America,* English Version of 1770, Edited by Adolph B. Benson, Wilson-Erickson, Inc., New York, 1937.

Moneypenny, Captain: *Orderly Book, 1755–1765.* Fort Ticonderoga Museum Library.

Pausch, Captain: *Journal,* Translated and Annotated by William L. Stone, Joel Munsell's Sons, Albany, 1886.

Pell, Joshua: *Diary, 1776–1777,* Bulletin, Fort Ticonderoga Museum, Vol. I, No. 6.

Rogers, Major Robert: *A Concise Account of North America,* London, 1765.

Rogers, Major Robert: *Journals,* London, 1765.

Schuyler, Major General Phillip: *Report to the Congressional Committee, November 6, 1776,* Bulletin, Fort Ticonderoga Museum, Vol. III, No. 6.

Starke, John: *An Open Letter to Captain Pringle,* Bulletin, Fort Ticonderoga Museum, Vol. I, No. 4.

Thacher, James, M.D.: *Military Journal of the American Revolution,* Hurlbut, Williams & Co., Hartford, Connecticut, 1862.

Trumbull, Reverend Benjamin: *Diary*, Bulletin, Fort Ticonderoga Museum, Vol. I, Nos. 1, 2, 3, 4.

Trumbull, John: *Orderly Book, Ticonderoga, 1776*, Bulletin, Fort Ticonderoga Museum, Vol. III, Nos. 1, 2, 3.

Trumbull, John: *Autobiography, Reminiscences and Letters*, Wiley and Putnam, New York and London; B. L. Hamlen, New Haven, 1841.

Unknown: *Attack and Repulse at Ticonderoga, July, 1758*, Unsigned Letter in the Bancroft Manuscripts, New York Public Library, Bulletin, Fort Ticonderoga Museum, Vol. VII, No. 1.

Wayne, Colonel Anthony: *Orderly Book, Fort Ticonderoga, 1776*, Bulletin, Fort Ticonderoga Museum, Vol. III, Nos. 4, 5, 6.

Webster, Robert: *Diary*, Bulletin, Fort Ticonderoga Museum, Vol. II, No. 4.

Wells, Bayze: *Journal*, Collection of the Connecticut Historical Society, Vol. VII, 1899.

SECONDARY SOURCES

Akweks, Arens: *The Formation of the Ho-de-no-sau-ne, or League of the Five Nations*. Akwesasne Counselor Organization, St. Regis Mohawk Reservation, Hogansburg, New York.

American Archives (Fifth Series), Edited by Peter Force. Published by M. St. Clair Clarke & Peter Force, Washington, 1851.

American Biography, Dictionary of, Edited by Allen Johnson and Dumas Malone. Charles Scribner's Sons, New York, 1930.

Baldwin, Leland DeWitt: *The Story of the Americas*. Simon and Schuster, New York, 1943.

Beirne, Francis F.: *The War of 1812.* E. P. Dutton & Co. Inc., New York, 1949.

Bishop, Morris: *Champlain: The Life of Fortitude.* Alfred A. Knopf, New York, 1948.

Brady, William N.: *The Kedge Anchor, or the Young Sailor's Assistant.* D. Appleton and Company, New York, 1872.

Company of Military Collectors & Historians: *Journal,* Vols. I–XI. Washington, 1949–1959.

Chapelle, Howard I.: *History of the American Sailing Navy,* W. W. Norton & Co. Inc., New York, 1949.

Chapelle, Howard I.: *History of American Sailing Ships,* W. W. Norton & Company, 1935.

Cook, Joseph: *Historical Ticonderoga.* Sentinel Press, Ticonderoga.

Crockett, Walter Hill: *A History of Lake Champlain, 1609–1909.*

Hobart J. Shanley & Co., Burlington, Vermont, 1909.

Cuneo, John R. *Robert Rogers of the Rangers.* Oxford University Press, New York, 1959.

DeCosta, B. F.: *Notes on the History of Fort George.* J. Sabin & Sons, New York, 1871.

de Roos, Lt. The Hon. F. Fitzgerald, Royal Navy: *Travels in the United States and Canada.* William Harrison Ainsworth, London, 1827.

Fort Ticonderoga Museum Bulletin, Volumes I through IX; Volume X through No. 3, 1927–1959.

Gifford, Stanley M.: *Fort Wm. Henry, a History.* Bullard Press, Glens Falls, New York, 1955.

Hagglund, L. F.: *A Page from the Past: The Story of the Continental Gundelo "Philadelphia" on Lake Champlain, 1777–1949.*

Haigis, John W., Jr.: *The Deerfield Massacre: A New Appraisal.* Deerfield Alumni Journal, Vol. XV, No. 1.

Jackson, Lt. Col. H. M.: *Rogers' Rangers: A History.*

La Farge, Oliver: *A Pictorial History of the American Indian.* Crown Publishers, Inc., New York, 1956.

Lewis, Charles Lee: *Famous American Naval Officers* (Revised Edition). L. C. Page & Co. Inc., Boston, 1944.

Lodge, Henry Cabot: *A Short History of the English Colonies in America* (Revised Edition). Harper & Brothers, New York, 1881.

Lossing, Benjamin J.: *Pictorial Field Book of the Revolution.* Harper & Brothers, New York.

Lossing, Benjamin J.: *Pictorial Field Book of the War of 1812.* Harper & Brothers, New York, 1869.

Maclay, Edgar Stanton: *A History of the United States Navy from 1775 to 1901.* D. Appleton & Company, New York, 1901.

Manucy, Arthur: *Artillery Through the Ages.* U.S. Government Printing Office, Washington, 1949.

National Geographic Society (Editors): *Indians of the Americas.* Washington, 1957.

Nickerson, Hoffman: *The Turning Point of the Revolution, or Burgoyne in America.* Houghton Mifflin Company, Boston, 1928.

Osler, Edward: *The Life of Admiral Viscount Exmouth.* Bulletin, Fort Ticonderoga Museum, Vol. II, No. 5.

Patterson, Captain Howard: *Patterson's Illustrated Nautical Encyclopedia* (Revised and Enlarged Edition). Marine Review Publishing Company, 1901.

Pell, John: *Ethan Allen.* Houghton Mifflin Company, Boston and New York, 1929.

Pell, Robert: *John Brown and the Dash for Ticonderoga.* Bulletin, Fort Ticonderoga Museum, Vol. II, No. 1.

Pell, Robert: *The Champlain Valley in King William's War.* A Lecture given at Fordham University, 1959.

Pell, S. H. P.: *Fort Ticonderoga: A Short History Compiled from Contemporary Sources.* Reprinted for the Fort Ticonderoga Museum, 1954.

Raddall, Thomas H.: *The Path of Destiny.* Doubleday & Company, Inc., Garden City, 1957.

Reid, W. Max: *Lake George and Lake Champlain, and the Mohawk War Trail.* G. P. Putnam's Sons, New York and London, 1910.

Riesenberg, Felix: *Standard Seamanship for the Merchant Service.* D. Van Nostrand Company, Inc., New York, 1936.

Roberts, Kenneth: *Rabble in Arms.* Doubleday & Company, Inc., Garden City, 1946.

Rutledge, Joseph Lister: *Century of Conflict.* Doubleday, Canada, Ltd., Toronto, 1956.

Sautai, Maurice: *Montcalm at the Battle of Carillon.* Translated by John S. Watts. Printed for the Fort Ticonderoga Museum.

Stark, Maj. Gen. John: *Reminiscences of the French War.* Luther Roby, Concord, N.H., 1831.

Stone, William L.: *Washington County, New York: Its History to the Close of the Nineteenth Century.* New York History Company, 1901.

Tower, Lawrence Phelps: *The Untold Story of Our Flag*. The United States Flag Foundation, Oceana Publications, 1956.

Unknown Author: *The Romance of the Revolution*. Published by G. G. Evans, Philadelphia.

Wallace, Paul A. W.: *The White Roots of Peace*. University of Pennsylvania Press, Philadelphia, 1946.

Ward, Christopher: *The War of the Revolution*. The Macmillan Company, New York, 1952.

Watson, Winslow C.: *The Military and Civil History of the County of Essex, New York*. J. Munsell, Albany, 1869.

Wilson, Lt. Col. A. W.: *The Story of the Gun*. Royal Artillery Institute, Woolwich, England, 1944.

Index